Photo*Secrets*

SAN FRANCISCO
and Northern California

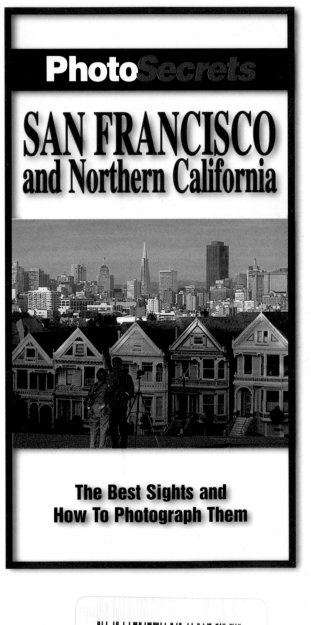

The Best Sights and
How To Photograph Them

SAN FRANCISCO
and Northern California

The Best Sights and How To Photograph Them

By Andrew Hudson

Foreword by Bob Krist

With articles by
Galen Rowell
and Dianne Brinson

A compendium of the most visually distinctive
places in and around San Francisco that you
can easily and dependably photograph.

-Photosecrets Publishing -

San Francisco

The Golden Gate Bridge, icon of the city, from the Marin Headlands. Best at mid-afternoon and dusk.

Northern California

The majestic faces of El Capitan and Half Dome, symbols of Yosemite Valley. This shot is taken from a turnout on Highway 120 (Big Oak Flat Road). Best in the late afternoon.

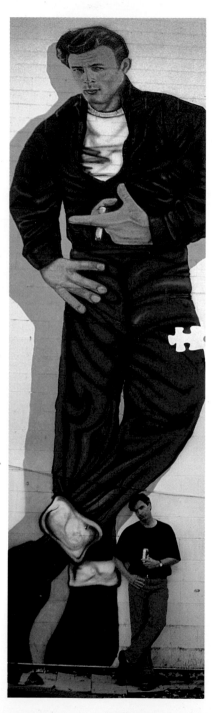

PhotoSecrets San Francisco and Northern California - The Best Sights and How To Photograph Them.
ISBN 0-9653087-1-5   First Edition © 1997
Author: Andrew Hudson   Foreword: Bob Krist
With articles by: Galen Rowell; Dianne Brinson
Printed in Korea.

PhotoSecrets books are distributed to the trade by National Book Network ☎800-462-6420. For other inquiries contact Photosecrets Publishing (address below).

Publisher's Cataloging in Publication
Hudson, Andrew, 1963-
    PhotoSecrets San Francisco and Northern California: the best sights and how to photograph them / Andrew Hudson.
    p. cm.   Includes index.
    Preassigned LCCN: 96-92366
    ISBN 0-9653087-1-5
    1. San Francisco (Calif.)--Guidebooks. 2. California, Northern--Guidebooks. 3. Travel photography--San Francisco (Calif.) 4. Travel photography--California, Northern. I. Title.
    F867.5.H84 1997   917.94'604'53
                QBI96-40391

The information in this guide is intended to be accurate however the author and publisher accept no responsibility for any loss, injury, inconvenience, or other unfortunate consequences arising from the use of this book.

We greatly appreciate your comments and suggestions. If you discover a new angle or sight let us know and we may include it in the next edition. We reward all good input with a free copy of the next edition. You can contact us at:
    Mail: PhotoSecrets. P.O. Box 13554,
            La Jolla, CA 92039-3554 USA
    E-mail: feedback@photosecrets.com
        Visit our web site:
        http://www.photosecrets.com

Left: "Rebel With A Cause."
On the road at the Brookdale Lodge, Felton.

Photo by Jennie Van Meter

"Take only photographs, leave only footprints."

Thank you for picking up this copy of PhotoSecrets. As a fellow fan of travel and photography, I know this book will help you find the most visually stunning places and come home with equally stunning photographs.

With beautiful architecture, steep hills, clanking cable cars, and the atmospheric morning fog, San Francisco is often considered America's most beautiful city. Certainly it has the best location. The surrounding region of Northern California offers rugged coastline, towering redwoods, inspiring mountains, and spectacular scenery. If you enjoy using a camera, you've come to the right place!

PhotoSecrets is designed to quickly show you all the best sights. As you travel, we'll show you the best places to take photographs. We'll show you ideas for compositions, describe the unique history of the location, highlight the best times of day for lighting, and give you tips to create your own unique shots. It'll be like travelling with a location scout and a pro-photographer in your pocket.

Now, pack some extra film and start exploring!

Andrew Hudson

Golden Gate Bridge

Muir Woods

Grace Cathedral

Resources | Yosemite | East | South | North | Other | Top Ten

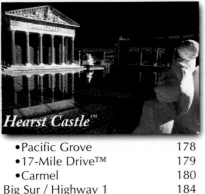

Hearst Castle™

The Gold Country

Yosemite Valley

Foreword

By Bob Krist

A **great travel photograph,** like a great news photograph, requires you to be in the right place at the right time to capture that special moment on film. Professional photographers have a shorthand phrase for that uncanny ability to be in just the right spot when it counts, "F8 and be there".

There are countless books that can help you with photographic technique, the "F8" portion of that equation. But until now, there's been no help available for the other, more critical portion of that equation, the "be there" part. To find the right spot, you had to expend lots of time and shoe leather to essentially re-invent the wheel.

In my career as a professional travel photographer, well over half my time on location is spent seeking out the good angles. It's time consuming, dull, and very frustrating.

Andrew Hudson's PhotoSecrets does all that legwork for you, so you can spend your time photographing instead of wandering about. It's like having a professional location scout in your camera bag. Hudson has thoroughly scoured the city and will tell you where and when to go to get the best possible pictures of San Francisco and the environs. I wish I had one of these books for every city I photograph on assignment.

San Francisco is one of the most beautiful cities in North America and PhotoSecrets can help you capture that beauty on film with a minimum of hassle and a maximum of enjoyment.

Bob Krist writes the photography column for *National Geographic Traveler*. His photographs regularly appear in *National Geographic*, *National Geographic Traveler*, *Travel/Holiday*, *Travel & Leisure*, and *Islands*.

Left: Where can you combine these two icons of San Francisco? See page 33.

HOW TO USE THIS BOOK

- A compendium of the classic views of the most visually distinctive places in and around San Francisco that you can easily and dependably photograph.

"Whether it's a major travel assignment or a family vacation, the more specifics you know about the location, the better your pictures will be."
Bob Krist, National Geographic Traveler

Why do you Need this Book?

To see the most interesting sights before you leave and thereby plan the most effective trip; to see the classic shots - what's been done before - and see how you, too, can take them; to get ideas for good locations and angles; to use as an idea book, a springboard to your unique interpretations and new creative heights.

All the photographs are original (no stock images). They were taken with standard 35mm equipment (nothing expensive) and from accessible places (no helicopters or special permission required) so you *can* take every shot in this book.

Organize Your Trip

1 Plan.

Decide which sights to visit by reviewing the pictures. Use the 'When' information (best in morning; best in afternoon) to plan your day.

2 Visit.

For each sight, text describes what it is and why it's interesting. 'Where' tells you how to get there and 'When' tells you the best time of the day.

3 Photograph.

Start by taking the photographs in the book. The italicized paragraph and 'Tip' paragraph tells you how. Then branch off with your own interpretations. Try different angles, work the subject. Use the accompanying pictures for ideas.

What's **Not** in this Book:

Places to stay; places to eat; museums (unless there's something worth photographing); pictures of festivals and events (you can't photograph them year-round); great photographs which are mainly of people or the weather (you can't dependably photograph them); places that you need to hike a long way to (we're lazy); places more than half-a-day's drive from San Francisco; nature & wildlife photography (this is just travel).

What's Next?

PhotoSecrets is intended as a 'community of interest' reference book. When you find other places or better angles, let us know for the next edition and others can benefit from your experience. Send us your photographs (slides or PhotoCDs preferred) and, if they fit the criteria above, we may print them in the next edition. If so, you'll receive a free copy with your name in the acknowledgements and you'll be a published photographer!

"Planning a shooting itinerary will vastly enhance the number and quality of the photo opportunities you encounter."
Jeff Wignall, Kodak Guide to Shooting Great Travel Pictures

Visit Our Web Site:

http://www.photosecrets.com

Title Listed in the contents and index.

Slide The Top Ten most photogenic sights are shown first. This is sight 7 of 10.

Scene-Setter Small photo shows you what the area is like.

Quote Creates atmosphere and historical relevance.

Italics Describes the picture.

Tabs Show you the general location.

What Describes what the sight is and why it is interesting.

Where How to get there.

When The best time to visit for good lighting. Usually east-facing subjects are best in the morning, and west-facing ones are best in the afternoon.

Clock Summarizes the best time for photography:

⊕ Morning

⊕ Afternoon

⊕ Late Afternoon

Tip On-the-spot tips and ideas.

Nearby Places to go afterwards.

Map Shows the best camera locations. Maps are always to scale and always point vertically North. Maps are for illustration only - you will need a good road atlas.

Photo A maximum size 'classic' shot for you to emulate, or use as an idea for something new.

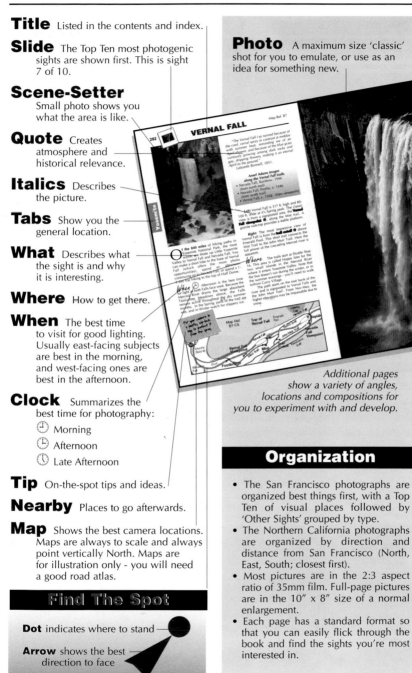

Additional pages show a variety of angles, locations and compositions for you to experiment with and develop.

Organization

- The San Francisco photographs are organized best things first, with a Top Ten of visual places followed by 'Other Sights' grouped by type.
- The Northern California photographs are organized by direction and distance from San Francisco (North, East, South; closest first).
- Most pictures are in the 2:3 aspect ratio of 35mm film. Full-page pictures are in the 10" x 8" size of a normal enlargement.
- Each page has a standard format so that you can easily flick through the book and find the sights you're most interested in.

Find The Spot

Dot indicates where to stand ●

Arrow shows the best direction to face ◣

Design © 1997 Photosecrets Publications

PhotoSecrets **Top Ten** sights of

San Francisco

1

Golden Gate Bridge
page 22

Gracefully spanning the entrance to San Francisco Bay, the Golden Gate Bridge is the icon of San Francisco. There are at least a dozen classic viewpoints from which to photograph it.

2

Cable Cars
page 30

Clanking steadily over the city's famously steep hills, San Francisco's cable cars are the nation's only moving national landmark. They provide a moving foreground for a variety of shots.

3

Lombard Street
page 34

"The Crookedest Street In The World", is also one of the most photographed. Hairpins, houses, hardbricks and hydrangeas pose for your camera.

Alamo Square
page 36

The Six Sisters of *"Postcard Row"* contrast the city's modern skyline with it's gingerbread Victorian heritage.

Transamerica Pyramid
page 42

The *"Great Alien Ring Toss"* tapers into the heavens and is the most distinctive building on San Francisco's skyline.

Coit Tower
page 46

Crowning Telegraph Hill, there are many terrific views of, and from, this famous landmark.

The Palace Of Fine Arts
page 52

Rising like an oasis in the city, this *'melancholic evocation of vanquished grandeur'* is a beaux-arts visual delight.

Alcatraz
page 58

Al Capone and "Machine Gun" Kelly came here. Now you can too. Let's Rock!

Fisherman's Wharf
page 60

It may be called *tacky* and *artificial* but it's fun. Ships, shops, seal lions and sourdough prove that 12 million tourists a year can't be wrong.

Golden Gate Park
page 66

One of the great city parks, this verdant retreat harbors a diverse collection of sights and extends almost half the width of San Francisco.

Introduction

With a city as beautiful as San Francisco, how can anyone select the 'Best' sights?

There are probably as many opinions about the Top Ten 'Best' sights of San Francisco as there are visitors or residents. Some people rave about the museums, others champion the wealth of arts and restaurants, many relish the quaint districts and shops. San Francisco is a varied, cosmopolitan city and there is a Top Ten for every taste.

Our selection - the PhotoSecrets 'Best' sights - is considered from the viewpoint of the camera. What are the most iconographic and visually stunning places that you can easily and dependably photograph? Places that make the viewer of your photographs say: *"Wow! Where's that? I want to go there!"*

We selflessly scoured the city on your behalf. Someone had to do it. Most of San Francisco's excellent museums and other indoor shots were excluded since they require more flash equipment (and permission) than a tourist would likely have. Also excluded are festivals, since they are seasonal. Instead, colorful events are listed at the back of the book.

That said, let's review our Top Ten 'Best' sights.

At number one is the most widely recognized symbol of San Francisco - the **Golden Gate Bridge**. Claimed to be the most photographed bridge in the world, this graceful structure makes a great photograph from almost any angle, at any time of day. You can get a great shot from the north or south, east or west, a high viewpoint or low, on a clear day or in fog, at sunrise or sunset. There are nine different viewpoints to explore and we show you each one.

The next four slots are taken by other enduring emblems unique to San Francisco: the roving **Cable Cars** (the country's only moving national monument), the hydrangea-lined, 'crooked' **Lombard Street**, the distinctive **Transamerica Pyramid**, Telegraph Hill's firehouse-shaped **Coit Tower**, and the Victorian 'painted ladies' of **Alamo Square**. They make great backgrounds behind your companions for those 'we are here' shots. Start by copying our classic 'postcard' views, then branch off for a fresh approach by changing the angle or composition. For a twist, combine two icons, such as Coit Tower and the Transamerica Pyramid from Pier 39, or a Cable Car at the top of Lombard Street.

We pause at this point for a short digression on the Queen Ann Victorian residences. Dotted around the city, these ornate, elegant and colorful houses warrant a book to themselves.

Sight number seven is the "indescribeably beautiful" **Palace of Fine Arts**. As the New York Times said: "it gives you a choky feeling in your throat as you look at it". This is the most romantic structure in a romantic city. Wander through the corinthian columns, exercise the swan-graced reflecting lagoon, and introduce your audience to this little-known oasis.

The eighth sight is the popular **Fisherman's Wharf**. 84% of visitors to San Francisco come here so you probably will too. Regularly chastised for being tacky and brash, this area of growing attractions offers a wealth of people shots, as well as howling sea lions, dungeness crabs, ships, a submarine, and an aquarium.

At nine is **Alcatraz**. More than one columnist has remarked that, in such a vibrant city, it's a waste of half a day to visit a deserted prison. But hey, where else can you see such a legendary prison? Explore abandoned buildings, and contrast the dull, drab landscape with the lively city, only one mile away. Alcatraz has atmosphere.

Rounding out the top ten is **Golden Gate Park**. The park may be smaller, and less central, than it's progenitor, New York's Central Park, but it is certainly more varied. Windmills, lakes, waterfalls, an English garden, a Japanese garden, a botanical garden, two major museums, and numerous sporting activities create a world within a world.

To simplify the many remaining sights, we have grouped them under 'Skylines', 'Districts', 'Places of Worship', 'Architecture', etc. Additional space is given for bustling **Chinatown** as this is a highlight for many visitors. There are few 'sights' here but it's a great area to explore.

Northern California

No American city has more varied and fascinating surroundings than San Francisco. Discover towering redwoods, the plunging coastline of Big Sur, pristine Lake Tahoe, and the majestic Sierra Nevada mountains. Visit the artistic colonies of Carmel and Mendocino, resort towns of Santa Cruz and Monterey, the future-forming Silicon Valley, historically rich Gold Country and palate-enticing Wine Country. Tour aesthetically-bizarre millionaire's mansions like Winchester Mystery House and Hearst Castle.

Explore the hexagonal basalt columns of Devil's Postpile NM, strange tufa formations of Mono Lake, or 1,200-foot-high spires of Pinnacles National Monument. Design a trip visiting the numerous lighthouses, Spanish Missions or steam trains. And this is in addition to California's crowning glory, Yosemite National Park - a photographer's paradise.

Whereas a week is sufficient for San Francisco, three to four weeks are needed for all of Northern California. If you're not a vacationing student, teacher, or lottery-winner, concentrate on one area rather than everything. To help, we have grouped sights by their direction from San Francisco - north, south or east, in increasing distances, up to about 200 miles radius (a half-days' drive).

It doesn't matter how wet you get, as long as you get the perfect shot!

Resources

At the back of the book is a brief selection of practical information. In order to focus on photography, and, since it is so well covered in other books, we have not included a lot of general travel information such as recommended hotels and restaurants. For this you will still need a general travel book.

What is included are contact numbers, a list of festivals and events, weather information, and tips to improve your photography. The section ends with a how-to section on making an album or journal to remember your trip.

Weather

The greatest effect on your photographs will be the weather. Blue skies usually give the most rosy views but don't be disheartened if it's not sunny. The low-contrast light of overcast days is better for green foliage. Rain is great for moods (many of Ansel Adams most-famous shots were taken before or after a storm), and fog adds atmosphere, particularly to the Golden Gate Bridge and Muir Woods.

To plan your trip, check our accompanying web site for the latest information and links to weather reports and live cameras around the Bay Area. You'll also find a list of revisions and updates to this book, more tips, and other reader's advice.

Feedback

Travel is fun because things always change. You'll no doubt find some sights that are new or that we've overlooked. If so, please let us know. There's a postage-paid reply card at the back of this book or send us an e-mail to feedback@photo-secrets.com. We want to hear from you and reward original ideas and photos that we use with a free book and an including your name in the next edition of this book.

I hope you have as much fun using this book as we did making it. Happy shooting!

The Golden Gate Bridge from Baker Beach and (inset) Hawk Hill.

PhotoSecrets   **San Francisco**

Top Ten Sights

GOLDEN GATE BRIDGE

"To pass through the portals of the Golden Gate is to cross the threshold of adventure." Allan Dunn

Left: The bridge leaps elegantly over Fort Point before crossing the Golden Gate.
Right: The best place for orientation is the **Visitors Center** ☉. There is a gift shop for information and ideas, a section of the 3 ft (1m) thick cable that suspends the bridge (which makes a good foreground with your companions) and a statue of the bridge's designer, Joseph Strauss.

To get a good view, find some height. The classic postcard view (left) is taken at mid-morning from the bus stop above the car park, using a 70mm lens.

Nothing conveys more the romance of the Bay Area than the Golden Gate Bridge. It is the most recognized symbol of San Francisco and looks stunning from any angle, and at any time. No wonder it is the nation's most photographed structure.

When completed in 1937, it was the longest single-span bridge in the world (1.7 miles). While that honor was taken by the Verrazano Narrows Bridge in 1964, the Golden Gate Bridge is still the tallest suspension bridge and remains one of the Seven Wonders of the modern world.

The bridge is named for the strait it crosses, where the expansive San Francisco Bay meets the Pacific Ocean. This was the entrance for most of the fortune-seekers to the gold and silver mines of California and Nevada, which financed the new city. In his 1848 *Geographical Memoir of California*, explorer John C Fremont predicatively recorded this strait as the "Golden Gate".

What Color Is The Bridge?

Although many shades of gold were tried, this color was chosen as it is most easily distinguished in fog. It is called 'International Orange'. 43 people work year-round painting the bridge to keep its color fresh.

When Anytime and every time. Mid-morning is preferred for views from the east, such as from Vista Point, the Marina, the Visitors Center, and Fort Point. Mid-afternoon favors the west views, such as Baker's Beach and Marin Headlands, which are also best at sunset. The weather is the most determining factor. Like the city, it is often clear from October to March, but densely foggy in the summer. In the fog, your best bet is from Marin Headlands for an evocative shot of the towers rising through the clouds.

Where The Golden Gate Bridge starts at the north-western tip of the city, in the Presidio and Golden Gate National Recreation Area, 5 miles from downtown. It is the only link north and connects San Francisco to beautiful Marin County, the Wine Country, and the Redwood Empire.

The best place to start your exploration is at the Visitor Center (☎ 415-556-1693), which is the exit just before the toll booths on the south (San Francisco) side (bus 28 & 29). From there you can walk east down to Fort Point, west to Baker's Beach, then walk or drive 1.7 miles across the bridge to Vista Point (east) and the Marin Headlands (west). ☎415-921-5858.

Nearby There's not much near the bridge, although from the south side you can explore Fort Point, drive east to the Palace of Fine Arts and the Marina district, or south west to the Legion of Honor. From the north side you can drive west to Point Bonita lighthouse, or north east to Sausalito and Tiburon.

Where to Photograph The Golden Gate Bridge

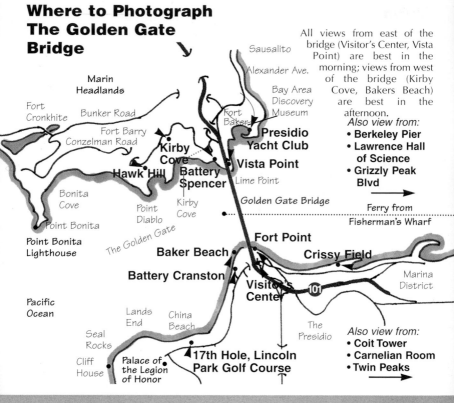

All views from east of the bridge (Visitor's Center, Vista Point) are best in the morning; views from west of the bridge (Kirby Cove, Bakers Beach) are best in the afternoon.

Also view from:
- Berkeley Pier
- Lawrence Hall of Science
- Grizzly Peak Blvd →

Sausalito
Alexander Ave.
Marin Headlands
Bay Area Discovery Museum
Fort Cronkhite
Bunker Road
Fort Barry
Conzelman Road
Fort Baker
Presidio Yacht Club
Kirby Cove
Vista Point
Hawk Hill
Battery Spencer
Lime Point
Bonita Cove
Point Diablo
Kirby Cove
Golden Gate Bridge
Point Bonita
The Golden Gate
Ferry from Fisherman's Wharf
Point Bonita Lighthouse
Fort Point
Baker Beach
Crissy Field
Battery Cranston
Marina District
Pacific Ocean
Visitor Center
Lands End
China Beach
The Presidio
Seal Rocks
Cliff House
Palace of the Legion of Honor
17th Hole, Lincoln Park Golf Course
101

Also view from:
- Coit Tower
- Carnelian Room
- Twin Peaks →

Marin Headlands

There are many classic views of the bridge, but the three best ones are from the northwestern side, on the **Marin Headlands**. Crossing to the north side of the bridge, take the second exit (after Vista Point) on Alexander Ave towards Sausalito. At the end of the off-ramp, turn left and go under the freeway, then just before the road joins 101 S, take the only right turn up Conzelman Road. Until 1972, this area was military property and closed to the public.

Battery Spencer ⏱ *Page 2*

Park at the first pullout on the left, by the disused gun emplacement, and walk 100 yards to the
point. You're
surprisingly
close to the
north tower
here. This is the
best view in the
summer fog.

Below: This stunning view is from **Hawk Hill** ⏱. To make this 10" x 3" panorama shot, take a normal photograph with the bridge in the center. When you get your film developed, ask for a 10" x 8" enlargement. Trim off the top and bottom 2.5 inches, and mount in a 10" x 3" frame.

Kirby Cove ⏱

Cover and p22.

Right: 3/4 of a mile further up Conzelman Road is a small pullout with a tree and bench, overlooking Kirby Cove. This is where you can get a tight shot with the Transamerica Pyramid behind. You'll need a 300mm lens (or a 210mm with a 2x adapter), and a tripod. This is the best place to watch the bridge at sunrise and sunset.

For a different perspective, you can hike down to the Cove's beach from Battery Spencer.

Hawk Hill ⏱

Below: At the top of Conzelman Road, near a tunnel, is a fabulous panorama with a full view of the bridge and city behind. On a clear day, this is the best view of San Francisco and it would be almost a crime not to see it.

Pages 2-3: The clean, elegant lines and bold color of the bridge make this shot. Notice how the roadway leads the eye from left to right, deep into the background, emphasizing depth. 50mm from above **Kirby Cove** ⏱. Mid-afternoon & polarizer for the rich blue sky.

Left: The view from **Kirby Cove** ⏱. The Golden Gate Bridge and the Transamerica Pyramid, two of San Francisco's most recognizable landmarks. In this classic view from the Marin Headlands, the north tower of the bridge provides a striking foreground to the city's distinctive skyline. Whilst dependent upon a (rare) clear day, this view is spectacular at the first light of dawn (front cover) and sunset (left). A 300mm and a good tripod will help you.

Fort Point

From the Visitor Center, a pleasant path leads down the hill to Fort Point. If you have a car, it's best to drive to avoid the Visitor Center's well-patrolled parking meters. Take the left exit from the car park, then the first left (sharp turn) down to Fort Point.

Right: Get low and use a wide angle (35mm) to give the foreground impact. This shot at right is taken from the north-eastern tip of the point. The South Tower is anchored 1000′ into open ocean. All the concrete in the foundation used would pave a five-foot wide sidewalk from San Francisco to New York.

Page 22: The three-story **Fort Point** ⏱ was built in 1853 to protect the city during the Civil War. It was modeled after Fort Sumter in South Carolina. Fortified with 126 cannons, it never saw action and now houses a small Civil War museum (Wed-Sun, 10-5pm, free).

Below: Horsehoe Cove and the boats at **Presidio Yacht Club** ⏱ provide several foreground opportunities.

Battery Cranston

Above: You've probably realized by now that the Golden Gate was a well-fortified area. Emplacements were first built by the Spanish in 1776, and progressively enlarged to defend the city during the Civil War, Spanish-American War, and WWII. On the north shore are Forts Cronkhite, Barry, and Baker; on the south shore lies The Presidio, Fort Point and Fort Mason. Alcatraz was also a fort.

Battery Cranston ◷ has a good view, and a trailhead down to Baker Beach. From the Visitors Center, drive under the highway towards South 101. Turn right onto Merchant Road, then right onto a small lane - Battery Cranston Road. From the parking lot a trail leads north to an overlook.

Spring flowers on Baker Beach

Baker Beach

Page 20, above and both below.

If you're tired of the crowds and want a view all to yourself, take a hike down to **Baker Beach** ◷. The trail starts at the wooden stairs near Battery Cranston. Head for the north end where sand and rocks glow in the setting sun. Baker Beach is a popular nude beach so you have plenty of foregrounds to choose from!

Tip Notice how the shots above and to the left emphasize depth. The surf and flowers seem just inches away and contrast with the distant hills. The bridge sweeps our eyes deep into the picture. To create this effect, use a wide angle (28mm), a small aperture (f22 - for wide depth-of-field) and get low and close to an interesting foreground.

Top Ten

Golden Gate Bridge

The Golden Gate Bridge was built in the 1930's as a depression-era work project, like the larger Oakland-Bay Bridge and the Coit Tower murals. It took 4 1/2 years to build and 11 people lost their lives in the process.

The bridge stretches 1.7 miles across the bay and is literally suspended from the towers by cables, each a yard thick. There are enough strands of steel wire in the cables to encircle the equator three times. It links San Francisco with Marin County, forming part of US Highway 101 which stretches from Mexico to Canada along the Pacific Coast. There is a $3 toll when entering San Francisco.

The Golden Gate Bridge is deliberately flexible, to absorb the force of an earthquake or a furious gale. In a 100 mph wind the bridge will sway about 27 feet. Don't walk across it on a windy day if you get seasick!

Lincoln Park

Above: One of the most beautiful golf shots in the US is of the 17th hole green in the **Lincoln Park Municipal Golf Course** ⊕. The best light is one or two hours before sunset, as the sun later disappears behind the trees. Wait for some players to reach the green.

On the other side of the green is a romantic ocean overlook. A coastal trail leads west round to Lands End - the best place to watch the sun set.

Nearby is the California Palace of the Legion of Honor (see *Architecture-Classic*).

Crissy Field

Below: From Fort Point you can drive north to the Marina along Mason Street. This area, **Crissy Field**, is a popular spot for windsurfers and joggers. Use a long lens to emphasize the distant bridge. This shot was taken with a 210mm lens just after sunset.

Similar views can be taken from Angel Island, Treasure Island and Berkeley Pier.

CABLE CARS

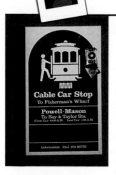

There are few cities in the world where the tourist sight actually comes to you. Clanking around at a steady 9.5 mph (15.5 km/h), the Cable Cars conquer the steep hills of the city and the hearts of it's visitors alike.

Introduced in 1873 by Andrew Hallidie, an English mining engineer who made wire rope, the Cable Cars relieved overworked horse-drawn trams and opened up the hills of San Francisco for development. Nob Hill and Russian Hill became the height of opulence with residents able to commute in these unpowered carriages. By 1906, five companies operated 600 cars on 115 miles of track.

The earthquake and electric trolleys put the system into decline and the cars were abolished in 1947. But sentiment prevailed and parts of the system were rebuilt. Now over 40 cars run on three routes carrying 12 million passengers a year - half of whom are residents. Cable Cars are now protected by the city charter and they are the nation's only moving national landmark. They are the last urban cable car system in the world.

Cable Cars cost $2 per ride, or $6 for all day.

Where

There are over 12 miles of track running across downtown San Francisco. The routes are perfect for tourists, mainly linking Fisherman's Wharf to the business district via North Beach, Russian Hill, Nob Hill, and Chinatown. The three routes are named after the major roads they follow:

Powell-Hyde: Links Union Square and the main Information Center to Lombard Street and Fisherman's Wharf. Understandably the most popular route.

Powell-Mason: Union Square to North Beach (and a few blocks from Fisherman's Wharf)

California: Embarcadero/Ferry Building to Van Ness Ave, via Chinatown and Nob Hill.

"A little cable car climbing halfway to the stars." Tony Bennett

Right: A Cable Car crests Nob Hill, reflecting the setting sun. In the background is he Oakland Bay Bridge. For this shot, stand on California Street, just west of **Jones Street** ☉, but watch out for traffic. Alternatively, stand east of Jones near Grace Cathedral and shoot a silhouette, into the sun.

When

Since you're capturing a general scene, anytime is fine. Infact, unlike most other subjects, mid-day is best as you get sunlight at street level in the canyons between the tall buildings.

Tickets

Tickets can be bought at terminus machines, shops, Visitor Center, or just pay the conductor. For information, call 673-6864.

Tip

The Hyde Street terminus by Fisherman's Wharf is the worst place to catch a car. In the summer the wait can be several hours. Try the Mason line instead, at Taylor/Bay, or walk part of the route to a street stop.

How Do Cable Cars Work?

The unpowered Cable Car is pulled along by a cable that runs just under the street. This cable, 2" thick and lying in a trough in the road, forms a loop which is continuously pulled by the massive engines at the Cable Car Barn on Mason Street. The operator, the 'gripman', starts the car by using a large handle to clamp onto the cable. To stop, he or she releases the clamp from the cable, and applies iron brakes to the wheels and wooden blocks to the track. The cables have to be replaced every three months and cost $20,000 each.

Nearby

Almost everything is nearby. For a fascinating behind-the-scenes look, visit the Cable Car Barn & Museum. This is the powerhouse of the system where you can see the engine and cables. 1201 Mason/Washington, 10-5/6pm, free. ☎415-474-1887.

Top Ten

Where to Photograph Cable Cars

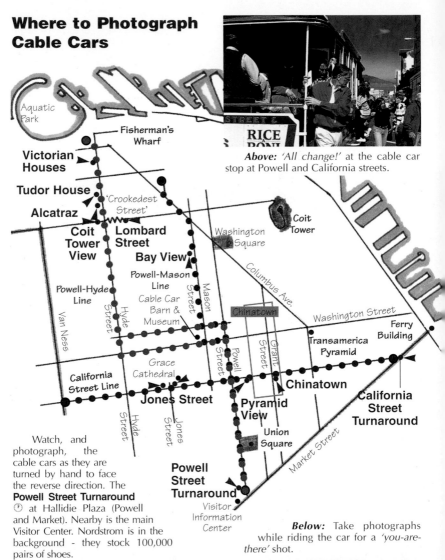

Above: 'All change!' at the cable car stop at Powell and California streets.

Watch, and photograph, the cable cars as they are turned by hand to face the reverse direction. The **Powell Street Turnaround** 🕐 at Hallidie Plaza (Powell and Market). Nearby is the main Visitor Center. Nordstrom is in the background - they stock 100,000 pairs of shoes.

Below: Take photographs while riding the car for a *'you-are-there'* shot.

Top Ten

The best area for photography is a walk up Hyde Street. At North Point is a backdrop with **Victorian Houses** ⊕ (wait for a downhill car) and, at Francisco Street, a **Tudor House** ⊕ (uphill car). The most famous view is with the prison-island of **Alcatraz** ⊕ and Aquatic Park in the background. Stand on the SW corner of Hyde/Chestnut, wait for an uphill car to crest the hill and use a long lens (100mm or 'tele') to flatten the image and bring out Alcatraz. Further up at Lombard St. is a great view of **Coit Tower** ⊕ (p46).

Left: The California Street car crosses **Chinatown** at Grant Street, allowing you to combine two icons of San Francisco.

Right: At California and Powell Streets you can include the Transamerica Pyramid.

At twilight, the **California Street Turnaround** at Market Street has views with street lights (not pictured).

Left: The apartments at 717 Bay Street, near Hyde, are so steep that they have their own private cable car.

3 LOMBARD STREET

"The Crookedest Street In The World."

Tip A scene like this needs a high vantage point but unfortunately there isn't one (or at least not one open to the public).

The best you can do is shoot from the driveway just off Leavenworth (left and right). Wait for a downhill cable car to stop at the top, and use a long lens to compress the shot and enlarge the cable car.

Lombard Street is known for the short section on Russian Hill that is so steep it makes eight turns in one block, and has become known as *"The Crookedest Street In The World."*

The turns, known as *switchbacks*, were added in the 1920's so that cars could descend the hill. In the 1950's, resident Peter Bercut added Hydrangeas. The flowers, red brick street, and a passing cable car make this section of Lombard Street one of the most unique and colorful streets in the country.

The Crookedest Street?

Lombard may be known as the "Crookedest Street" but there are other contenders:

Lombard St.:   8 turns in 412'
Vermont St.(20th/22nd): 6 turns in 270'
Twin Peaks Blvd: Six 180˚ turns and
                      eleven other curves in 1 mile.

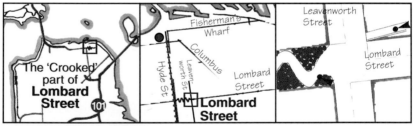

Where Lombard Street is several miles long but the famous section is between Hyde and Leavenworth. The Powell-Hyde Cable Car conveniently stops at the top, where you have a great view of Coit Tower. This area is known as Russian Hill, after some Russian fur-trappers who were reputedly buried here in the early 1800's.

When 🕐 Early morning is best as the hill faces the rising sun. Springtime (May) sees the Hydrangeas in full bloom.

Nearby Two blocks south is the steepest street in the city. **Filbert Street**, also between Hyde and Leavenworth, is 31.5˚ - and there are no turns! 22nd Street between Vicksburg and Church, near Mission Dolores, also shares this honor. At 1067 Green Street is the **Feusier Octagon House**, one of two such odd shaped houses in the city. It is not open to the public.

4 ALAMO SQUARE

One of the most photographed views of San Francisco, is "Postcard Row", a delightful set of six Victorian Houses facing Alamo Square. The tightly escalating terrace, with it's elaborate Victorian woodwork, contrasts with the modern skyline background, crowned by the Bank of America building, and the distinctive Transamerica Pyramid peaking over the valley beyond.

Designed by Matthew Kavanaugh and built in 1895, the "Six Sisters" and the adjoining park are a travel photographers dream. There are so many other majestic Victorian Houses nearby, that the surrounding 12 blocks have been designated an Historic District.

Where "Postcard Row" is on the 700 block of Steiner Road, between Hayes Street and Grove Street, on the east side of Alamo Square. Muni bus 21 and 22. Take Geary Blvd to Divisadero, turn south for eight blocks then east on Hayes.

The best vantage point is near the Ida B Wells School by Hayes and Pierce Street.

"Postcard Row"

When This view is best in the late afternoon as the houses face west. The park's trees can cast a shadow on the houses at sunset (below) so arrive a few hours before. In the winter, when the office lights are on at night, a dusk shot can work well. Hope that someone is home to switch on a front room light for you!

Nearby The surrounding area, particularly Birch Street and McAllister Street, is blessed with Victorian Houses and makes a pleasant walk or drive.

One-and-a-half blocks south, on the corner of Steiner and Fell, is **601 Steiner**, a large yellow Queen Anne (p39, top left). On the diagonal corner of Alamo Square, at 1198 Fulton (with Scott Street), is the **Westerfield House** (p39, bottom right).

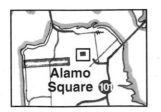

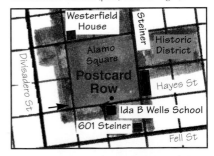

Victorian Houses

During the great boom years of 1850-1900, with the Sierra gold rush, Comstock silver-rush and the excitement of the transcontinental railroad the city flourished. Extravagant mansions sprang up, exploiting every flamboyance of various Victorian styles. Within fifty years, over 300,000 people had moved to San Francisco, making it the largest city west of Chicago.

Sadly the 1906 earthquake and ensuing fire destroyed over 500 blocks of houses, particularly around Nob Hill, but a surprising amount remain. Today there are still over 14,000 gingerbread Victorian Houses in San Francisco, mainly in the Pacific Heights, Western Addition, Haight-Ashbury and Mission districts.

Victorian Styles

Whilst most houses are generally similar - wooden frames decorated with carved ornamentation and built on a narrow square plot - there are three general styles:

Italianate 1850-1875. Inspired by classical Rome, these houses used Corinthian columns in tall, narrow row houses with angled bay windows and flat roofs.

Stick-Eastlake 1875-85. The columns were replaced with sharp, angular posts which today are often brightly painted.

Queen Anne 1885-1905. The most graceful style which unabashedly combed turrets and towers, gabled roofs and bay windows, and spindles on every porch and roof truss. It had nothing to do with Queen Ann but was developed from a style popular in 1860's England.

Facing Page

Top left: 601 Steiner Street. A large Queen Anne near Alamo Square

Top right: Painting enhances architecture on this Stick-Eastlake in the Mission district. 24th Street near South Van Ness.

Lower left: A Stick-Eastlake house with an unusual Persian dome

Lower right: The Westerfield House. Built in 1889, this is the city's most attractive Gothic/Stick Italianate Villa, similar to the Carson House in Eureka.

Haas-Lilienthal House ⊕

Left: The most interesting Victorian in San Francisco is the Haas-Lilienthal House because it is the only one open as a public museum. Original period furniture and an informative tour provide a rare glimpse into this historic time (Wed noon to 3:15, Sun 11 to 4:15,$5/3, ☎415-441-3004).

The Haas-Lilienthal House is at 2007 Franklin Street, between Jackson and Washington, and is best photographed in the morning from the southeast side.

The house was built in 1886 for William Haas, a Bavarian wholesale grocer. His daughter Alice married Samuel Lilienthal and when she died the house was donated. Family members still return every Christmas and the house has a lived-in feel.

The Haas-Lilienthal House

Top Ten

McElroy Octagon House

Above: One of the most distinctive designs is this eight-sided house. In his 1848 book, *"A Home For All"*, New Yorker Orson Squire Fowler claimed this octagonal design was more healthy for it's owners as each room received maximum sunlight.

About five such houses were built, two of which still remain. The Feusier House on Russian Hill (not pictured) is at 1067 Green Street, near Jones. It is not open to the public. The one above, the McElroy Octagon House in the Cow Hollow district, is occasionally open to the public. It is difficult to photograph as there's no high vantage point or open space nearby.

2645 Gough Street, open 2nd & 4th Thu, and 2nd Sun of each month, noon-3pm, $3. ☎415-441-7512

This Page:

Above: It's featured on many brochures but has since fallen into disrepair. This otherwise nondescript house, built in 1892, is at 1597 Fulton Street, near Lyon Street between Haight-Ashbury and Alamo Square.

Bottom Left: A detail from a row of colorful houses on Delmar Street in the center of Haight-Ashbury

Near Left: Although more noted for its modern condominiums, the Marina district is graced by this elegant French-inspired balcony. Chestnut Street near Divisadero.

Facing Page:

Top Left: The Edward Coleman House, now safely maintained by the law offices of Choulos, Choulos, and Wyle, is on California Street (1701 Franklin Street) just west of Van Ness Ave.

Top Right: The Mission district has a surprising amount of Victorians. This one is at 17th Street at Eureka, near the murals.

Bottom Left: Also in the Mission district is this earthen-colored stick house with a rare third floor.

Bottom Right: There are many Queen Anne residences in Haight-Ashbury which are lovingly painted. This one is on Waller Street.

"The Great Alien Ring Toss"

Right: The classic shot of the Transamerica Pyramid. The green building in the foreground, at 916 Kearny Street, is known as **Columbus Tower** ⏰ although it's officially called the Sentinel Building. The oscar-winning director of the *Godfather* films, Francis Ford Coppola, owns this building. It is home to his production company, Zoetrope Studios. Columbus Tower was one of the first skyscraper's in the city. The green color is oxidized copper.

San Francisco's most distinctive building, and it's tallest, is the Transamerica Pyramid. Towering 853 ft (256 m) above sea level, the pyramid can be seen all around the city.

The unique design, a triangular tapered spire, was supposedly chosen because it casts a smaller shadow than a rectangular building. The upper 212-foot (64m) peak is purely decorative and is hollow.

Although the only popularly recognized building on the city's skyline, the Transamerica Pyramid was fiercely disliked by many residents when it opened in 1972 and it was called "The Great Alien Ring Toss". Fortunately the later "jukebox" Marriott took off the heat.

Where The Transamerica Pyramid is located at the base of diagonal Columbus Ave, where North Beach meets the Financial district.

The classic view (right) is from two blocks away, at Kearny Street and Columbus Ave. Here, on the edge of Chinatown, you can include the contrasting Columbus Tower/Sentinel Building.

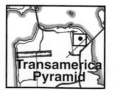

When ⏰ Mid-afternoon is the best time as the all views are of the western face.

Nearby This is a very historic area. Next door at Merchant Street was the western terminus of the Pony Express which, for it's brief existence, rode to Sacramento and St. Joseph, Missouri. The Wells Fargo Museum on Montgomery and California recalls these days. Across Washington Street is the Jackson Square Historical District which includes the Golden Era Building on Montgomery Street. It was here that Mark Twain worked, after having established himself in Virginia City.

You can walk up up Washington to Portsmouth Square and Chinatown (one block), down Montgomery to the Pacific Stock Exchange (4 blocks, then to the Embarcadero Center, the Market Street terminus of the California Cable Car line, and the Ferry Building), up Columbus Ave to Washington Square (six blocks), or up Montgomery to Coit Tower (eight blocks).

Left: Walking up Columbus Ave provides many opportunities. The **Stinking Rose** ⏰ and Vesuvio's Coffee House are popular foregrounds. In this shot, taken near sunset, you can see the full scale of the Transamerica Pyramid, compared to the now diminutive Columbus Tower.

Facing Page: A great view of the Transamerica Pyramid, in fact the best elevated view of the city, is from the nearby Bank of America building at 555 California Street. On the 52nd floor, 761 feet high, is a cocktail bar and the renowned **Carnelian Room** ⏰ restaurant.

Bank of America no longer occupies the building. They sold it in 1985 for $660m, making it the most expensive building bought in the US. There are 48-stories housing 1,500 people. On the eastern plaza is a small grove of redwoods.

You can photograph through the window but remove your polarizer lens as it will only reveal the stress marks in the glass. On a clear day, you also have a good view of the Golden Gate Bridge from here. Best at about one hour before sunset on a clear day, 50mm.

Right: Here's a famous view, seen in many TV shows and films. This is taken from near Coit Tower, on **Montgomery Steps** ⏰. The steps are on Montgomery Street, 1/2 block up from Green Street. The road is too steep for cars and is broken by a wall and some Venetian stairs. Most of the time the sun will be behind the pyramid giving a flat look to your shot. So wait for late afternoon when the north face of the pyramid, and the west facing row houses are nicely lit. 50mm polarizer.

Like most of the financial district (and the Marina district), the ground beneath the Pyramid is actually landfill, reclaimed from the Bay. The building sits on a large concrete and steel block sunk 52 ft (15.5m) into the ground. During an earthquake, the building is designed to sway on this foundation and there are gaps around the exterior panels to allow movement.

The two shoulder-like wings house a smoke-stack, stairs, and 18 elevators. Half way up on the 27th floor is an observation area. You can see Coit Tower from here but the view is otherwise unexceptional. The building was designed by William Pereira & Associates as the headquarters of the Transamerica Corporation, a large insurance company.

Left: Standing stoutly above North Beach, Coit Tower is an elegant and romantic landmark. This shot is taken from **Hyde Street** ⏱ at the top of "crooked" Lombard Street, and benefits from the golden light of the setting sun. Use a long lens (210mm/tele). A tripod will help although there are railings on Hyde Street to lean against.

Right: The postcard view includes the handsome **statue** ⏱ of Christopher Columbus in the foreground for depth and interest. Sit on the circular wall of the flower bed and get low, resting on the small white rail. 35mm.

Coit Tower is on the top of Telegraph Hill. The hill was named after an optical telegraph station, built here in 1853, that communicated with ships sailing through the Golden Gate.

Like Rome, San Francisco is built on seven hills, and on the top of the most famous one, Telegraph Hill, stands the landmark of Coit Tower.

Funded by Lillie Coit, an unconventional Victorian woman who relished firefighting, the 1933 tower combines art deco and classicism in a simple fluted pillar. Despite the rumors, it's only by coincidence that Coit Tower resembles a fire hose.

The observation deck and car park/plaza offer great views of the Golden Gate Bridge, North Beach, Lombard Street, Transamerica Pyramid, and the Oakland Bay Bridge. You can even hear the sea lions down at Fisherman's Wharf.

When ⏱ With such a view, hope for a clear day. The classic shot (right) is best at mid-afternoon, when the sun lights the west-facing Columbus statue.

Open 10-7:30. ☎415-362-0808

Where Coit Tower is located at the top of Telegraph Hill in North Beach. Car access is only from the west via Lombard Street. Bus no. 39.

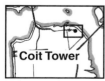

Coit Tower

How Much Parking and entrance to the tower and murals is free. The observation deck costs $3 per person. The deck has a 360° view but if you're short of time, the view from the parking lot is just as good. Tripods are not allowed on the deck.

Who Was Coit?

Lillie Hitchcock Coit was born in France in 1844. She first saw San Francisco at age seven when her wealthy parents moved into the Oriental Hotel. The following year, she was rescued from a fire by Knickerbocker Engine Company No. 5 and instantly fell in love with firefighting. Thereafter she followed the volunteer firemen to almost every blaze and became their mascot - *Firebelle Lillie*.

Lillie married gambler Howard Coit. Her parents bought him a seat on the Pacific Stock Exchange, of which he later became Chairman, and the excited speculation of Comstock silver made the Coits wealthy. But the marriage failed and they separated in 1880.

Charismatic Lillie moved to Napa, then Paris, then back to San Francisco. When she died in 1929, she left $100,000. "to be expended in an appropriate manner for the purpose of adding to the beauty of the city which I have always loved". It was decided to build a memorial to all the city's volunteer firefighters, and a competition selected the designer.

Below: From the pedestrian bridge at **Pier 39** you can see Coit Tower and the Transamerica Pyramid.

Above: The most elegant view is from **Hyde Street** ⊙ at Lombard.

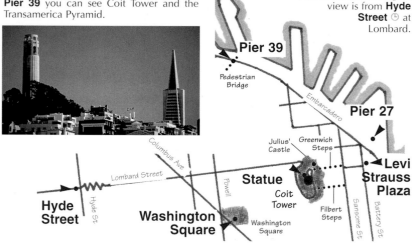

Left: Inside the tower is a fascinating collection of murals. 25 artists painted various scenes of California life in the 1930's. They were funded by a government program to employ artists during the depression. The technique used, called *fresco*, is an ancient art-form where color is applied to wet plaster as it dries.

"City Life" by Victor Arnautoff depicts a robbery in progress. Elsewhere in the picture is a man wearing a fur hat and collar -a self-portrait of the artist.

Right: Coit Tower with **Julius Castle**, a famous Italian restaurant, in the foreground. This view is best in the morning and is taken from **Pier 27** ⊕, northeast of the tower.

Below-Right: The tower is gently lit at night, making for a good dusk shot. The parking lot at **Pier 27** ⓘ makes a good platform for a necessary tripod.

Below-Left: Nearby is **Levis Strauss Plaza** ⓘ, (also called *Pioneer Park*), headquarters of jeans-maker Levi Strauss. The plaza has a lighted waterfall, although it's difficult to squeeze that in the shot.

From Levi Plaza, Greenwich steps leads up to the tower. A more scenic stairway is rustic Filbert Steps on Montgomery Street.Local resident Grace Marchant turned Filbert Steps into a luscious garden with bougainvillaea and rhododendrons.

The concrete tower is something of an optical illusion. To create the effect of a tall tower, while on a limited budget, designer Henry Howard utilized forced perspective. The 210-foot (63m) tower is 18″ (50cm) wider at the base than at the top.

Coit Tower and Washington Square.

"Indescribeably beautiful. It gives you a choky feeling in your throat as you look at it." New York Times

The Beautiful City

After the 1906 earthquake, civic design was propelled by the *City Beautiful* movement, a successful attempt to make San Francisco an attractive city. Their hallmark is the Beaux-Arts style, inspired by classical roman and greek architecture.

The **romantic** Palace of Fine Arts rises like a mirage from it's landscaped lagoon and casts you to some faraway land. It is the city's most unique sight and rightly revered as it's "*most vibrant celebration of the art of architecture*". The fake Roman ruin consists of a main rotunda surrounded by a peristyle of ornate Corinthian columns topped with maidens mourning the loss of art.

Designed for the 1915 Panama-Pacific International Exposition, the neo-classical Palace represents a '*melancholic evocation of vanquished grandeur*'. Visitors were ferried across the lagoon by gondola.

This is the only survivor of the exhibition, the original plaster and wood having been replaced with concrete. The building is just for effect and has no real purpose other than as a frontage to the Exploratorium museum behind.

Where The Palace of Fine Arts is located where the Marina district meets the Presidio, where Lombard Street heads toward the Golden Gate Bridge. Buses 28 and 30. There is a parking area behind and street parking all around.

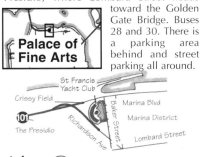

When ⏰ Morning is best as the Palace faces east. Get there early (or late in the afternoon) as the low light enhances the colors of the pillars (at midday it looks washed out). Dusk is a popular time to capture the artificially-lit rotunda.

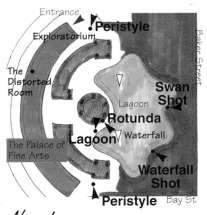

Nearby Behind the Palace is the **Exploratorium**, an interactive science museum fun for kids. Once called the *"finest science museum in the country"* by Scientific American, it feels like an aircraft hangar stocked with 650 hands-on science exhibits. The "Distorted Room" is an optical illusion that, when photographed from the right point, makes the person on the left three times the height of the person on the right. Use your camera's automatic flash and a 28mm lens.

The Exploratorium was founded in 1969 by Frank Oppenheimer, brother of Robert who helped design the atom bomb. There is also a theatre here (☎ 567-6642).

3601 Lyon St. at Marina Blvd. ☎ 415-563-7337. Closed Monday.

East is **Chestnut Street** with it's funky selection of shops, coffee houses and hip restaurants. North is the **Marina Promenade** (where people jog and walk their dogs) offering fine views of the Golden Gate Bridge, windsurfers, and moored yachts.

Beaux Arts

In the early 1900's, eager to show its resurrection from the earthquake, and its supremacy over rivals New York and Los Angeles, San Francisco embraced the romantic, flamboyant architecture of Beaux Arts. Developed in Paris at the 'Ecole de Beaux Arts', this strictly neo-classical style can be seen at the Civic Center, the Ritz-Carlton hotel, and the Spreckels Mansion on Lafayette Park.

The Palace of Fine Arts has been called a "Beaux Arts hallucination" and was designed by Bernard R. Maybeck. Born in New York in 1862, Maybeck studied architecture at the Ecole des Beaux Arts, and moved to Berkeley in 1889. He was a mentor of Julia Morgan, the first woman to graduate from the Ecole, who later designed Hearst Castle.

The Panama-Pacific Exposition

In August 1914, the first ship to sail from the Atlantic to the Pacific without going around Cape Horn made its way through the brand-new Panama Canal. The steaming distance between New York and San Francisco was thus shortened by 7,873 miles, more than enough reason for an official celebration.

The ensuing 1915 Panama-Pacific International Exposition was designed to be the most extravagant world's fair ever held. One visitor described it as "a miniature Constantinople". The fair's impressive pavilions were donated by all the states and by 25 foreign countries and lined a concourse 1 mile (1.6 km) long. Ansel Adams spent almost every one of the 288 days the fair was open exploring and learning from the exhibits. It was here he first learned of the power of photography.

The fair cost $15 million to build but generated enough profits to pay for the building of the Civic Auditorium (still in use) and leave a million-dollar surplus.

Pictured: The late afternoon brings warmth to these shots of the rotunda (top-left) and the peristyle (top-center). Include one or two people for to emphasize the immense scale. The lit rotunda and peaceful lagoon make an excellent dusk shot (top-right). You'll need a tripod and long exposure (3-15 seconds). Most shots use a 24mm or 35mm lens.

The lagoon of the Palace of Fine Arts, from the Rotunda.

O ne-and-a-half miles from Fisherman's Wharf lies the world's most legendary prison. Now empty and desolate, "The Rock" provides a fascinating glimpse into the bleak lives of some of its notorious past inhabitants, such as Al Capone, "Machine Gun" Kelly, and "Birdman" Robert Stroud.

Between 1933-63, the maximum-security prison of Alcatraz was home to an average of 264 criminals, moved here for disobedience at other jails. Each prisoner was kept alone in a 5'x9' (1.5m x 2.7m) cell for between 16 and 23 hours a day. Four out of five of them never received a visitor. No one is known to have escaped.

Alcatraz (the name means 'Pelican' in Spanish, after its earlier residents) was first developed as a military fort. Alongside Fort Point, Fort Spencer and others, the fort protected San Francisco Bay from 1859 to 1907. After a period as a military prison, Alcatraz was converted to its most famous role. Today the island is part of the Golden Gate National Recreation Area.

Where Alcatraz is located in San Francisco Bay, north of the city. Access is only via Red & White Ferries (☎415-546-2700). Ferries leave from Fisherman's Wharf, Pier 41 between 9:30am and 2:45pm. $5.75/3.25, or $9/4.50 with an audio tour (recommended). Additional information is provided at the ranger station on the island (☎415-705-1042). This is one of the most popular tours in San Francisco and the summer ferries are sold out days in advance, so book as early as possible.

When ⏰ Anytime is good although mid-afternoon provides the best light. Much of the tour is indoors so this is a good option for a foggy day.

"You are entitled to food, clothing, shelter, and medical attention. Anything else you get is a privilege."
Alcatraz Prison Rule No. 5.

Clockwise from top-left:

The main **cellblock** is a popular shot. Switch off your flash (it won't reach so deep) and hold the camera steady. Use the flash only for close shots, such as your companions locked in a cell. There are four free-standing blocks of cells. No cell has an outside wall or ceiling.

The **Post Exchange** and Storehouse. A polarizer brings out the deep blue sky.

The **old cells** are photogenic but were not used for maximum-security prisoners.

The **Lighthouse** was built in 1909. From the parade ground you can include the jagged rocks. 50mm. Alcatraz is a barren rock so, to make gardening plots for the prison guards, soil was shipped from Angel Island.

Power Plant
Water Tower
Storehouse
Post Exchange
Old Cells
Exercise Yard
Dock
Cellblock
Giftstore
Lighthouse
Parade Ground
View of City
Alcatraz Island
Ferry

The water tower and exercise yard.

Left: The huge 'Fisherman's Wharf' sign is at Jefferson & Taylor.

Right: Ghiradelli Square is at the west end of Fisherman's Wharf by Beach/Larkin. In 1852, Domenico Ghiradelli made chocolate here which became famous around the world. The factory has moved across the bay to San Leandro and the square with its trademark clock tower is now lined with boutiques. A Ghiradelli store with original chocolate-making is the prime draw.

This classic view marries the mermaid fountain in the red-brick courtyard as a foreground, to the rooftop sign in the background. A daytime photograph is best in the morning, but the scene is also great at dusk.

Nearby

For photographers, there's nothing better than a walk up **Hyde Street** from Jefferson to Lombard. In these six blocks you can capture Fisherman's Wharf, Alcatraz, Cable Cars, crooked Lombard Street and a fine view of Coit Tower.

Many ferry trips leave from Pier 43, including those to Alcatraz, Sausalito, Tiburon, under the Golden Gate Bridge, and to Marine World/Africa USA.

For National Park lovers, don't mis the park store on PIER 39.

From PIER 39 it's a half-mile walk to Pier 29 for a nice view of Coit Tower. Washington Square and Columbus Ave also make good destinations.

When

Since these are mainly street scenes, anytime is fine. The many restaurants and attractions can occupy you for several hours; coupled with a visit to Alcatraz (book ahead) and a walk to Lombard Street, this makes a full 'touristy' day.

Fisherman's Wharf is tourist central for San Francisco. 84% of the city's visitors, 12 millions tourists, flock here annually. Despite being derided as tacky and devoid of local culture, the area boasts many attractions and deserves its popularity.

In the 1880's, fishermen from Sicily and Genoa moved here, at the edge of the Italian district, and built a fishing industry. Small boats still return to the harbor each morning with a catch of fish and crab but tourism is now the main industry.

The Fisherman's Wharf area stretches from the National Maritime Museum, Ghiradelli Square, and The Cannery, down Jefferson Street to PIER 39. Try the famous Dungeness crab (Nov-June) straight from steaming cauldrons or sourdough bread at the many restaurants, enter a submarine or a rigged clipper, or visit the many shops. Children will love the noisy sea lions, the arcades, Venetian Carousel, Laser Maze, Medieval Dungeon, Ripley's Believe It or Not! museum, the Guinness Museum of World Records, and Underwater World.

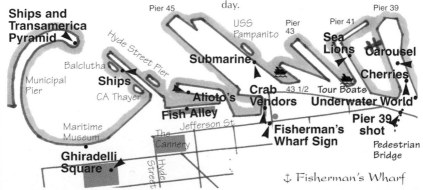

Fisherman's Wharf

Below: The huge **'Fisherman's Wharf' sign** ☼ (left) is at Jefferson & Taylor and makes a great *'we are here!'* shot. Noon, 50mm

Left: Across the street is a small boardwalk packed with **crab vendors** ☼ (below). Lean over the counter, include some crabs in the foreground, and capture the flavor of San Francisco. 28mm. To see the fish being landed, be at **Fish Alley** ☼ at the base of Leavenworth Street, early!

Where Fisherman's Wharf is a one-mile long area in North Beach at the northern edge of the city. The Cable Cars make make a great arrival (Hyde line at Hyde/Beach and the Mason line at Taylor /Bay). Bus 15, 32, 42. There are a few expensive parking areas; street parking is metered.

Underwater World on Pier 39.

Pier 39

Above: The newest and most interesting set of shops is on **Pier 39** ⏰. Redeveloped in 1978, the Pier contains many arcade rides and a large Venetian Carousel. You can view Alcatraz from the end of the pier. The postcard view is from the pedestrian bridge over Jefferson to the parking lot.

Far left: A major development on the Pier is **UnderWater World**, a $40 million aquarium. A moving walkway passes through an acrylic tunnel through an aquarium of leopard sharks, spiny dogfish sharks, and bat rays. (☎415-623-5300). Use a fast film (800 or 1600) and switch off the flash.

Sea Lions

Below: From a mile away you can still hear the noisy **sea lions** ⏰ of K-Dock. In 1990, the seals, most of them male, started wintering here. Now they're a year-round sight (and sound) and have driven the boats away! They can be seen from Pier 39 but a better view is just west, from Pier 41.

Fresh red cherries make a bold foreground. Use a wide angle (28mm), get low, and place the horizon high in the shot.

Above: The actual Fisherman's Wharf is best photographed from the base of Pier 45 near the Fisherman's and Seaman's Chapel. Famous **Alioto's** ⏲ restaurant is in the background. 35mm, afternoon or dusk.

Left: The USS Pampanito is a WWII **submarine** ⏲ (on Pier 45). You can tour through the tiny passageways to the command room and torpedo room. The Pampanito sank six Japanese ships and starred in the 1995 film *'Down Periscope!'*

Below: Street entertainers await your camera.

Maritime Museum

An interesting place to walk around is the **San Francisco Maritime National Historic Park**. The museum is at the foot of Polk Street (☎415-556-8177) but most of the ships have a separate entrance at Hyde Street Pier. 10-5/6 $2/1.

Right and below: The **Balclutha**, at the end of the pier, is a three-masted ship built in Glasgow in 1886. The ship brought coal and whiskey around Cape Horn, from Britain to the growing city of San Francisco, and returned with wheat. Being unstable in the hold, grain was a difficult cargo and only the best shippers could transport it. There's a good shot by walking around Aquatic Park to the end of Municipal Pier, and capturing Coit Tower in the background.

Adjacent is the 1985 *CA Thayer* that brought lumber, then Alaskan salmon, down the northwestern coast, and the sidewheel ferry *Eureka* that took passengers around the Bay from this pier.

During WWII, a huge shipbuilding plant was established across the bay in Sausalito. Over 2,700 Liberty Ships were built, each in less than eight weeks. The last one in working order, the Jeremiah O'Brien, is located south of the Oakland Bay Bridge.

Nearby is **The Cannery**, another redeveloped shopping center. Once the largest peach cannery in the world, the center now houses the Museum of the City of San Francisco (3rd Floor, ☎415-928-0289).

Ahoy shipmates! Aboard the Balclutha, with the Golden Gate Bridge in the background.

Left: You can rent boats on Stow Lake.
Right: Speedway **Meadow**, viewed from near Lloyd Lake. The overhanging tree provides a frame to the shot and the late afternoon sun provides depth with backlighting. Ansel Adams' childhood home was near here. After the 1906 earthquake, the park was home to 300,000 people. In 1967, 14,000 hippies were here for the *"Summer of Love"*.

Golden Gate Park is the largest man-made park, and one of the largest urban parks, in the world. It stretches from the Pacific Ocean to almost half way across the San Francisco peninsula, forming an oasis of greenery and calm in which to escape the hectic city life.

Three miles long and half a mile wide, the 1,000 acres are cleverly divided into a range of features, including an archery range, baseball and softball diamonds, a golf course, four soccer fields, 21 tennis courts, horseshoe pitching, lawn bowling, a stadium and polo field, an equestrian oval, a dog training field, botanical gardens, nine lakes, two major museums, a redwood grove, a waterfall, and two windmills.

Inspired by New York's Central Park, the Golden Gate Park was commissioned in 1866 and built with gold-rush wealth. The area was originally desolate sand dunes and had to be strengthened with cypress, eucalyptus, and pine trees before anything could be planted. Scottish-born John McLaren lovingly cared for the park from 1890 to 1943. He chose plants to provide color all year round.

Where Golden Gate Park is on the west side of San Francisco and is best approached from the city or 101 through Haight-Ashbury down Fell Street (Panhandle). Stop at the McLaren Lodge for visitor information (☎415-666-7200). There are free walking tours and you can rent bikes in Haight-Ashbury at Stanyan Street. Buses 5, 7, 21, 71 from Market St.

When ⏰ Spring and Fall is best; in the Summer the park is often covered in thick fog, particularly in late afternoon. In the morning photograph Japanese Tea Garden, Huntington Falls and the north windmill; in the afternoon photograph Speedway Meadow.

Nearby From the east side you can explore Haight-Ashbury (SE 0.4 mi), the University of San Francisco (NE 0.1mi), St. Ignatius Church (1 block), the Columbarium (N 0.3mi), the University of California at San Francisco (S 0.2mi) and Twin Peaks (SE 1mi). From the west side you can follow the Pacific Coast up to the Cliff House (0.5mi), round to the Legion of Honor (0.8mi) and the Lincoln Park Golf Course (1.1mi). Three miles south is the San Francisco Zoo and Fort Funston, where hang-gliders are launched over the ocean.

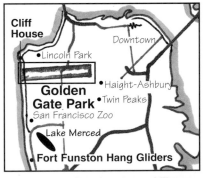

Cliff House
Downtown
• Lincoln Park
Golden Gate Park
• Haight-Ashbury
• Twin Peaks
San Francisco Zoo
Lake Merced
• **Fort Funston Hang Gliders**

Conservatory of Flowers
Dutch Windmill **Japanese Tea Garden**
Ocean Beach
Great Highway
Tulip Garden
Hwy 1
Spreckels Lake Lloyd Lake
Meadow
Stow Lake
Asian Art Museum
Music Conservatory
Strybing
Arboretum
McLaren Lodge
South Windmill
Hoover Redwood Tree & George Washington Grove
Shakespeare Garden
Huntington Falls & Taiwan Pavilion

Top Ten

The Conservatory of Flowers, in the
north-east section of Golden Gate Park.

Conservatory

The **Conservatory of Flowers** (previous page) was modeled after Kew Gardens in England. Designed in 1875 for the San Jose estate of millionaire James Lick, the glass building was shipped in pieces around Cape Horn. However, Lick died before it could be built and the Conservatory was donated to the park.

Currently closed for remodeling, the Conservatory faces south so any clear day is good. This shot is best in the Spring, with the flowers at full. Use a wide setting (35mm) and stand over the flowers so that they fill the bottom of the frame and create a colorful foreground. In the fall, a different foreground is needed, such as the trees.

Stow Lake

The most attractive area of the park is Stow Lake. Tumbling down an island in the lake, Strawberry Hill, is **Huntington Fall** ☺ (top-left). The fall was named after a millionaire benefactor. It faces east and is best photographed in the morning. Nearby is the Golden Gate Pavilion, also facing east. The structure was donated by Taiwan and is also known as the **Taiwan Pavilion** ☺ (top-right). You can rent rowing boats at Stow Lake for a pleasant afternoon (main page).

Music Concourse

The main development in the park is around the Music Concourse. Facing the open-air theatre is the De Young Museum, Asian Art Museum, and the California Academy of Sciences. The Academy, the west's oldest scientific museum, includes the National History Museum (with a simulated earthquake), the Steinhart

Aquarium (with a 180' fish roundabout) and a Gary Larson Gallery. 10-5 or 9-6 summer, ☎415-750-7145. $7/4.

To the right of the Academy, behind the statue of Beethoven, is the quaint **Shakespeare Garden** ☺ (not pictured). Shakespeare's plays and sonnets mentioned many flowers and plants, most of which are planted here. There are quotes in the back wall. The iron and red brick gateway provides a good foreground.

To the left of the Asian Art Museum is the **Japanese Tea Garden** ☺ (bottom-right). The waterfall and pagodas make a good photograph. Built for the 1894 Midwinter Fair, this is a popular spot for a refreshing drink and snack. April is stunning as the cherry blossoms are in full splendor. The Moon Bridge is steeply arched so that it forms a perfect circle with its reflection. Another photogenic subject is the bronze statue of Buddha.

That staple of chinese restaurants, the fortune cookie, was invented here in 1909 by the Japanese gardener Makota Hagiwara. He used them to attract people to the park. Like many Japanese, his family were interned during WWII, when the park was renamed the Oriental Tea Garden. Entrance to the garden is $2.

Windmills

On the west edge of the park are two windmills, built to pump irrigation water from an underground well to the reservoir of Stow Lake. They are no longer in use. The northern one, called the **Dutch Windmill** ☺ (bottom-left), is the most photogenic as it fronted by the Queen Wilhelmina Tulip Garden. In the Spring, co lorful tulips blossom here, all from Holland

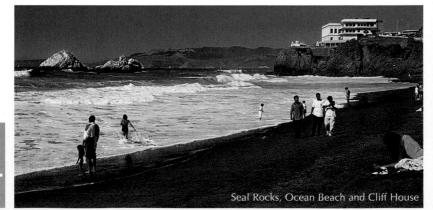

Seal Rocks, Ocean Beach and Cliff House

Huntington Fall, on Strawberry Hill.

Taiwan Pavilion and Stow Lake.

The Dutch Windmill.

The Japanese Tea Garden.

Other

The Rose Window of Grace Cathedral. Built in Chartres, France in 1964, the window is an explosion of color in the morning as the sun shines through it. Zoom tight and use a tripod. Other windows show Albert Finstein and astronaut John Glenn. Inset: City Hall.

PhotoSecrets **San Francisco**

Other Sights

A great signature shot of your trip is a skyline. This sets the scene, establishing location. Look at the cover of this book for example, it just says 'San Francisco'.

The skyline on the cover is the best general view and is taken from the **Marin Headlands**.

The most expansive skyline view is from Twin Peaks, near Haight-Ashbury. This is one hill with two peaks, originally called Los Pechos de la Chola (The Breasts of the Indian Girl). Twin Peaks is a good overview at anytime (sunrise, noon, sunset, at night), as long as it's clear.

The best peak is the northern one (elevation 904'), where you can see straight down Market Street to the Ferry Building. Nearby is Sutro Tower on Mt. Sutro, at 908'.

Best Skylines

1	Marin Headlands	p25
	(view of the Golden Gate Bridge)	
2	Yerba Buena Island	p78
3	Carnelian Room	p44
4	Marriott Hotel	Below
5	Alamo Square	p36
6	Twin Peaks	Above
7	Pier 7	p76
8	Coit Tower	p46
9	Treasure Island	Not shown
10	Hyde & Lombard Sts.	p48
11	Alcatraz	p58
12	East Fort Baker Pier	Above
13	Buena Vista Park	Right

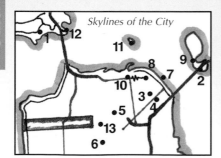

Skylines of the City

Other

Top Ten Rooftop Restaurants

	Rated by height	*floor*
1	Carnelian Room (p45)	52
2	Hilton	46
3	Marriott (this page)	39
4	Grand Hyatt	36
5	Westin St. Francis	32
6	Holiday Inn Union Sq.	30
7	Transamerica Pyramid	27
8	Fairmont	24
9	Sir Francis Drake	21
10	Top of the Mark	19
	(In the Mark Hopkins Hotel)	

Top: Twin Peaks. Six shots produce a wide panorama. *Left:* A fisherman surveys the Transamerica Pyramid and Coit Tower from the East Fort Baker Pier. *Above:* Buena Vista Park has a buena vista, looking southeast. *Below:* The View Lounge in the Marriott Hotel has a beautiful window and spectacular views of the Financial District.

The skyline view from Pier 7, in the rain.

Other

The Shot You Can't Take

Probably the best skyline shot can't currently be taken. This view of the Oakland-Bay Bridge at dusk is taken from **Yerba Buena Island**. However, when we went to press, access was prohibited so we don't recommend going there.

Should the situation change, take the Oakland Bay Bridge towards Oakland but get off half way, on Yerba Buena Island. This is mostly Coast Guard property. There is a small road which crosses above the bridge although no stopping or pedestrian access is allowed.

The same view but without the bridge can be photographed from adjoining Treasure Island (mostly US Navy property).

There is a small parking area on the main access road, by the guard station, with telescopes for viewing.

Arrive before sunset and set up beforehand. You'll need a tripod for a long exposure (1/2 - 10 seconds, depending upon film speed, light level and aperture). Try auto exposure plus one f-stop (+1) overexposure. The best time is 30-40 minutes after sunset, when there is still light in the sky. Winter is better as the office lights are still on (use an FL-D filter).

A similar shot but from under the bridge can be taken from the Oakland-San

Francisco Ferry. This is a 20-minute trip docking at the Ferry Building at the foot of Market Street in San Francisco and Jack London Square in Oakland (☎ 510-522-3300). However, you can only hope that the ferry is at the right place at the right time. The view is also good in the morning so, to avoid the commuters, board in San Francisco and ride to Oakland.

Yerba Buena Island is a natural island. Treasure Island, however, is completely man-made - notice its geometric shape. Like the Golden Gate and Oakland Bay bridges, the Island's construction was funded by the Works Project Administration in the depression.

Treasure Island (named after the Robert Louis Stevenson novel) was the built as the site the 1949 Golden Gate International Exposition. After the Exposition, the island was intended to become an airport, but when that proved infeasible, the Navy moved in. There is a museum at 410 Palm Ave (10-3:30, $3) with the luxury 'Golden-Age of Travel' airplane -the PanAm China Clipper. Some of the buildings have great Art Deco architecture.

The Oakland Bay Bridge may not carry the romance of the Golden Gate Bridge, but it does carry more traffic. At 8.5 miles, it is also five times longer and the second largest bridge in the world.

The Marina district.

Districts

District	Main Attraction
Civic Center	City Hall
Financial District	TrAmerica Pyramid
Haight-Ashbury	Hippie shops
Japantown	Japan Center
Marina	Chestnut Street
Mission	Mission Dolores & Murals
Nob Hill	Hotels & Grace Cathedral
North Beach	Coit Tower
Russian Hill	Lombard Street
SoMa	Moscone Ctr & SFMOMA
Western Addition	Alamo Square

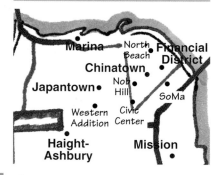

Haight-Ashbury

In 1967, the Haight-Ashbury district became "the vibrant epicenter of America's hippie movement", swelling from 7,000 to 75,000 inhabitants in six months. Embracing peace, love and understanding, and forsaking material possessions for social freedom, the 'junior hipsters' of the 1950's Beat movement became hippies. LSD, originally tested by the Government on volunteers at Stanford University, became popular, as did Jimi Hendrix, The Grateful Dead and Jefferson Airplane at the Summer Of Love. Within a year the movement collapsed but its flames still linger.

The **intersection of Haight and Ashbury Streets** is the symbolic center but, except for the signpost and passing hippies, there's little to photograph. A better shot is **Positively Haight Street**, one block east, at 1157 Masonic Ave.

Haight-Ashbury has many Victorian houses and Buena Vista Park.

Japantown

Near right: The 100' **Peace Pagoda** was gift from Japan in 1968 and is the landmark of **Japantown**. It is on the north side of Geary near Webster. Stand on the south side of Geary, armed with a 50mm lens.

Unfortunately Japantown lacks the color of Chinatown. Most of the second generation Japanese (Nsei) lost their property after being banished to detention camps during WWII and didn't return.

At 1750 Geary Blvd is **Kabuki Hot Spring**, a communal bath house, and **Webster Bridge** (over Webster Street) is a replica of the Ponte Vecchio in Florence.

Other

CHINATOWN

One of the favorite districts for many travelers is Chinatown - one of the largest population centers outside of Asia. Your camera will delight in its 24 blocks of narrow alleys, iron balconies, colorful bunting, hanging roast ducks, and mysterious products. A gentle whiff of incense transports you to another land.

Between 1849-1882, 25,000 Chinese crossed the Pacific to California, lured by the gold mines (10% of miners were Chinese) and the Trans-continental Railroad. Their hard labor made them valued employees but also many enemies. They were banned from towns, driven into isolated districts, and even specially taxed ($20 a month). From 1882 to 1965, Chinese immigration was banned with the "Yellow Peril" 'Exclusion Act'.

Things to Photograph

Below right: The best entrance to Chinatown is the **Chinatown Gate** ① (at Grant/Bush). This was a gift from the Republic of Taiwan and erected by the 'Chinatown Cultural Development Committee' in 1970. The dragons represent fertility and power, the fish prosperity, and the foo dogs scare off evil spirits.

The heart of Chinatown is **Grant Street** (left) ①. A good view looks south to the 'jukebox' Marriott Hotel. Grant Street was the main thoroughfare of Spanish San Francisco (Yerba Buena) in the 1830's; later it was more noted for gambling, prostitution, and opium dens.

The intersection of **Grant and California Streets** (see 'Cable Cars') ① is a great place to capture a combination of Cable Cars and Chinatown. On this corner is the red brick **Old St. Mary's Church** (1854), the West Coast's first Roman Catholic cathedral. The biblical quote on the clock tower, *'Son, observe the time and fly from evil'* was a response to the brothels that used to line the street.

The place to capture a sense of Chinese community is in the four tiny **Chinatown Alleys**, 1/2 a block west of Grant between Sacramento and Jackson. The best are

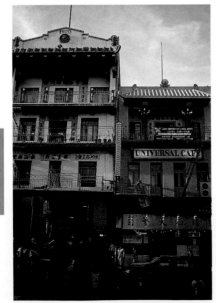

Waverly Place ⏲ (lower left, called *"The Street of Painted Ladies"* for it's colorful balconies) and **Ross Alley** (a popular movie location used in *Big Trouble in Little China*). At 56 Ross Alley (no sign) is a fortune cookie factory where you can watch the little treats being made. Nearby is the attractive Kong Chow and Tin How temples but they do not allow photography.

One block east is the concrete and characterless **Portsmouth Square**. There's not much to photograph (although it's a popular spot for games of Mah Jong and chess) but it was here that the American flag was first raised over the city in 1846. Two years later, newspaper publisher Sam Brannan stood here and announced the discovery of gold in the Sierra foothills.

The Mission district is famed for its more than 200 colorful murals. In a successful effort to beautify the district, the predominantly hispanic community sponsors public works of art painted on walls. These intriguing blends of art and politics are dotted around the area and reward casual exploration. 24th Street, 21st Street, and Balmy Street (between Treat and Harrison at 24th) are the best haunts.

Pick up a self-guided mural map ($2) at the Mexican Museum at Fort Mason (☎415-441-0445). Or take the Mission District Mural Walk (first and third Saturdays of the month, 1:30pm), an organized tour starting at Precita Eyes Mural Center (348 Precita Av, south of Army St., ☎415-285-2287).

This page: Above: "Music and Flowers" at 21st/Mission, by Barry Hazard and Susan Greene © 1991.

Upper right: "Culture contains the seed of resistance which blossoms into the flower of liberation" on Balmy Alley, by Brian Thiele, Mirand Bergman, Gayle Markow, Lori Kinolani © 1984.

Center right: "Friends don't let friends drink and drive", on Folsom/24th, by Ernesto Paul student workshops with RAP and MAS school © 1993.

Below right: "Dream", on Bartlett/21st, by Daniel Galvez © July 1996.

Opposite page clockwise from top-left: Untitled, Mission/21st, by © Juana Alicia 1988.

Cesar Chavez School, near South Van Ness/24th.

Untitled, on Balmy Alley, by Susan Cervarites and Mia Gonzalez © 1991.

Cesar Chavez School, near South Van Ness/24th.

Nearby The **Anchor Steam Brewing Company** gives tours at 2pm (1705 Mariposa St., ☎415-863-8350).

The **Levi Strauss Factory** at 250 Valencia Street, near Duboce, is their oldest and smallest factory, and offers free one-hour tours on Wed at 10:30am and 1pm. (reservations required, ☎415-565-9153). Levi Strauss came to the gold rush initially as a maker of tents, and later made durable trousers for the miners. He used a special material, Serge, from Nimes in France. 'Denim' is a contraction of the French "Serge de Nimes". Strauss founded the company in 1853 with his brother, and it is still family owned.

San Francisco was founded by the Spanish Catholics and the original Mission and Basilica still stand. Other Catholic, Russian Orthodox, Jewish, and Episcopalian places of worship display similarly impressive architecture.

Left: The Russian Orthodox **Holy Virgin Cathedral** (also known as St Mary-the-Virgin-in-Exile), built in 1909, boasts gorgeous golden Byzantine domes. 6210 Geary Blvd/26th, ☎ 415-221-3255. 100mm, taken from the Mayflower Seafood Restaurant.

Right and below: In the heart of of the University of San Francisco lies **St. Ignatius Church**, built in 1914. The view to the right, with the Golden Gate in the background, is from Buena Vista Park.

Not shown: The Jewish **Sherith Israel Synagogue** built in 1904, has a spectacular dome based on sixth century Sancta Sophia in Istanbul, however public photography is not encouraged. On California Street.

Below: The decorative **Mission Dolores Basilica**, was built in 1913. It towers over the adjacent Mission Dolores (next page). Officially called Mission San Francisco de Assisi, it was nicknamed Dolores after a nearby swamp, Laguna de los Dolores (Lake of Our Lady of Sorrows).

The Mission and its Basilica are in the Mission district, at 8203 Dolores St/16th. ☎415-621-8203, 9-4. Entrance is $1.

Other

Clockwise, from top-left:

The Catholic **St. Mary's Cathedral**, built in 1971, is the most stridently modern church in the city. It has been likened to a washing machine and nicknamed '*St. Maytag*'. The 190ft. roof tapers into a stained glass window shaped like a cross. Inside the open floor plan deliberately removes the traditional division between apse, nave and transepts. A good foreground is this bell on the NW corner. Geary Blvd. at Gough St., near the Japan Center.

The adobe **Mission Dolores** was the sixth in the chain of historic Spanish Catholic sanctuaries that linked Baja and Alta California. Founded by Father Junipero Serra in 1791, it is the oldest building in San Francisco. The large building to the right is the Basilica.

The Romanesque **Saints Peter and Paul Church** (1922-37) is the largest Catholic church in San Francisco. Joe DiMaggio and Marilyn Monroe had their wedding photos taken here (but, since they were both divorced, weren't allowed to be married here).

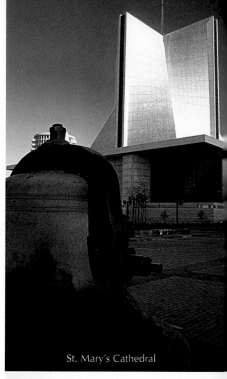

St. Mary's Cathedral

Episcopal Church

The neo-gothic **Grace Cathedral** is based on Notre Dame in Paris. It is the main Episcopal church. Designed in 1914 and not completed until 1964, the cathedral houses several interesting features, including a 1995 Alterpiece by Keith Harding, and stained glass windows depicting Albert Einstein and astronaut John Glenn. (☎ 415-749-6300, tours on the weekends). This shot is taken with a 35mm lens from Taylor Street.

Grace Cathedral stands stridently on Nob Hill at Taylor/California, facing Huntington Park. Nearby is the Pacific Union Club (the fire-surviving mansion of Comstock-millionaire "Bonanza King" James Flood and now a private club), the Fairmont Hotel, Chambourd Apartments, and the Cable Car Barn.

Another view of **Saints Peter and Paul Church**. For a foreground, come in the morning to see the Tai-Chi workout, or at the weekends when local artists display their work.

This castle-like **Episcopal Church** stands at Gough/Bush.

Other

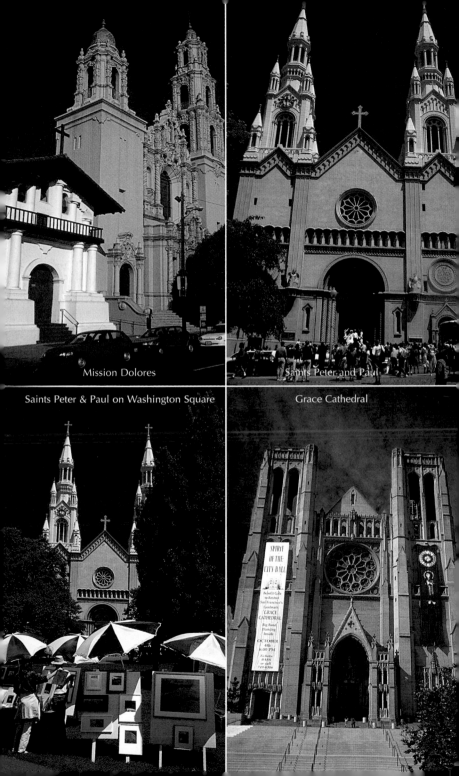

Mission Dolores

Saints Peter and Paul

Saints Peter & Paul on Washington Square

Grace Cathedral

Below: The **Hyatt Regency Hotel** is at the foot of California Street. This shot of the atrium is taken from the 12th floor (24mm). Below is a golden sculpture, *Eclipse*, by Charles Perry.

The films 'The Maltese Falcon' and 'The Conversation' (Hackman/Coppola) were set in the **Westin St. Francis** (on Union Square). The hotel has signed photographs by Ansel Adams in the Compass Room.

Don't miss the 'jukebox' Marriott Hotel (see Architecture - Modern), best viewed from Grant Street in Chinatown and Buena Vista Gardens.

The most famous of San Francisco's hotels are on Nob Hill, the "hill of the palaces" as Robert Louis Stevenson called it. The **Fairmont Hotel** (above, 1906) was built by Julia Morgan (of Hearst Castle fame) and hosted the initial meetings of the United Nations. It has a great porte cochere (for a tip the porters may pose for you) and a fabulously opulent red lobby (24mm). Ride the glass elevator to the city's highest bar, the Crown Room. The **Mark Hopkins Inter-Continental Hotel** (950 Mason St), built in 1923, has good views from its famous "Top of The Mark" cocktail lounge.

"Nob" was slang for a wealthy or influential person, possibly from the hindu Nawab in Colonial India. Nob Hill is the highest hill in the city center (338 ft) and when Cable Cars made it accessible in 1878, the four railroad and two of the four Comstock silver millionaires built ostentatious mansions here. The homes were all destroyed in the 1906 fire.

Other

Above: The **Garden Court of the Sheraton Palace Hotel** (633-56 Market St). Take Afternoon Tea (Lapsang Souchong or Darjeeling? Cucumber sandwiches or scones?) under ten crystal chandeliers and a leaded glass skylight, and surrounded by marble columns and palm trees. The original 1870's Grand Court was an entrance for evening guests in their horsedrawn carriages. Destroyed in the 1906 fire, it was rebuilt in 1909. Afternoon Tea is served from 2-4:30pm, wed-sat. The Ritz-Carlton (600 Stockton St) offers a two-hour tea etiquette class.

Below: The **Red Victorian** is in Haight-Ashbury (1665 Haight St). Each room has a theme, with names like "Redwood Forest" and "Flower Child" and there are four-poster beds with tie-dyed canopies.

The opulent lobby of the
Fairmont Hotel.

SHOPS

The expensive shops of San Francisco surround **Union Square**. Tiffany, Armani, and Chanel are here, so too is FAO Schwartz and the Virgin Superstore. Macy's is so large it requires two buildings.

It's difficult to photograph Union Square as there are no high public view points. This shot is taken through the 3rd floor window of Border's Books, at Powell and Post. The Powell Street Cable Car crosses into the foreground. You can also try the the Rotunda Restaurant in Neiman Marcus, diagonally opposite, and the glass elevators of the Westin St Francis hotel.

Union Square is named after the pro-Union rallies held here during the Civil War.

Below: The **Circle Gallery** is the only Frank Lloyd Wright building in the city. The famous spiral walkway of the Guggenheim Museum in New York was first tried here. 140 Maiden Lane, -east side of Union Sq.

The Shopper's Widow/Widower

Or: *Where To Go When Your Partner Is Shopping.*

• **Union Square** - Check out the skylight in Neiman Marcus (east), or follow the cable cars down Powell Street to the turnaround at Market St. (south). There's a good travel book store on Tillman Place (west), and the building at 450 Sutter Street (north) has a terrific Art Deco lobby.

• **Market Street** - *North:* The Pacific Stock Exchange on Pine at Sansome has a great Art Deco frontage; The Carnelian Room in the Bank of America building (California by Kearny) has great sky-high views; the Embarcadero Center has this 'downtown' view over Battery Street (below); and the Ferry Building is nearby. *South:* Rand McNally's travel store is on Market St.; The Sheraton Palace Hotel has a lovely tea room; SFMOMA and Yerba Buena Gardens are on 3rd by Mission; the Ansel Adams Museum of Photography is nearby at 4th and Howard; and if your camera need some shopping, stop at the Adolph Gasser photographic store at 181 2nd St., near Howard.

Above: City Lights Bookstore was the first all- paperback bookstore in the country and the birthplace of the Beats. Allen Ginsberg's poems were published by store owner Lawrence Ferlinghetti and when the poem 'Howl' was seized by US customs for being 'obscene', the alienated, counterculture movement took off. Drinking coffee, talking poetry, smoking marijuana, and generally dropping out of the mainstream became fashionable, eventually leading to the *'Free Love'* of the 1960's. Jack Kerouac, who had moved here with Ginsberg from New York, wrote *On The Road*. It has been claimed that legendary San Francisco columnist Herb Caen coined the phrase *'Beatnik'* after the then-recently launched Sputnik satellite.

City Lights Bookstore is at 261 Columbus Ave, adjacent to Vesuvio's.

Following pages:
Left: The **Crocker Galleria** has a great skylight, best photographed from the top floor near Post Street. 50 Post Street, ☎415-393-1505, between Sutter/Post and Kearny/Montgomery.

Right: This magnificent stained rotunda glass skylight is at **Neiman Marcus** at 150 Stockton Street (south-east corner of Union Square). It was inherited from the 1909 City of Paris store which used to be here. This shot is taken with a 35mm lens and a tripod helps. Consider an 81C filter to warm up the stonework.

Below: **Mollnari's Deli** (on Columbus in North Beach) overflows with Italian meats, pastas and cheeses. It dates from 1896 (the building, not the cheese).

Also try the **Victoria Pastry Company** (Italian cakes and pastries) at 1362 Stockton Street.

The Crocker Galleria.

The City of Paris rotunda skylight at Neiman Marcus.

Opposite: Clockwise from top left:

Mad Magda's Russian Tea Room is at 579 Hayes Street in Hayes Valley, and has an interior design called "Bedlam at the Kremlin".

The Franciscan Croissant is close to the Chinatown Gate, on Sutter and Grant.

To capture the style and underground culture of San Francisco, head for the city's many Coffee Houses. Chestnut Street in the Marina District (above) and Polk Street on Russian Hill are good hangouts.

Vesuvio's (on Columbus Ave at Broadway) is the most famous, being a popular haunt of the Beats. Jack Kerouac, Allen Ginsberg and Welsh poet Dylan Thomas all sipped here. It's rampant graffiti, bohemian atmosphere and steaming coffee welcome the over-traveled photographer.

Below: The unique **Brainwash Cafe** cleverly combines three student essentials - food, alcohol, and a laundromat. 1122 Folsom Street, between Langton and 7th. Nearby at Folsom/7th is a nightclub with an unusual cow sign (right).

Another old Beat hangout is **Caffe Trieste** on Grant/Vallejo.

Other well-known coffee houses include **Spec's** (12 Adler St.) and **Museum Cafe** (12 Sarayan St).

Other

S ome people like to *eat* at restaurants, but you and I know they're really meant for *photography*. The best viewing time is at dusk, when the lights are on but there's still some natural light in the sky.

Above: **Fog City Diner** has the best display of neon. It starred in a famous Visa® commercial. Use a tripod and a long exposure (4s and a 50mm lens). On Battery Street near the Embarcadero.

Below: The cluby **Tadich Grill** is often called the city's oldest restaurant. There has been a restaurant in this building since 1920; the Tadich Grill moved here in 1965.

Right: San Francisco is a hotbed of new restaurant concepts, the best being **World Wrapps**. Leading the Wrapps-craze, they serve international gourmet food in a tortilla. This one is at Polk, between Green/Vallejo.

Below: **Mels Drive-In Diner** on Geary/Beaumont (there's another on Lombard Street) has a great neon 1950's frontage. The **Stinking Rose** on Columbus serves garlic within sight of the Transamerica Pyramid. The **Carnelian Room** in the Bank of America Building (555 California Street) offers a spectacular view through it's 52nd floor windows.

Julius' Castle (more like *'Julius' Large Wooden Shack'*) is a popular Italian restaurant and provides a good foreground to Coit Tower. Shoot from Pier 29 (see page 49) or Greenwich St near Battery Street. The obligatory Hard Rock Cafe is on Van Ness Avenue at Sacramento Street.

Other

discovered in 1848, the city grew to a major international port, mainly in the Financial District around Market Street and today's Ferry Building. The Victorian Houses (see 'Alamo Square') are the chief jewels of this period. After the 1906 earthquake, a fire spread through the Victorian city, razing most buildings east of Van Ness, including Nob Hill and the Financial district. To rebuild the city, the citizens chose stone instead of wood, and adopted a flamboyant mix of greek and roman classicism.

Left and below: An original bronze cast of Rodin's is in the courtyard of the **California Palace of The Legion of Honor.** The Legion of Honor is a neo-classical museum modeled after its namesake in Paris. It was commissioned by Alma Sutro (wife of Adolph), a francophile. The recently renovated museum displays an eclectic mix of ancient and European art, and the parking area offers distant views of the city. In Lincoln Park, near 34th Ave and Clement St. (☎415-863-3330)

Right: The **Hobart Building** (582-92 Market St) has an unusual design, a square building with ornate oval ends. It was designed by San Francisco's most famous architect, Willis Polk.135mm from SW corner of New Montgomery and Market, next to the Sheraton Palace Hotel.

There's a lot of think about with San Francisco's architecture. The Bay was first explored by europeans in 1769 and the Spaniards soon built a fort (the Presidio) and Mission. Only the Mission remains from this time. After gold was

Other

City Hall (1913-15) is considered one of the most beautiful public buildings in the country, and is a fine example of French Renaissance Revival architecture. The gold dome, taller than that of the US Capitol, was modeled after St. Peter's Basilica in Vatican City. The design was picked by competition and it is said that the winning architects, Arthur Brown and John Bidwell, only submitted such a grandiose design as they thought they would never win.

The Van Ness side has statues representing Wisdom, Arts, Learning, Truth, Industry and Labor, while the Polk Street side has images of Commerce, Navigation, Californian Wealth and the city of San Francisco. The lobby, entered from Polk Street, makes a spectacular indoor shot but it is currently closed for an earthquake retrofit.

The classic view is photographed in the afternoon from Franklin and Fulton, between the Veterans Building (on the left; where the UN charter was signed) and the Opera House.

City Hall is the crown jewel of the Civic Center, a 14 city block area between Van Ness Avenue and Market Street. The Louise M. Davies Symphony Hall (Van Ness/Hayes) and the new Main Library (Larkin and Grove) are also attractive buildings.

Other

Above: Built in 1898, the **Ferry Building** is the oldest landmark of San Francisco. The famous clock tower was modeled after the Giralda Tower in Spain. At it's height, 200,000 people commuted by ferry each day. Now that the Oakland Bay Bridge exists, most ferries run to Sausalito and Larkspur.

The Ferry Building is at the foot of Market St on the Embarcadero. You can best photograph it on Market Street near the intersection of California Street (above left) and from the end of Pier 7 (above right).

Left: The Marina district may have many beautiful apartments, but none are as stylish as the 1921 Beaux-Arts **Chambourd Apartments** on Nob Hill (at 1298 Sacramento St, near Grace Cathedral).

Right: This is a detail from the **Spreckels Mansion** on Lafayette Park. Stand on Octavia Street, just north of Washington, and catch the late afternoon light. 100mm. Note that there is another Spreckels Mansion of differing design in Haight-Ashbury.

A good indoor shot can be taken at the Columbarium, a crematorium near the University of San Francisco. This is a Neo-Classical domed rotunda, brightly lit through stained-glass windows. In total there are 30,000 niches - places for urns of cremated ashes.

ARCHITECTURE MODERN

Above: This beautiful staircase in the **Embarcedero Center** looks like a flower from above. The Embarcadero Center, a "city within a city", fills three city blocks with 45 restaurants and 4 office towers. The staircase is at section 3EC, and this view is from the top floor with a 28mm lens.

Right: The entrance to the **Federal Reserve Building**, on Market Street.

Below: The **Vaillancourt Fountain** is in Justin Herman Plaza, on Drum and Market Streets, near the Embarcadero and the Ferry Building. It has been dubbed *"Aqueduct meets ventilation duct".*

Other

The glass palace **Marriott Hotel** was built in 1989 and has been likened to a jukebox. This view is from the top of a parking lot on O'Farrell, near Union Square.

Dusk is the best time for evocative shots of well-lit buildings. There is a very short window of time that is best for photography - 30 to 40 minutes after sunset. In this brief moment, the sky has some light for color but is dark enough to allow exposure of the building's exterior and interior lights. Plan your spot during the day and get set up in advance. There are only a few critical minutes to take a good dusk shot - after that the sky will appear black.

SFMOMA

The most impressive and attractive example of modern architecture in the city is, fittingly enough, **SFMOMA - the San Francisco Museum of Modern Art**. Unveiled in 1995, this bold $60M building designed by swiss architect Mario Botta, is photogenic from many angles. The main feature is a huge cylinder over the atrium with a diagonally-cut skylight.

SFMOMA is the second largest modern art museum in the US with more than 15,000 works from artists such as Jackson Pollock, Mark Rothko and Paul Klee. The fourth floor is devoted to photography with 9,000 photographs by Ansel Adams, Man Ray and others. Changing exhibits and a multi-media area make this a fascinating visual experience.

SFMOMA is in SoMa (South of Market Street), at 151 3rd St. Open Tue-Sun (closed Wed), 11-6, $7/$3.50, ☎415-357-4000. You can photograph the building but not the works. The Museum Store has a great gifts.

Above: This shot is taken from inside the museum, standing on the main stairway's balcony and looking down. Looking up you can take a picture of the main skylight (next page).

Left: The best place to photograph SFMOMA is from the adjacent **Yerba Buena Gardens** (part of the Moscone Center). This five-acre urban oasis (also called *Esplanade Gardens*) provides a myriad of photo opportunities and is a relaxing retreat from the city. This shot is taken from the plaza by the Center for the Arts, on Third Street. Behind SFMOMA is the Pacific Telephone and Telegraph Building. Use a telephoto lens and zoom right in for impact.

Right: The main feature of Yerba Buena Gardens is a sheer waterfall which makes a great foreground to SFMOMA behind. Stand on the balcony on the west stairway and get close to the falling water. Under the fall is a memorial to Martin Luther King displaying several of his quotes.

Next page left: Near the Center for the Arts Galleries is this classic juxtaposition of old and new. Through some artistically positioned rocks you can capture the traditional 1872 St. Patrick's Church and the modern 1989 Marriott Hotel.

Across Howard Street, the Moscone Convention Center (named after the late mayor George Moscone) includes a children's garden and an ice rink. At Fourth and Clementina is the **Ansel Adams Center for Photography**. The Center displays many of the masters works and changing exhibits by other inspiring photographers. (250 4th St., between Howard and Folsom, Tue-Sun, $4, ☎415-495-7000)

Other

The **San Francisco Museum of Modern Art** (SFMOMA) framed by the **Martin Luther King Waterfall.**

"No. No, we are not satisfied, and we will not be satisfied until justice rolls down like water and righteousness like a mighty stream" *Martin Luther King, Jr. Washington DC 1963.*

The Marriott Hotel and
St. Patricks Church, from
Yerba Buena Gardens.
Right: The San Francisco
Museum of Modern Art.

Muir Woods and (inset) the Sonoma Coast.

PhotoSecrets **Northern California**

Going North

Right: Three miles from the Golden Gate Bridge, guarding the entrance to San Francisco Bay, is **Point Bonita Lighthouse** ⏰. Barraged by winter storms and enveloped in summer fog, it was never a pleasant location and many lighthouse keepers resigned or went crazy. You'll need a rare clear day for a photograph. The lighthouse can be visited via a trail, tunnel and a 180' steel suspension bridge. This shot is taken from the parking and viewing area just north.

Southern Marin County

San Rafael
East Brother Lighthouse
Larkspur
Mt Tamalpais
101
580
Mill Valley
Muir Woods
1
Golden Gate National Recreation Area
Tiburon
Angel Island
Sausalito
Ferry
Point Bonita Lighthouse
Golden Gate Bridge

Marin County, immediately north of San Francisco, is one of the most desirable places to live in the Bay Area. With towns such as Larkspur, Mill Valley, Sausalito and Tiburon, Marin is home to many well-known Bay Area artists and entrepreneurs. But it's Marin's unspoiled landscape that is the main attraction. From the moment you cross the Golden Gate Bridge, most of the next 40 miles of coastline is wilderness protected as the Golden Gate National Recreation Area and Point Reyes National Seashore.

The southern Marin Headlands at Kirby Cove provide some of the best views of the Golden Gate Bridge, including our cover shot. See *Golden Gate Bridge.*

Right and previous page: The pride of Marin County is **Muir Woods** ⊕, the nearest natural grove of Redwoods to San Francisco. While not as impressive as Big Basin (south) or the Avenue of the Giants (north), it has a pleasant and free 2-mile walk. The woods were named after naturalist John Muir who helped establish the national park system. Open 8am-sunset, (☎415-388-2595).

Above: At 2571 ft, **Mount Tamalpais** ⏰ (above) is the highest point in the area and, on a fogless day, offers a 360 degree view including most of San Francisco Bay. Called "The Sleeping Maiden" for its curving landscape, this was the proving ground for the mountain bike, developed at Fairfax. Nearby at Muir Beach is the Pelican Inn, a favorite British Pub.

North

"Tiburon: Free of Vices and Vampires." An old advertising slogan encouraging San Franciscans to move across the Bay.

Left: Tiburon's commuters can walk off the **ferry dock** straight into restaurants. ☉

Sausalito (Spanish for "little willow") is a charming, affluent, Mediterranean-like waterfront town with a main street (**Bridgeway Blvd**) lined with boutiques, galleries and restaurants. If you're trapped in the cold summer fog of San Francisco, drive or take the ferry (from Pier 43 1/2) into the warm sunshine of Sausalito which is protected by the coastal hills. The town came to prominence as a port for lumber, brought from the northwest by steam train, and in WWII became a massive shipyard, building tankers and Liberty Ships. Little remains of either industry but there's a display museum (and tourist information ☎415-332-0505) at 777 Bridgeway.

One mile north is the mildly interesting **Army Corps of Engineer's Bay Model** (2100 Bridgeway, ☎415-332-3871, 9-4, Tue-Sat/Sun), a two-acre scale model of San Francisco Bay used to study tidal patterns. On the way you'll pass an area of numerous residential houseboats, called **'Ark Row'**.

Tiburon (Spanish for 'Shark'), across Richardson Bay, is another affluent seaport village, with less boutiques but as many restaurants as Sausalito. The heart of Tiburon is narrow Main Street and the dockside restaurants near the commuter ferry dock (above). The ferries, from Fisherman's Wharf (Pier 43 1/2) and the Ferry Building in San Francisco, are an excellent way to reach Sausalito and Tiburon (30 mins, about $5).

Nearby Reached by ferry from Tiburon, **Angel Island** is a protected State Park good for hiking & biking.

Across the San Pablo Strait, near Richmond, is the **East Brother Light Station**. Built in 1873, this is now a romantic B&B ($295 per couple, ☎415-233-2385).

The county capital of San Rafael has the expansive and futuristic **Marin County Civic Center**. Interesting to see but almost impossible to photograph, this is the most memorable of the 25 buildings Frank Lloyd Wright designed for California. Further north in Lucas Valley, at 5858 Lucas Valley Road, is Skywalker Ranch, where George Lucas is busily developing the next set of *Star Wars* films. Seven miles NW is **Nicasio**, a small town (complete with church and post office) based around a baseball diamond.

Above: Sausalito's **Plaza de Vina Del Mar Park** on Bridgeway Blvd has an attractive palm-flanked fountain. This view is from the stairs opposite.

Below left: Coastguard houses in **East Fort Baker**. The adjacent **Bay Area Discovery Museum** (☎415-332-7674) is popular with children. Nearby are several photo opportunities around **Horseshoe Cove** and the Presidio Yacht Club. **Battery Yates** overlooks Alcatraz and San Francisco.

Above: In Tiburon, one mile north from the dock and perched on a hill, is **Old St. Hilary's Church** ◷. A polarizer filter provides the deep blue sky, contrasting the stark white building. The surrounding area is a wildflower preserve.

Below: Sausalito's **Bridgeway Blvd** ◷ is lined with shops and has a relaxing view of the Bay. Always look for a high vantage point for such a shot, this one is taken from a 2nd floor restaurant window.

Left: This fence straddles the San Andreas fault. During the 1906 earthquake, the west half moved 16 feet north, separating it from the east half. A local myth says that a cow was swallowed by the fault. The fence is along **The Earthquake Trail** ☻, at the Point Reyes Visitor Center off Bear Valley Rd, 1 mile north of Olema (☎415-663-1092).

Right: **Point Reyes Lighthouse** ☺ is a short 16-sided iron tower, reached by 308 stairs. Getting back is like ascending a 31-story building. Built in 1870, the lighthouse is open Thu-Mon, 10-4:30.

Point Reyes is the windiest place in North America and the trees on the approach road grow diagonally. It is also the second most foggy place in the US, making a clear photograph a rare possibility.

The lighthouse is 21 miles from the Visitor Center near Olema. Jutting so far out into the Pacific Ocean, Point Reyes is the best place for whale watching (Dec-Feb). The rocks here are covered in red patches from an algae called "rock violet".

North

Point Reyes is the largest peninsular on the northern California coast. It is home to the Point Reyes National Seashore, a large wilderness area popular for hiking. The San Andreas fault runs into the ocean here (passing through Tomales Bay) and Point Reyes is gradually moving northwest at 2″ per year. It used to be part of Los Angeles and is on its way to Alaska.

The first European visitor to California, the English adventurer Sir Francis Drake, landed near here in 1579. His log records anchoring his ship the *Golden Hind* (he left England with five ships and lost four) just north of the bay for 36 days of repairs. Drake, in the service of Queen Elizabeth I, named the land Nova Albion (New England) and may have left a brass plaque.

Drake's Estero is a good haunt for landscape photographers, particularly at dawn or dusk. Sculntured Beach and Arch Rock make good hiking destinations

There are two waterfalls in California that empty onto a beach - McWay Cove Fall in Big Sur and **Alamere Falls** on Point Reyes National Seashore. The 50 ft falls can be reached on a 8.4 mile hike from Palomarin, near the Bird Observatory north of Bolinas.

Below:
Tomales Bay

Point Reyes Lighthouse

Map labels:
Tomales Bay
Tomales Bay
Abbotts Lagoon
Point Reyes Beach
Point Reyes National Seashore
Drake's Estero
Pt. Reyes Station
Olema
Drake Monument
Sculptured Beach
Earthquake Trail
Sea Lion Overlook
Arch Rock
Drake's Bay
Alamere Falls
Bird Observatory
Bolinas
1

Tip Placing the lighthouse in the corner, rather than the center, of the frame emphasizes its long stairway and thus remoteness. The stairs become a 'leading line', sweeping the eye into the picture.

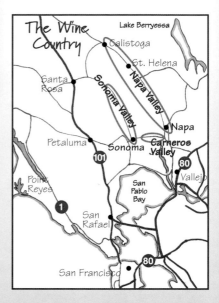

"Such a place as I would like to live and die." George Yount, 1831.

One of the most fun and romantic places to spend a San Francisco weekend is in the Wine Country. Less than an hours drive from the city are the towns of Napa and Sonoma, gateways to their famous parallel valleys. Napa Valley is the longest (25 miles long) and has the most wineries. The 'big' names like Mondavi are here offering extensive tours. Shorter Sonoma Valley (11 miles long) is a more charming, family-run affair.

Where The Wine Country is 55 miles (1 hour and 20 mins) from San Francisco. There are one-day bus tours (ask at your hotel or Fisherman's Wharf) but a weekend tour by car is better. Visitor information is just before you enter Sonoma.

When The best photography is in the Spring, with blooming wildflowers and roses and bright yellow mustard, or in the Fall (Sept/Oct - the 'Crush') when the grapes are their fullest and being harvested. Summer weekends are hot and busy (try to come during the week) and in the Winter the vines are pruned back for the next year.

Most wineries generally face the north-south main roads, so that the ones west of the road (Beringer, Mondavi) are best in early morning, and the ones east (V. Sattui) are best in the late afternoon.

North

Below and right: Visual art abounds in the Wine Country. **Clos Pegase** (right) has striking shapes and colors. Don't miss the

Hess Winery (left) with its wonderful museum of modern art - **The Hess Collection** ⊕. You can't photograph the works here but the huge painting *Johanna II* by Frantz Gertsch is stunning. 10-4, 4411 Redwood Rd, Napa.

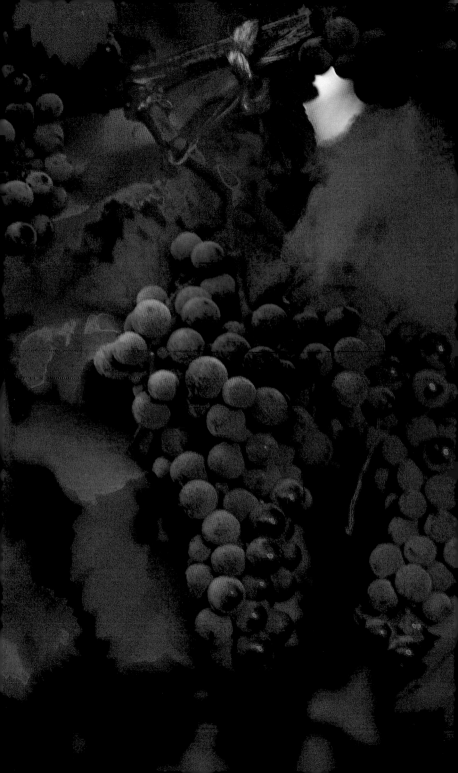

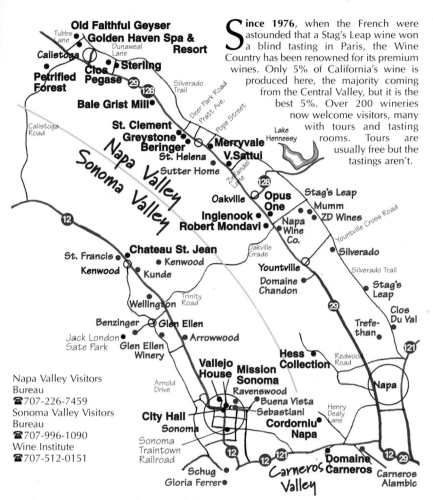

Since 1976, when the French were astounded that a Stag's Leap wine won a blind tasting in Paris, the Wine Country has been renowned for its premium wines. Only 5% of California's wine is produced here, the majority coming from the Central Valley, but it is the best 5%. Over 200 wineries now welcome visitors, many with tours and tasting rooms. Tours are usually free but the tastings aren't.

Napa Valley Visitors Bureau
☎707-226-7459
Sonoma Valley Visitors Bureau
☎707-996-1090
Wine Institute
☎707-512-0151

Left: The most spectacular winery is the Louis XV style chateau of **Domain Carneros** ⏲. Built in 1988 and partly owned by the French champagne maker Tattinger, the building is modeled after the Tattinger's family home, the *Chateau de la Marguetterie* in Champagne, France.

Domain Carneros is not in Napa nor Sonoma Valley but in the small Carneros Valley which connects the two. It is easily found on Route 12/121 at 1240 Duhig Road. Their premium sparkling wine can be tasted 10:30-6pm (☎707-257-0101).

Nearby is the **Carneros Alambic Distillery**, the only brandy distillery in US, where you can get drunk in the aging room just by breathing the aroma.

Tip Use a long lens (210mm) to 'contract' the image, bringing the background closer to the foreground and making the chateau more significant.

✖ Short lens, 35mm. Chateau is small.

✔ Long lens, 210mm. Chateau becomes more prominent.

North

Sonoma is the entry point for most visitors. This small city is centered around a beautiful plaza, in the middle of which is **Sonoma City Hall** ⏰ (above). The building has identical sides because all the local businesses that funded it wanted to face the front.

The Visitor Bureau, on the east entrance of City Hall, has maps and a walking tour brochure. The nearest winery is Sebastiani Vineyard, a short walk east from the plaza. There are about 32 wineries in Sonoma Valley and 100 in Sonoma County. Highway 12 is the main route but Arnold Drive is quieter and less congested.

On the NE corner of the plaza, near the Mission, is a small monument celebrating the Bear Flag Revolt which occurred here. At dawn of June 14, 1846, thirty men arrived from the Sacramento Valley, overtook the Mexican Presidio, and claimed California an independent Republic. A flag was made using a picture of a bear. A month later, in the Mexican-American War, the US captured the Mexican capital of Monterey and, on hearing the news, the republic chose to join the United States.

At the northern end of Sonoma Valley is **Santa Rosa**. Look for an unusual building in Julliard Park (Sonoma Ave/Santa Rosa Ave). The **Church of One Tree** was built from a single redwood tree and was painted bright red. It houses Robert Ripley's 'Believe It or Not!' museum, a collection of strange oddities from around the world (10:30-3:30, $1.50/75c). Ripley's column is still syndicated, even though he died in 1949.

Another famous cartoonist resident is Charles Schultz, the creator of Snoopy. His gallery is at 1667 W Steele Lane, two miles north of the town center, off Hwy 101. Open 10-6.

"The Valley of the Moon." Named by resident author Jack London (1876-1916). This was also the title of his 1913 novel.

Top right: On the north-east corner of the plaza is **Sonoma Mission** (*San Francisco Solano de Sonoma*). This was the last and most northern of the 21 missions built by the Spanish. During its construction, Mexico took control of California, ending 300 years of Mission history.

The original mission fell into disrepair after secularization in 1834, and this replacement was built in 1840 by General Vallejo as a church for his soldiers. 10-5, $2/$1.

Top left: Chateau St Jean ⏰ has beautiful grounds and a grape-laden fountain. The tower behind has an observation deck. Tastings are offered 10-4:30.

South of here is **Benziger Winery**, with a good tram tour and a free open-air museum demonstrating the techniques of wine growing.

Just up the road is the remains of **Wolf House**, the magnificent mansion that author Jack London had built. It mysteriously burnt down a few days after completion and only the foundations are left.

Near right: A gothic winery near Chateau St Jean.

Right: On the northwest edge of town is General Mariano G **Vallejo's house** ⊕, a rural New England Gothic built in 1851. It is called "Lachryma Monits", latin for "Tears of the Mountain", after the nearby hillside springs. General Vallejo was the Mexican commander during the Bear Flag Revolt but he supported the change of nationality and became one of the first state senators.

Vallejo persuaded a Hungarian, Agoston Haraszthy, to tour Europe in search of vine cuttings and start a winery in Sonoma. There had been vineyards in Los Angeles since the 1830's but it was Haraszthy's cuttings that raised the quality and he is known as "the father of California wines". His last trip was to Nicaragua where he was unfortunately eaten by an alligator.

Haraszathy's winery, Buena Vista, lies on the east side of town and still has great wine.

Napa Valley has the greatest number and variety of wineries. Highway 29 is the main access route although the Silverado Trail just east is quieter.

The town of Napa has little of interest (except the Robert Louis Stevenson Silverado Museum at 1490 Library Lane) so head straight for the hills. More interesting towns are Yountville (quaint), St. Helena (with 1870's building) and Calistoga (with spas and mud baths).

Above: The best place for a picnic is **V Sattui** ⏲. They have large gourmet deli, with over 200 cheeses, and in the summer a barbeque. ☎707-963-7774.

Below: clockwise from top left:
A church near the Hess Winery; Looking like a flying saucer buried in the vineyards, **Opus One** ⏲ is opposite Robert Mondavi; **St Clement Vineyards** ⏲, just north of Beringer; The **Culinary Institute of America** ⏲ and Greystone Restaurant was

North

formerly the Christian Brothers winery. It was originally built as the Greystone Winery by W.B. Bourn Jr, inheritor of the rich Empire Mine near Grass Valley.

Above: Napa's best known wine comes from **Robert Mondavi** ⏱. Robert Mondavi was the first to uncork science and technology and pour it into winemaking. The main building is in the adobe Mission-style and there is an extensive tour.

Below: You can't find a better 'haunted house' than the gothic mansion of **Beringer** ⏱. Built in 1883, the house was inspired by the German home of brothers Frederick and Joseph Beringer. This is the oldest continuously operating winery in the valley and is now owned by Nestlé. Good tour.

Next page: **Merryvale Winery** ⏱ is housed in a large, windowless brick building but contains this spectacular dining area. This shot was handheld but bringing a tripod would be smarter.

Merryvale Winery

Above: This strikingly modern architecture belongs to **Clos Pegase** ⊙. The main column (right) provides good fodder for photographers.

The San Francisco Museum of Modern Art held a competition to design the winery. It was won by this 1987 design from Michael Graves, an architect now famous for his work for Walt Disney Company.

Below: The 'Most Unique Entrance' award is won by **Sterling Vineyards** ⊕. The white stucco monastery-like building sits atop a 300' hill and is linked to the parking area by an aerial tramway. It's recommended to be seen *"veiled in morning fog, starkly white against storm clouds, or pale rose at sunset"*.

Sterling is adjacent to Clos Pegase at 1111 Dunaweal Lane, 1mi S of Calistoga. ($6, 10:30am-4:30pm, ☎707-942-3359).

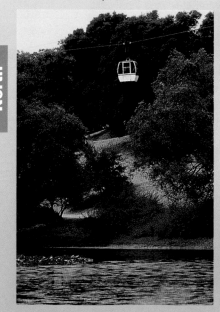

Below: The **Bale Grist Mill** ⊕ is a preserved water-powered mill. It was used to turn grain into flour, and was built in 1846 for Dr. Edward Turner Bale. There is a park and picnic area here.

This photograph is taken from the base, near Highway 29.

Above: The **Petrified Forest** ⏱ is an odd area full of redwood trees made naturally into stone ('petrified'). The size of the trees and the variety of petrification makes it unique in the world.

Three million years ago, redwood trees were blown over by a volcanic blast and buried with volcanic ash. Water seeped down, bringing silica from the mineral-rich ash. As each wood cell decomposed, it was replaced with an identical cell of crystallized silica until an identical stone tree was made. the tree became stone. Even insects were turned to stone. Discovered in 1870, more trees are still being unearthed.

4100 Petrified Forest Rd, W of 128 1 1/2 N of Calistoga (1-6, $3/1).

Above right: The **Old Faithful Geyser of California** is one of only three truly 'faithful' geysers in the world that erupt on a regular basis. The geyser shoots a 60 ft plume every 40-50 minutes. Water from an underground river runs over hot magma, superheats, then explodes through a narrow hole. The height, interval, and duration all depend on the weather, the moon, and the earth's tectonic movement, making the geyser a good predictor of earthquakes. If the interval between eruptions gets very long, get very worried!

1299 Tubbs Lane, Calistoga. It's the area walled off by thick bamboo shoots and plumed pampas grass. (9-5/6, $5/2, ☎707-942-6463).

Right: The **Golden Haven Spa and Resort** ⏱ (1713 Lake St Calistoga 9-9).

In 1859, millionaire publisher Samuel Brannan developed this area as the Saratoga (a New York spa town) of California. **Calistoga** has since been known for its hot-water mineral spas. Take a mud bath, then rest that weary shutter-release finger in the soothing waters.

Owning San Francisco's newspaper in 1849, Sam Brannan reputedly delayed publishing the news that gold had been discovered until he had bought all the mining equipment in the area and could mark it up 100%. Calistoga, however, wasn't such a success and he died penniless.

Nearby is huge Lake Berryessa, good for hiking and boating.

SONOMA COAST

Left: One mile north of Bodega Bay is a postcard shot of the **Sonoma Coast** 🕐. This is a popular surfing spot.

Center: The inland route of 101 is faster but far less scenic than the coast road. Stop off at Cloverdale, however, for the **Cloverdale United Church** 🕑, almost entirely covered in Ivy.

Below: **Bodega** 🕑, five miles east of Bodega Bay, was the setting for Alfred Hitchcock's 1962 film, 'The Birds'. The famous schoolhouse, built in 1873, is now a private home.

North

FORT ROSS

"The hope of extending the sea-otter business was the principal motive for the foundation of a factory in California."
Capt. Lt. Frederick Lutke, c.1829.

Right: Overlooking the Pacific, **Fort Ross** ⏲ was a well-defended Russian Fort. A 300 ft quadrangle, enclosed by a redwood wall, contains several buildings including this Russian Orthodox chapel.

Fort Ross is a preserved Russian stockade (Ross is an archaic named for Russia). For thirty years, the Russians operated a fur trapping empire from Alaska to Fort Ross, supplying Russian and Chinese markets. This was their southernmost base on now-American soil.

In 1790, the fur of a sea otter (the thickest fur of any mammal) could fetch $100 in China - a year's income for a Pennsylvania farmer. The Russian influence grew through Alaska where they used the native Aleut Indians to catch the relaxed animals. In 1812, 25 Russians along with 80 Aleuts established this outpost, on the edge of Spanish territory. With a good view of the ocean and formidable defenses, the Spanish considered the Fort impregnable.

Within 16 years however, the aggressive hunting by Russians, British and Americans had reduced the defenseless sea otter herds to near extinction (the Spanish had laws prohibiting them from catching fur bearing animals). A change to agriculture and logging wasn't successful and the loss-making fort had to be abandoned. In 1841, everything (livestock, hardware, furnishings and building materials) was sold for $30,000 to John Sutter for his pioneer fort in Sacramento. Today's Fort Ross is a reconstruction.

The sea-otter is now making a gradual comeback and otters and whales can occasionally be seen around the cove.

When ⏲
The most distinctive building is the chapel which faces west, so mid-afternoon is the best time. Open 10-4:30, $5 per vehicle.

Where
Fort Ross is 8 miles north of Jenner, near Santa Rosa and Point Reyes. ☎707-847-3286.

Point Arena.
Mendocino 60 miles

Fort Ross

Kruse Ranch Road

Kruse Rhododendron State Reserve

Fort Ross State Historic Park

Jenner

116

Scenic Road to Santa Rosa 42 miles

San Francisco 70 miles

Bodega Bay

Bodega

Tip
The classic view (right) uses one of the cannons for a powerful foreground and contrast of war and peace. Walk up to the second cannon from the right, get close (about two feet) and align the chapel above the cannon. Use a wide angle (35mm) for impact and 'overflow' the bottom of the frame.

This is a popular place for school-children to dress in period costume (above left), making for a good foreground.

Nearby
Ten miles north of Fort Ross is **Kruse Rhododendron State Reserve** ⏲. Years ago a fire swept through this small redwood-lined canyon, allowing 317-acres of sun-loving Rhododendrons to flourish. The pink blooms are best seen in April, May and June.

From Hwy 1, near milepost 43, take Kruse Ranch Rd east. (☎ 707-847-3221)

North

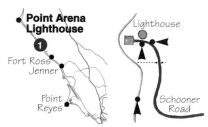

Point Arena Lighthouse is the tallest lighthouse on the west coast. It was featured in the closing scenes of *Forever Young* with Mel Gibson. A private group maintains the elegant lighthouse and makes it a joy to tour. They provide free daily tours (donation requested) and rent nearby vacation homes.

The original lighthouse was built in 1870 but was irreparably damaged in the 1906 earthquake. The company chosen to replace it had more experience building factory smokestacks, hence the tubular design.

The top is crowned with a magnificent first-order Fresnel lens, over six feet in diameter. It contains 666 individual prisms, all hand-polished, which had to be shipped from France around the treacherous Cape Horn. The design is so exact that a single flame could be seen almost to the horizon, about 25 miles away. Each prism had to be cleaned every day. The lens weighs over two tons and floats in a tub of mercury. It rotated via a descending weight, which had to be hand cranked every four hours.

The Lighthouse is three miles south of Point Arena (the nearest part of mainland US to Hawaii), on Schooner Road.

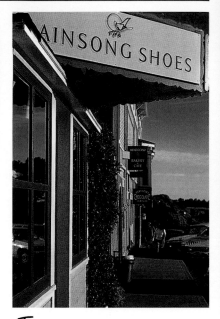

Mendocino is a small bohemian coastal town, a mini-Monterey. It was the setting for *East of Eden* (with James Dean, from the John Steinbeck novel) and *Murder, She Wrote* (this is Cabot Cove!).

The most distinctive building is the **Presbyterian Church** ☺ (below), one of the oldest Protestant churches in continuous use in California. Dedicated in 1868, the church is built from redwood trees and is on the south shore. In the center of town is a church painted in red.

When Like most of the coast, Spring and Fall is best. Summer is cold and foggy; Winter is cold and rainy. Around February you can watch for migrating whales.

Tip The headlands park at the end of the peninsula is a popular place to watch whales and the sunset.

To photograph a sunset, set up your camera on a firm surface (a wall, car top, or tripod) and wait for the sun to get low on the horizon. Unless you're capturing a reflection in the water, put the horizon at the bottom of the frame to emphasize the sky. Switch off the flash. Automatic metering usually works fine.

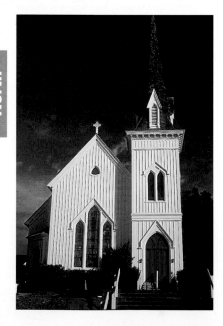

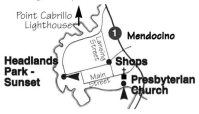

Following page: A few miles north of Mendocino is **Point Cabrillo Lighthouse** ☺. Turn left off Hwy 1, then immediately right onto Point Cabrillo Drive. The gateway to the lighthouse is 1.3 miles from this junction, just after "Ocean View". The lighthouse is a ten-minute walk from the road and there's a small display museum.

This shot, using a 100mm lens, benefits from the dense coastal summer fog.

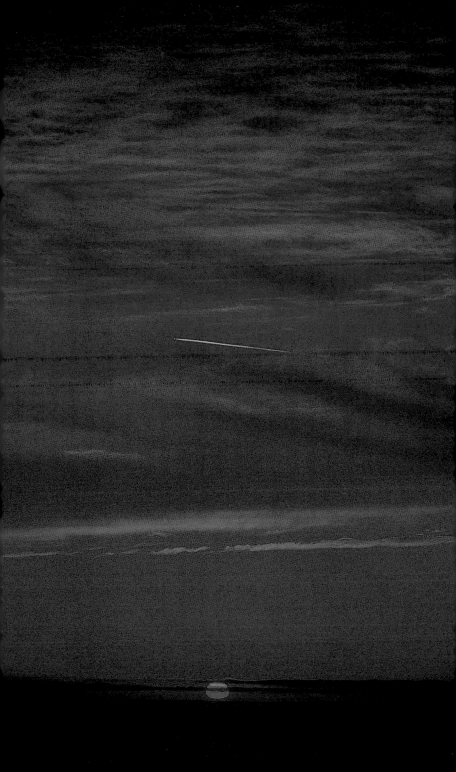

Point Cabrillo Lighthouse

FORT BRAGG SKUNK TRAIN

The **Skunk Train** ☻ is the longest and most popular steam train ride in California. Riding 40 miles of original track between coastal Fort Bragg and inland Willits, the former logging train carries eager daytrippers through towering redwoods. The line has more than 30 bridges and two deep tunnels.

One-way and round-trip rides start from Fort Bragg and Willits. The steam train usually only runs on Saturdays (during mid-week, the less photogenic diesel trains are used) so plan your schedule accordingly. Call 707-964-6371 for train times and reservations.

Fort Bragg was a military base named after Colonel Braxton Bragg. Today it is the largest coastal town between San Francisco and Eureka. Near the station is an historic house, a brewery, and several shops and restaurants.

"You can smell 'em before you can see 'em."

North

The major industry of Northern California was, and in several places still is, logging. In the 1880's, trains and ships would carry the timber down the coast to San Francisco and the gold mines. At it's height in the 1940's, almost 50 sawmills operated between Point Arena and Fort Bragg.

The Skunk Train originated in 1885 as the California Western Railroad. It was built to bring trees from the forest to Fort Bragg. Each huge, ancient redwood took up an entire train, with the tree's trunk sawn into carriage-sized chunks and loaded unceremoniously onto the waiting flatbeds. In 1925, gas-powered trains were introduced which smell so bad that the line was soon nicknamed the 'Skunk Train'. Today's passengers are transported by stink-free diesel or coal-powered-steam trains.

> *"When a tree takes a notion to grow in California, nothing in heaven or earth will stop it."*
> *Lillian Leland Stanford, 1890.*

The **Avenue of the Giants** is a spectacular 32-mile drive through magnificent redwood trees. Several old-growth groves containing 17,000 acres overwhelm you with these "ambassadors of another age".

The two most interesting groves are the Founder's Grove (with the 'Founder's Tree' and the 'Dyersville Giant', a fallen [1991] 362' tree which you can walk around) and the Rockerfeller Grove (with the 'Tall Tree', 'Giant Tree', and the fallen [1995] 'Flatiron Tree'). The Avenue is spiced with a quirky selection of 1950's-style attractions, including four 'room-inside' trees and two 'drive-thru' trees.

Where The Avenue of the Giants is a scenic highway running alongside the 101 freeway, 200 miles north of San Francisco. A free map is available at either entrance.

Nearby is the 'Lost Coast' of California, a 56-mile undeveloped coastline, too steep and wet for road access.

When Choose your mood! Early morning carries a light mist and fog, noon brings daylight down to the forest floor, and late afternoon catches golden light breaking through the branches.

Right: This tree is so large you can drive through it! The **Chandelier Drive-Thru Tree** is 315 ft (96m) high and about 2,400 years old. The tunnel was cut in 1920 by Charles Underwood, and is still run by his family. There's also a swan-graced lake and 200 acres of park. $3 entrance. A 35mm lens captures most of the tree; use a 50mm to photograph just the tunnel and car.

The **One-Log House** is inside a 2,000 year old, 40-ton log. It's mounted on wheels (?!). The **Living Chimney Tree** has a 9'x12' room carved into its base and a natural chimney for campfires. The **World Famous Tree House** also sports an electric lightbulb.

Myers Flat has the barely-alive *Shrine Drive-Thru Tree*, a *Step-Thru Stump* and the can't-miss *Drive-On Tree* (with a ramp to drive your RV up!). If you're short of some good burl wood, this is the place to get it.

Scotia Redwood Mill
To Eureka 40 miles
101
Avenue of the Giants North Entrance
Pepperwood 10
Eternal Tree House
Rockerfeller Grove
Founder's Grove
Humboldt Redwoods SP 6
Myers Flat
Avenue of the Giants
Shrine Drive-Thru Tree
10
Phillipsville
One-Log House
Living Chimney Tree
Avenue of the Giants South Entrance
To Shelter Cove and the 'Lost Coast'. 21 miles
Garberville
101
26
Confusion Hill
World Famous Tree House
Chandelier Drive Thru Tree
Leggett
101
To Fort Bragg 45 miles
To Willits, 46 miles

'Eureka!' James T Ryan, on rediscovering the Humboldt Bay. It is the only town whose name appears on the Seal of California, as t he phrase is also the State's motto.

T he **Carson Mansion** ◷ (right), in Eureka, is the Queen of California's Victorian houses. Lumber magnate William Carson commissioned the mansion in 1885, it is said, to keep 100 millworkers busy during a slow year. This fabulously ornate house is at the east end of 2nd street at M Street. Unfortunately it is now a private men's club and cannot be toured.

The mansion faces west, making for a good afternoon or sunset shot. This photograph is taken from 2nd Street, two blocks west from the mansion, with a 100mm lens.

Eureka is on the Humboldt Bay, California's largest bay north of San Francisco, first discovered by sea otter fur traders in 1806, then rediscovered by whalers in 1850 with the popular Victorian cry *'Eureka!'*, Greek for *'I have found it!'*

A short walk west is '**Old Town**', a 16-block area of restored Victorian buildings, shops and galleries. Nearby is **The Fantastic Museum**, complete with a petrified space-man, a *Hitler Is Alive!* skull and Liz Taylor's dressing room. (You can't beat that). The original 1854 **Fort Humboldt**, is off 101 on the southwest edge of Eureka.

Further north is **Redwood National Park** (tallest redwood), **Klamath** (known for the 'Trees of Mystery') and **Crescent City** (with Battery Pt. Lighthouse). East is idyllic **Burney Falls** and **Lassen National Park**.

Above: **Scotia** is famous for the **Pacific Lumber Company Mill** ◷, the world's largest redwood sawmill. You can take a fascinating self-guided tour of the mill (mon-fri 8-2pm). Get a permit at the museum, or at the guard shack at the front of the mill. This shot is taken from a public bridge which crosses the log flume/river, by the museum. The town itself is charming and is one of the few company-owned towns in America.

Below: **Ferndale** ◷ is a quaint dairy-farming Victorian village including this gingerbread Bed & Breakfast. Nearby is the Loleta Cheese Factory. Besides its elegant inns, the town is famous for the Kinetic Sculpture Race in May.

Trinidad Lighthouse 🕐, a squat metal tower, overlooks a beautiful cove. The lighthouse is in the small town of Trinidad, at the end of Main Street. The tower is only for display - a more modern lighthouse stands one mile west on a peninsula.

The Big Sur coastline and (inset) Hearst Castle™.

PhotoSecrets Northern California

Going South

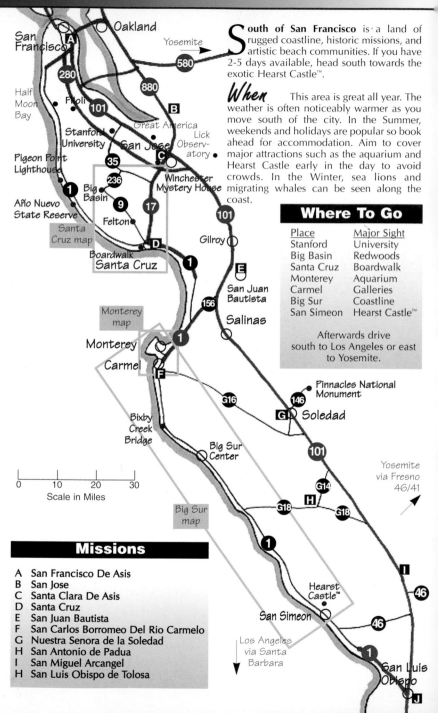

South of San Francisco is a land of rugged coastline, historic missions, and artistic beach communities. If you have 2-5 days available, head south towards the exotic Hearst Castle™.

When

This area is great all year. The weather is often noticeably warmer as you move south of the city. In the Summer, weekends and holidays are popular so book ahead for accommodation. Aim to cover major attractions such as the aquarium and Hearst Castle early in the day to avoid crowds. In the Winter, sea lions and migrating whales can be seen along the coast.

Where To Go

Place	Major Sight
Stanford	University
Big Basin	Redwoods
Santa Cruz	Boardwalk
Monterey	Aquarium
Carmel	Galleries
Big Sur	Coastline
San Simeon	Hearst Castle™

Afterwards drive
south to Los Angeles or east
to Yosemite.

Missions

A San Francisco De Asis
B San Jose
C Santa Clara De Asis
D Santa Cruz
E San Juan Bautista
F San Carlos Borromeo Del Rio Carmelo
G Nuestra Senora de la Soledad
H San Antonio de Padua
I San Miguel Arcangel
H San Luis Obispo de Tolosa

San Francisco
Oakland
Yosemite
280
580
880
Half Moon Bay
Filoli
101
B
Stanford University
Great America
Lick Observatory
San Jose
C
Pigeon Point Lighthouse
35
Winchester Mystery House
236
Big Basin
9
17
Año Nuevo State Reserve
Felton
101
Santa Cruz map
D
Gilroy
Boardwalk
Santa Cruz
1
E
San Juan Bautista
156
Salinas
Monterey map
1
Monterey
Carmel
F
Pinnacles National Monument
G16
146
G
Soledad
Bixby Creek Bridge
101
Big Sur Center
Yosemite via Fresno 46/41
G14
H
G18
G18
Big Sur map
1
I
Hearst Castle™
46
San Simeon
46
Los Angeles via Santa Barbara
1
San Luis Obispo
J

0   10   20   30
Scale in Miles

Silicon Valley is the nickname of the Santa Clara valley, once farmland and now home to the world's first and largest concentration of high-tech companies. Silicon, a cheap, silver-colored material grown from sand, is the basis of semiconductors.

An outgrowth of Stanford University, there are now over 7,000 high tech companies spread among 15 cities. San Jose is the defacto capital and it's population exceeds that of San Francisco.

Silicon Valley started in garages. In the 1930's, an engineering professor at Stanford University, Dr. Frederick Terman, asked his graduating students not to work for the big firms of the east but to start their own companies in the valley. William Hewlett and David Packard were the first to be persuaded and started building audio test equipment in this garage in 1939. When

Walt Disney bought eight units for $34,000 for his *Fantasia* film, Hewlett-Packard was in business.

In 1976, a HP employee, Stephen Wozniak, developed a basic minicomputer and showed it to his friend, Steve Jobs. Selling a VW Microbus, they raised $1,300 and formed Apple Computer in the garage of Job's parents. Within three years, sales of the Apple II had grown to $200M, and to $1B three years later. By age 23, Jobs was worth $1M. By 25 he was worth $100M.

Unfortunately this is not Wine Country mentality; there are no tours available and little corporate architecture worth photographing. The valley itself has little form - the photograph above was taken from Page Mill Road, near Route 35. The **HP garage** 367 Addison Ave (off Alma St), near Waverly is five blocks south of University Ave in Palo Alto. **Jobs' garage** is at 2066 Crist Dr, Cupertino.

The Birthplace of Silicon Valley:
Hewlett-Packard's garage.

The Birthplace of Apple Computer:
Steve Job's parent's garage.

The Winchester was the "Gun that won the West", but the spirits of the men it killed terrified the heiress to the fortune, Sarah Winchester. After her husband and daughter died, Sarah Winchester was persuaded by an occultist that she would only live if she continuously built a house to confuse the spirits. If work was ever stopped, she would die.

For the next 38 years, using her $1,000 a day in royalties, carpenters worked day and night enlarging her eight-room farmhouse. Now it has 160 rooms, 40 staircases, 2,000 doors and 10,000 windows. It was so complicated that even the owner and servants needed maps to navigate it. There's a window built into the floor, secret passageways, and doors opening onto blank walls. The heart of the mansion is the seance room with only one way in but three ways out, including one that drops down to the kitchen sink on the floor below.

Tours: $12.50. ☎408-247-2101.

When 🕐 The house is open 9-4pm. The best view is from the front garden (east side) which has the best light in the morning. The fountains here make good foregrounds. A popular magazine shot of the many roofs is taken from water tower, but there's no public access.

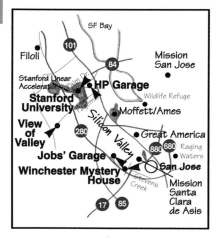

"Do you know the way to San Jose."
Songwriter Burt Bacharach.

Where The Winchester Mystery House is at 525 S Winchester Blvd in San Jose. From San Francisco, take Hwy 101 to 880 south. Exit on to Stevens Creek, then turn left onto Winchester Blvd. The house is on your right.

Nearby Filoli Mansion is a 654-acre country estate with an English-style house and magnificent gardens. Built in 1916-19 for William Bowers Bourn Jr, inheritor of the Empire Mine in Grass Valley, it was used in TV's *Dynasty* and the film *Heaven Can Wait*. The name 'Filoli' is a contraction of the Bourn's code: *'Fight, Live, Love'*. The house and gardens are interesting to walk around.

Filoli Mansion is at Crystal Springs,10 miles NW of Palo Alto and 25 miles South of San Francisco. Take the Edgewood exit from I-280, then west to Canada Rd. Open Feb-Nov, 10-1pm, $8, ☎415-366-4640.

Mountain View is home to NASA's **Ames Research Center**, in Moffett Field AFB (visible from I-101). The 2.5 tour takes you inside the world's largest wind tunnel, huge hangars, flight simulators, a centrifuge, and past the U2 spy plane. (Free, 9-4:30pm, ☎415-604-6497, advanced reservations required).

Paramount's **Great America** is a small theme-park in Santa Clara. The most unique shot is of *Top Gun*, an inverted looping rollercoaster. Take 101 to the Great America Parkway exit, or catch the light rail from San Jose. $27.95, ☎408-988-1776.

Mission Santa Clara is now a chapel at Santa Clara University.

Mission San Jose is a replica of the 1797/1809 sanctuary. 4300 Mission Blvd, south of I-680 and 4 miles east of I-880.

Near San Jose is a popular summer waterpark, **Raging Waters**. Take 101 east for 13 miles to Lake Cunningham.

Millionaire James Lick wanted to see life on the moon so he built one of the world's largest telescopes, the **Lick Observatory**. Take 101 east to Alum Rock Rd, then take Mount Hamilton Road for 18 miles. There's a good view of the valley here, when it's not smoggy.

Stanford University, on Palm Drive in Palo Alto, has a beautiful campus. The best photograph is of the romanesque Memorial Church, fronted with a large colorful mosaic. You can photograph it from the quadrangle (designed by Frederick Law Olmstead, designer of Central Park in New York) or through the roman arches by the Rodin sculptures. Built in 1903, the church has stained glass windows and a pipe organ with 7,777 pipes. Also climb the 285 ft. Hoover Tower for a panoramic view of the campus (10-4, $2). The tower is named after Herbert Hoover, a graduate of Stanford's first class in 1891, who later became US President in 1929.

Stanford University was founded in 1891 by Leland Stanford, with his untold wealth from the Transcontinental Railroad. It is still a private institution. The university is in memory of Stanford's only son, who died of typhoid in 1884, and built on the family's horse farm. Research here helped develop the IQ test, the pill, heart transplants, and the microprocessor. The Stanford Linear Accelerator Center (SLAC) burrows two miles into the foothills and makes a good tour for quantum-fans. 2575 San Hill Road, ☎408-926-2204, free but advance reservations required). Stanford receives $5m each year from patents. There are one-hour tours at 11 and 3:15 leaving from the Visitors Center. ☎408-723-2560.

It was on Leland Stanford's Horse Farm that Eadweard Muybridge (1830-1904) developed the first moving photograph. In 1877, Stanford gave the English-born Muybridge $40,000 to answer an age-old sportsman's argument - When a horse gallops, is there an instant when all four hooves leave the ground? Muybridge made a series of consecutive photographs with multiple cameras tripped by strings and rubber bands, and proved the answer was yes. Muybridge became an instant celebrity and, due to hundreds of similar motion studies, is known as the "Father of the Motion Picture".

Nearby

Palo Alto has a lively main street. At 210 Oak Grove Ave. is the eye-catching Church of the Nativity. The Barbie Hall of Fame is at 433 Waverly Street ☎408-326-5841. Acres of Orchids is at 1450 El Camino Real.

Pigeon Point Lighthouse ☉ is one of the west's most photogenic lighthouses. Built of brick in 1872, and in continuous use since, it is the second-tallest lighthouse in the US. Tours are given on Sundays between 11am and 3pm, and there is a small hostel (☎415-879-0633).

The south fence near the lightning mast makes a great 'leading line' (leading your eye into the subject). A good landscape shot is taken about a mile south from the road.

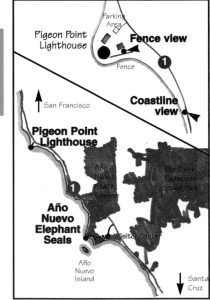

Nearby Nearby is **Half Moon Bay**, famous for its October Pumpkin Festival. **Point Montara Lighthouse** 20 miles north, is a 30' stubby tower built in 1928 and also has a hostel (☎415-728-7177).

Año Nuevo State Reserve

The best place to see Northern Elephant seals is **Año Nuevo State Reserve** ☉. Over 3,000 seals come here each year to molt, fight for domination, breed and give birth. Named for the male's distinctive inflatable nasal sac, Elephant seals can grow to 16 feet in length and weigh 3 tons. They can be seen all year but breeding season (December to March) is best. To minimize disturbance at this sensitive time, visits are only allowed on a pre-arranged basis. Call MISTIX two months in advance, ☎800-444-7275 for tickets.

The breeding grounds are a 1.7 mile walk from the Visitor's Center so expect to spend around 3 hours here.

In the early 1800's, the elephants were hunted for their oil-rich blubber. Not naturally afraid of humans, they made easy targets and were wiped almost to extinction within 40 years. A small group managed to survive in Mexico and is now repopulating the original breeding grounds.

In December, the bulls fight to determine a dominate male that gets to mate with all the females. The females come ashore in midwinter to give birth, then leave after four weeks, abandoning their offspring on the beach. These 'weaners' fast for 8-12 weeks before attempting to learn to swim. Once in the sea they feed on sharks, squid and rays. The seals separate, with the females swimming to Hawaii and the males going north to the Aleutian islands. They come ashore in the Summer to fast and shed a top layer of fur and skin.

Elephant seals at Año Nuevo.

BIG BASIN & FELTON

Left: The coast redwood is a relative of the giant sequoia (sometimes called the Sierra Redwood). It gets it's name not from the color of the bark, but of the heartwood, a much-sought-after building material.

Outside of the Redwood Empire around Eureka and Klamath, **Big Basin Redwoods State Park** ☺ is the best place to see magnificent redwoods, the tallest of trees. There are 19,000 acres and over 100 miles of hiking trails.

A leisurely self-guided 1/2-mile stroll from the car park takes you past the park's widest tree (Santa Clara, 17' diameter at the base), tallest tree (Mother-Of-The-Forest, 329') and oldest tree (Father-Of-The-Forest, around 2,000 years old). You can also stand inside a living tree which is completely hollow, and see the sky through the top. A short hike on Sequoia trail takes you to the delightful **Semperivens Falls**.

Big Basin is California's oldest state park and was created from the efforts of a photographer, Andrew Hill. Hill led the campaign to save these redwoods from logging - 96% of California's redwoods have been cut down for timber.

The park headquarters is easily found along SR 236, 9 mi N of Boulder Creek. (8-dusk, $5 per car, ☎408-338-6132).

Nearby **David Bruce Winery**, an impressive stone chateau with terra cotta roofing and lush views of vines and mountains beyond. Take Bear Creek Rd out of Boulder Creek. 2 miles north of Felton is a large painting of James Dean on the **Brookdale Lodge** (see title page).

Felton ☺ is home to the tallest **covered bridge** in the country, built in 1892.

Boulder Creek is a delightful historic town which, in the 1880's, used to have a 14-mile-long log flume down to the railhead at Felton.

The most colorful steam train operating in California is at _____. This renovated 'skunk' train was built in the 1880's for logging but now takes visitors on a slow but scenic six-mile roundtrip ride (1.25 hours) through a redwood forest up to Bear Mountain. From the 1880's-themed station area, the approaching train sounds like a dragon as it winds its way back down the hill. A narrow-gauge railway operates to Santa Cruz (2 hours) and there's even a Moonlight Steam Train Dinner Party.

Roaring Camp is in Felton, 6 miles north of Santa Cruz on Graham Hill Rd/Mt. Hermon Road. $13/$9.50, more for inclusive barbeque. ☎408-335-4484.

SANTA CRUZ

Santa Cruz (Spanish for 'sainted cross') is a major beach resort town, best known for it's **boardwalk**, the 'Coney Island of the West'. The boardwalk is a half-mile long amusement park along the beachfront and was built in 1906, making it the oldest in the west. The highlights are the 1911 Looff Carousel and the 1923 Giant Dipper, a wooden rollercoaster towering over the other 26 rides. Most of the year the boardwalk is open on weekends and holidays, but from June to August it is open every day, 11am-10pm. Free entrance; ride tickets are $1.50-$4. 400 Beach St. ☎408-423-5590.

Santa Cruz claims the best surf in California (disputed by Huntington Beach) and it was here that Jack O'Neill developed the neoprene wetsuit in 1956. There's a surfer statue at the end of Pelton Ave.

Where Santa Cruz is 75 mins south of San Francisco on I-280 and 17 via San Jose, or scenic Hwy 1 through Half Moon Bay. A longer tour takes you on I-101 and 84 to Stanford University in Palo Alto, 35/9/236 to Big Basin, 9/35 to Felton, then 9 to Santa Cruz.

Visitor Information is at 701 Front Street, ☎408-425-1234.

Above: The classic shot of the **boardwalk** ◔ is taken from the beach, at the waters edge, looking inland. A good dusk shot can be taken from the end of the pier.

When ◷ The area is good all year. Santa Cruz is popular in the summer as it's warmer than in SF. The boardwalk and Wilder Beach are best in late afternoon.

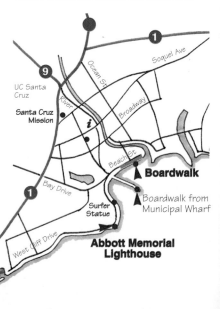

Soquel Ave
Ocean St.
UC Santa Cruz
River
Broadway
Santa Cruz Mission
i
Beach St.
Bay Drive
Boardwalk
Boardwalk from Municipal Wharf
Surfer Statue
West Cliff Drive
Abbott Memorial Lighthouse
Wilder Ranch State Park
Natural Bridges State Park

South

Above left: **Santa Cruz Boardwalk**. ***Above right:*** The coastline north of Santa Cruz used to have some spectacular natural rock bridges but most have washed away. The only remaining bridge is at **Natural Bridges State Beach** ☽, at the end of West Cliff Drive. Wilder Ranch State Park used to have an arch, but still offers a nice beach shot.

Below: Further east on West Cliff Drive at Lighthouse Point is the **Mark Abbott Memorial Lighthouse** ☽ (12-4, Thur-Mon, ☎408-425-7278). To remember their son who died in a surfing accident, the parents of Mark Abbot had this brick lighthouse built. It overlooks a favorite surfing spot, Steamers Lane. At the end of Pelton Ave is a surfing statue.

volcano. Jagged earthen spires reach 1,200 above the chaparral-covered canyon floor and talus caves await intrepid hikers.

You can enter the park from the east or west, but there's no through road. The west entrance is best as you are closer to the pinnacles. There are good views from the parking area but hiking is the main attraction. In the Summer it is exceedingly hot so bring a hat and water - there are no stores nearby. ☎408-389-4485.

S alinas was the birthplace of John Steinbeck, writer of *Grapes of Wrath*, *Of Mice and Men*, *East of Eden*, and winner of the Pulitzer Prize and Nobel Prize for Literature. His childhood home, a large Victorian house, is now a delightful restaurant (lunch only, ☎408-424-2735, 132 Central Ave at Stone St.).

Salinas was Steinbeck's for "East of Eden" and is known as the "salad bowl of the world" due to the amount of lettuce grown nearby.

Just north is **Gilroy**, famous for it's Garlic Festival. **Castroville**, towards the coast, is the 'artichoke capital' and Marilyn Monroe was once crowned the 'artichoke queen'.

PINNACLES

If you're looking for a strange, distant-planet-like environment, try **Pinnacles National Monument** ☺. This little-visited area is the weathered remains of an ancient

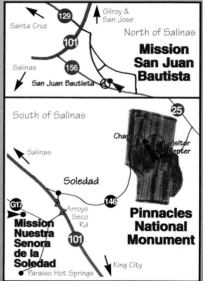

SAN JUAN BAUTISTA

The **largest**, and one of the most attraction, of California's Missions is **Mission San Juan Bautista**, ☺ in the equally delightful town of San Juan Bautista. Built in 1797, this was the 15th in the chain of 21 missions and, unlike many of the others, was never abandoned. The missions, each about a day's ride apart, were linked by one road, El Camino Real (the Kings' Highway), used from 1797-1850 and now the basis of Highway 101. The road was named after King Carlos III of Spain who ordered the settlement of Alta California to thwart the encroaching Russians. On the north side of the mission's cemetery you can see a part of El Camino Real.

You can also see (by the ridge) the San Andreas fault, culprit of San Francisco's 1906 earthquake. The San Andreas fault system, where the Pacific Plate rubs against the North American Plate, is 800 miles long and up to 10 miles deep and reaches the ocean at Point Reyes.

There are other restored buildings nearby and the town is a joy to explore.

Mission Nuestra Senora de la Soledad

"A poem, a stink, a grating noise."
J Steinbeck.

Left: The old Monterey Canning Company, now full of shops and restaurants, is the most distinctive part of **Cannery Row** ☉.

Facing page: (from top left):
Another view of Cannery Row; boats in the Monterey Marina; the morning catch can be caught on the **Municipal Wharf** ☉. In the park on El Estero is the **Dennis The Menace Playground**, part-designed by Dennis' creator Hank Ketcham. The colorful playground includes a full-size steam train to climb over, various slides and a maze. (10-dusk, free. ☎408-646-3866).

The **Monterey Peninsular** is arguably the most beautiful coastal area of California. Renowned as a luxury destination (mainly due to a marketing campaign of the Southern Pacific Railroad for their Hotel Del Monte in the 1880's), the area has 18 golf courses, three of which are ranked in the top ten internationally. It is home to the cities of Monterey, Pacific Grove and Carmel, and the famous 17-Mile Drive™.

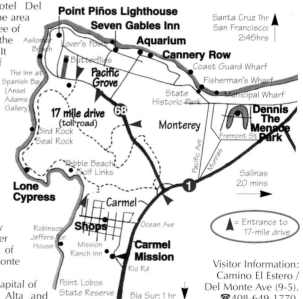

Point Piños Lighthouse
Seven Gables Inn
Santa Cruz 1hr
San Francisco: 2:45hrs
Asilomar Beach
Lover's Point
Aquarium
Butterflies
Cannery Row
Coast Guard Wharf
The Inn at Spanish Bay (Ansel Adams Gallery)
Pacific Grove
Fisherman's Wharf
State Historic Park
Municipal Wharf
17 mile drive (toll road)
68
Monterey
Dennis The Menace Park
Fremont St
Bird Rock
Seal Rock
Pacific Ave
Munras
Lone Cypress
Pebble Beach Golf Links
1
Salinas 20 mins
Carmel
Ocean Ave
▲ = Entrance to 17-mile drive
Robinson Jeffers House
Shops
Mission Ranch Inn
Carmel Mission
Rio Rd
Point Lobos State Reserve
Big Sur: 1 hr
Visitor Information: Camino El Estero / Del Monte Ave (9-5). ☎408-649-1770.

MONTEREY

Monterey is California's most historic city. First discovered in 1542 by Juan Rodriguez Cabrillo, it was named in 1602 by Sebastian Vizcaino after his patron, the viceroy of Mexico, el Counte de Monte Rey.

Monterey was the capital of Spanish and Mexican Alta and Baja California for 76 years. The Customs House was the only legal port of entry for foreign ships. In 1846, three American ships under Commodore John Drake Sloat captured the port and thereby a huge Mexican territory, now most of today's seven southwestern states. In the 1849 Gold Rush, most of the population left for the gold fields but was repopulated by the whaling industry (1854-1900's) and, with the 1880 Hotel Del Monte, tourism. After depleting the whales, Monterey became the world's largest sardine port.

Monterey Bay, fed by cold currents bring nutrients from the deep, is one of the richest and most varied marine environments in the world. Only a hundred yards out from Moss Landing, the Monterey Canyon plummets to a depth of 10,000 feet. A former sardine-processing plant has been converted to one of the world's greatest aquariums, the **Monterey Bay Aquarium**

Where Monterey Bay Aquarium is located on the northern edge of Monterey at 886 Cannery Row by David St. ($14.75/$11.75/$5, ☎408-648-4888).

When Anytime is fine. The aquarium is open between 10am and 6pm (9:30am in summer). About 1.8 million people a year visit this non-profit private organization. It's busy in the Summer so try to line up one hour before opening, or buy tickets in advance (☎800-756-3737).

Plan on spending about 3 hours here. Most of the exhibits are indoors so it's a good fallback for a rainy day. Divers feed fish in the Kelp Forest at 11:30am and 4pm, and the Sea Otters at 10:30am, 1:30pm and 3:30pm.

Monterey Bay Aquarium is one of the largest, and certainly most visually delightful, aquariums in the world. Over 300,000 marine creatures, all native to the area, are dramatically displayed in 100 galleries. Touch silky bat rays, sea stars and other tide pool creatures. Watch sea otters play in their two-story exhibit. See sharks and sardines swim together in a three-story living kelp forest.

Outside is Monterey Bay, the country's largest Marine Sanctuary with an area as large as Connecticut and an undersea canyon deeper and wider than the Grand Canyon. The Outer Bay exhibit recreates this environment with one million gallons of seawater behind a 54'x15' acrylic panel, the largest window in the world.

Tip The golden rule here is to turn OFF your camera's flash. Hold the camera steady, and include people for scale. Using a fast film (800 or 1600 ISO) and a tripod will help greatly.

Below: *The most bewitching exhibit is the Jellyfish, the country's largest collection of these oceanic drifters.*

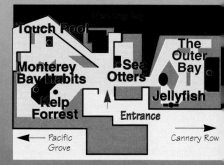

Above: Stealthy sharks patrol the Bay Habitats. *Right:* The Outer Bay exhibit allows you to get nose-to-gill with Ocean inhabitants, including the ocean sunfish. This shot is taken from the balcony.

South

With Flash	Without Flash

How To Photograph An Aquarium

1. **Turn off your flash.** It will only reflect in the glass. Use natural light instead.

2. **Use fast film** (ISO 800 or 1600). This reacts quicker in low light levels, allowing you to take hand-held shots. (With ordinary ISO 100/200 film you'll just get blurry images). You can buy film at the giftstore, so rewind your existing roll, remove it, and put in a new fast film.

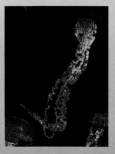

Sea Otters are elusive but fun subjects. Use a zoom lens.

Jellyfish are naturally lit. Use a fast film.

The **Kelp Forest** is best photographed from the balcony. Automatic exposure is fine, or meter off the center.

3. **Include People.** It's tempting to put the camera against the window, but don't. It can scratch the glass and you'll loose an important factor - a sense of scale.
   Stand back from the window and include a few people in your shot. This will show the size of the animals, and the wonder of the viewers. Children pointing make the best subjects.

4. **Hold The Camera Steady.** In low light it's easy to get blurry pictures so keep the camera steady. Hold the camera with both hands, keep your feet slightly apart, and breathe slowly. Rest on someone's shoulder for added support.

5. **Look For Height.** In the large exhibits, the best views are from high up. At the **Kelp Forest**, climb the stairs to the second-level. The **Outer Bay** is best viewed from the balcony - wait for the sunfish or turtle to swim by.

6. **Look for Details.** Capture individual animals by zooming in. At the **Touch Pool**, get your companions close to the tide-pool animals as they touch them. At the **Sea Otters**, zoom in to one or two otters (this is difficult as they move fast - you'll need a steady hand). Bird lovers will like the **Sandy Shore Aviary**.

7. **Exposure.** Most shots will be fine with an automatic exposure. Dedicated SLR users can meter off the main subject - the face of a fish or shark for example. Use the widest aperture for maximum light.

South

I n the 1930's, Monterey was home to the largest sardine factory in the world. The area was immortalized in John Steinbeck's 1945 novel "Cannery Row", when over 250,000 tons of sardines were processed. The industry died out in 1951 and the factories have become tourist shops, wine tasting rooms, restaurants and the Monterey Bay Aquarium.

Today the fishing industry resides around the Municipal Wharf, at the foot of Figueroa Street. Arrive very early to watch the day's catch being brought in. The breakwater near Coast Guard Wharf has been overrun with noisy sea lions, and Fisherman's Wharf is overrun with restaurants and whale watching tours (Dec-Jan).

Facing Fisherman's Wharf is the original 1827 Custom House, California's oldest government building. The Spanish Presidio, Royal Chapels, and 40 other buildings form the Monterey **State Historic Park**. Guided tours are offered between 10-4 ($5, ☎408-649-7118).

PACIFIC GROVE

Pacific Grove is a Victorian village on the northern tip of Monterey Peninsula. It was settled in 1875 by the Methodists as a religious and cultural retreat. Dancing, drinking and public bathing were all regulated. The town has over a thousand Victorian homes and cottages.

Color photographers will love the bright purple flowers of the **Royal Carpet,** while black and white photographers will prefer the colliding currents of **Asilomar Beach**.

Above: The 1855 **Point Piños Lighthouse** is the oldest continuously operating lighthouse on the West Coast. For 40 years it was operated by women. There are free tours on Thur, Sat & Sun (1-4pm, ☎408-648-3116). Good views are available all around the lighthouse - this one is taken from the south side.

Below: Pacific Grove has an abundance of delightful Victorian Bed & Breakfast inns, the most famous being **The Seven Gables Inn** ☺. Located at Bayview and 17th, it is best viewed from Lover's Point (below) or the Shoreline Bike path (left). Nearby at the base of 5th is the **Green Gables Inn**.

Butterfly Town USA

Pacific Grove is known as "Butterfly Town USA" for the millions of Monarch butterflies that migrate here from Canada and Alaska each year (Nov-Mar). It takes four or five generations of butterfly to fly the 2,000 miles north to Canada. The return journey South is made by one generation of butterfly (with a longer lifespan), covering 100 miles a day.

The butterflies are best seen from November to March at George Washington Park and Monarch Grove Sanctuary on Grove Acre Ave. "Butterfly molestation" carries a fine of $1,000. The Buttery Habitat Grove is between Short and Lighthouse (☎408-373-7047). Monarchs can also be seen at **Natural Bridges State Beach** in Santa Cruz and **Pismo Beach** in San Luis Obispo.

South

The **17-Mile Drive**™ is a private scenic road that features one of California's most famous natural landmarks, **The Lone Cypress Tree**™ ⏱.

In the 1880's, the luxurious Hotel Del Monte (now the Naval Postgraduate School) began offering it's guests a horse-drawn carriage ride around the area. A 17-mile long loop was created and known as the "Circle of Enchantment".

Today the area is still private land, operated by the Pebble Beach Company, and a toll is charged ($7 per car, ☎408-625-8426).

There are several sights besides the tree. Just south is **Ghost Tree**, a victim of so much sea spray and wind that it's trunk has turned white. Just north is **Cypress Point Lookout** which, on a good day, has a 20-mile view down to Big Sur Lighthouse. **Fanshell Overlook** is home to Harbor Seals and is curtained off during breeding season.

Off **Point Joe**, you can see a rare sight - colliding ocean currents. Even on calm days this is a 'Restless Sea'. Just south is a one-mile guided nature walk where you can photograph birds (on **Bird Rock**), sea lions and harbor seals (on **Seal Rock**).

Nearby Along the drive are deer, wildflowers, two luxury hotels (the Inn at Spanish Bay and The Lodge at Pebble Beach), expensive homes, seven restaurants, and several renowned golf courses (including Pebble Beach).

"Like ghosts fleeing before the wind."
A description of Monterey Cypress trees by Robert Louis Stevenson.

The **Lone Cypress Tree**™ ⏱ is a Monterey Cypress, growing from the cracks of a small rocky peninsula. It is thought to be about 500 years old. A small wall has been built to protect its location and access to the tree is prohibited.

The classic view is from a small turnout on the 17-Mile Drive™. Late afternoon is best as the rocks are lit by the golden light.

At The Inn at Spanish Bay is the **Ansel Adams Gallery**, with an inspiring collection of prints and books.

✍ PEBBLE BEACH, SPYGLASS HILL, SPANISH BAY, 17-MILE DRIVE, the LONE CYPRESS TREE and images thereof are trademarks of Pebble Beach Company. Photography for publication requires written permission.

In 1986, the Academy Award winning director, and actor, Clint Eastwood served one term as mayor. His restaurant, the Hog's Breath (left, on San Carlos and 6th), is a popular hangout and his hotel, the 31-room Mission Ranch (☎408-625-9040), claims "some of the best views in California".

Visitor Information is above Hog's breath. (9-5, closed Sundays and hols, ☎408-624-2522).

Nearby Three miles south of Carmel is **Point Lobos State Reserve** ⏱. Called "the greatest meeting of land and water in the world", it is said to be the model for Spyglass Hill in Robert Louis Stevenson's "Treasure Island". Discover seals, whales, otters, sea lions, cormorants and pelicans, and the Devil's Cauldron blow hole. 2hrs min., 9-5, $6 per vehicle, ☎408-624-4909.

The man who charted Monterey, Sebastian Vizcaino, named this valley after his patron saint, Our Lady of Carmel. In the 1880's, Carmel-by-the Sea became a planned seaside resort and you could buy a lot for $20. In 1906, the San Francisco earthquake made many people homeless, so many artists, musicians and writers moved here to establish a bohemian community.

Valuing their rustic environment, the residents of Carmel fought modern encroachment. Today there are no billboards, neon signs, stoplights, parking meters or fast-food outlets. There are no sidewalks or streetlights in residential areas, no house numbers, and no home mail delivery. Residents collect their mail from the Post Office, making it a social meeting spot. Even high heels are outlawed. Within the one-square mile city there are over 70 art galleries and studios and 60 restaurants.

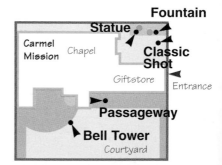

South

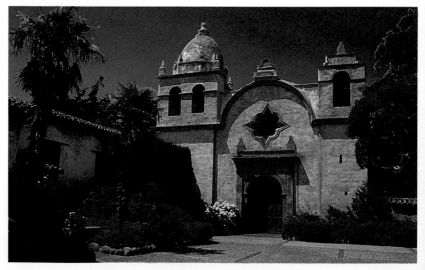

CARMEL MISSION

Established in 1770, **Mission San Carlos Borromeo Del Rio Carmelo** ☉ is the best restored and one of the most picturesque of California's Missions. It was reputedly Father Junipero Serra's favorite and he was buried here in 1784. The gardens, moorish bell tower and courtyard make good camera subjects.

10:30-4:30, $2.

☎408-624-3600.

Tables in Carmel

THE SALMON BAGEL SANDWICH $4.50
SMOKED SALMON ON A BAGEL WITH CREAM CHEESE

THE SMOKED SALMON CLUB $5.50
SMOKED SALMON, CREAM CHEESE, LETTUCE, ONION & TOMATO ON A FRESH FRENCH ROLL

THE CRAB DELUXE $6.00
CRABMEAT, MAYO, LETTUCE, TOMATO & ONION ON A FRENCH R...

THE SHRIMP DELUXE $5...
SHRIMPMEAT, MAYO, LETTUCE, TOMATO & ONION ON A FRENCH RO...

THE COMBO SUPREME $6.00
CRABMEAT, SHRIMPMEAT, MAYO, LETTUCE, ONION & TOMATO ON A FRENCH ROLL

SMOKED SALMON BY THE PIECE $11.00 lb

Fish on Fisherman's Wharf

Point Lobos State Reserve

Monterey

5

Carmel

Garrapata SP

Rocky Point Restaurant

San Francisco: 2:45 hrs from Monterey (1 hr to Santa Cruz on 1)

Bixby Bridge 34 / 105

25

Coast Road

Point. Sur Lighthouse

Andrew Molera SP

Big Sur Center

Pfeiffer Waterfall

Pfeiffer Big Sur SP

Pfeiffer Beach Arch

Big Sur Ranger Station

Nepenthe Restaurant

Sycamore Canyon Rd

McWay Cove Waterfall 54 / 85

Partington Cove

Julia Pfeiffer Burns SP

Esalen Institute

21

1

Lucia

Mileages from Monterey / Mono Bay

36

Ragged Point

Turquoise Ocean

Lime Kilns

Pt. Piedras Blancas Lighthouse 106 / 33

Arroyo Laguna

Hearst Castle 112 / 27

San Simeon

Cambria

> "Like the steep necks of a herd of horses, ... the mountain ridges pitch to the sea, the lean granite-boned heads plunge nostril-under."
> Robinson Jeffers

Bixby Creek Bridge ① *is one of 38 bridges between Carmel and San Simeon and one of the world's highest single-span concrete bridges. It was built in 1932 by convicts, like most of Highway 1, and was originally called 'Rainbow Bridge'.*

Above right:
The turnout one mile south offers the most classic view of Highway 1. This is a good place to view the steep, rugged cliffs. Place the horizon high in the shot to emphasize the rocky headlands. 50mm, late PM.

Lower right:
A powerful shot of the 320' concrete arch can be taken from the parking area immediately north of the bridge. Again place the horizon high in the picture to emphasize the height of the supports.
In the Summer the route can be cloaked in fog, but this can add mystery to your photographs.

The 90-mile section of State Highway 1 between Carmel and San Simeon, often called *Big Sur*, is considered the most dramatic coastal road in the US. As the road twists and turns, it caresses wild headlands, and clings to cliffs that plunge almost vertically into the Pacific Ocean. Nearly a hundred turnouts allow you to sample the scenery.

The area was named by the Spanish of Monterey as the Big Country of the South, *El Pais Grande del Sur,* and became home to poet Robinson Jeffers and novelist Henry Miller.

Where Start from Carmel in the north or San Simeon in the south. The drive alone takes 2-3 hrs but double that for sightseeing. Most of the views (including the classic one of Bixby Bridge) are from turnouts. There is no town of Big Sur - it's a region.

When ① Late afternoon is generally best as it brings a warm, golden light to the west-facing headlands. It can take five hours to drive from Carmel to Hearst Castle and its busy in the Summer.

Any season is great. Spring brings out the wild roadside flowers which make a good foreground. Summer sees fog in the morning but it dissipates by lunch. In Winter, (Nov-Feb) Gray and Humpback whales can be seen migrating south.

Yosemite: 6 hrs from San Simeon (3 hrs to Fresno via 46 & 41, + 3 hrs on 41)

Los Angeles: 5 hrs from San Simeon via 1 & 101. 3 hrs to Santa Barbara.

South

Bixby Creek Bridge and the Big Sur Coastline

McWay Cove Waterfall

Nepenthe Restaurant

"It was always a wild, rocky coast, desolate and forbidding to the man of the pavements." Henry Miller

"If there is a restaurant on earth more beautifully situated than Nepenthe, I have yet to find it." Kenneth Brower, National Geographic Traveler.

The Arch Rock at Pfeiffer Beach

South

The **Big Sur section** of Highway 1 was chosen as the country's first Scenic Highway in 1966. The remote, cliff-hugging road took 18 years to build, mainly by prisoners, and was unveiled in 1937. Dynamite blasting during construction has weakened the surrounding rocks and winter storms can wash away parts of the road. So watch for temporary traffic lights.

Point Sur lighthouse was built in 1899 on a volcanic rock. It lies within military property and can only be accessed on Wednesdays and weekends. Hurricane Point, 3 miles north of Naval Point Sur. ☎408-625-4419.

***Right:* Pfeiffer Beach Arch Rock** ⏱ is a small natural arch on an attractive beach. During the winter you can catch the setting sun through the arch. Access is from a narrow downhill lane, Sycamore Canyon Road, 1-mile south of Pfeiffer Big Sur State Park. There's a tiny street sign and a few mailboxes, but no sign for the beach. ☎408-667-2315.

Next page: The exotic **Pfeiffer Waterfall** ⏱ is in Pfeiffer Big Sur State Park. The fall faces west, so afternoon is best (this shot with 35mm), and is reached along a short hike through the woods from the north parking area. The region is named for Michael and Barbara Pfeiffer who became the first first european settlers in 1869.

Left: Perched 880' above sea level on a prominent cliff, **Nepenthe Restaurant** ☉ has a spectacular panoramic view of the coastline. There is great food here and a good bookstore.

Nepenthe is Greek for 'sorrow-banisher', an ancient potion used to give forgetfulness of pain. Orson Welles used to own a cabin here. It was built for his wife, Rita Hayworth, but they divorced before sharing it. Just south is the cultural Henry Miller Memorial Library ☎408-667-2574. Henry Miller, who wrote *Tropic of Cancer*, lived nearby at an abandoned convict labor camp in Anerson Creek. The rent was free. Partington Cove has a wooden footbridge and tunnel built in the 1870's.

"There are mountains which seem to reach the heavens and the sea beats on them. Sailing along close to land, it appears as though they would fall on the ships." Juan Cabrillo, sailing past Big Sur, 1542.

Previous page: McWay Cove Waterfall ☾ is a hidden treasure where a slender, idyllic waterfall plunges 50 ft into the ocean like milk from a pitcher. It is the one of two waterfalls In California that flow into the ocean (the other, Alamere Falls, is in Point Reyes). Of the two, this is the easiest and most attractive to photograph. It is best viewed in the late afternoon at low tide.

The fall is in Julia Pfeiffer Burns State Park. From the parking area, take the trail take the trail under the highway, along a boardwalk to the overlook. You can just about see it from Highway - stop at the pullout 100' north of the Park's entrance, on the west side. ☎408-667-2315. 50mm.

From November through February, California Greay Whales can be seen on their annual migration south to Baja California. Watch the ocean about a mile offshore for the occasional spout.

Below: Sea Lions near Arroyo Laguna.

The **Esalen Institute**, named after the original indian tribe of the area, is a famous New-Age health center. They encourage holistic body/mind potential through acupuncture, meditation and yoga. There's no public access except from 1:30am to 3:30am when you can bathe nude in the hot-spring baths overlooking the moonlit ocean.

More cost-conscious hedonists will prefer **Sykes Hot Springs**, an 11-mile hike into the Ventana Wilderness. The natural hot mineral pools are enclosed by towering redwoods. Take the Pine Ridge Trail from the Big Sur Ranger Station.

Past Lucia the coastline gradually becomes less dramatic. The **Lucia Lodge Restaurant**, at 500' above sea level, has a good coastal view. **Lime Kiln State Park** has four old circular kilns (entrance fee and hike). A one mile hike takes you to the pretty **Lime Kiln Falls**. The highway around here (1 mile S of **Ragged Point**) has views of the **turquoise ocean** ☉ (next page), colored by the limestone. Don't use a polarizer here as it will reduce the turquoise color.

Below: Around **Piedras Blancas Lighthouse**, the rugged northern coast gives way to the gentler southern coast. Two miles north of Hearst Castle is **Arroyo Laguna** ☉, a beach popular with windsurfers. A long lens is required.

◄ Pfeiffer Waterfall ▲ Turquoise Ocean near Ragged Point

I f you like people, places and their stories, there is not a more visually and historically fascinating place in California than Hearst Castle™. Perched on a remote hill overlooking the Pacific Ocean, like a scene from a fairytale, the beloved home of publishing magnate William Randolph Hearst justifies the long drive. It harbors wild tales of riches, power and fame and is one of the most expensive and extravagant private residences built during America's Gilded Age that is open to the public.

As the sole inheritor of an enormous mining wealth, and an insatiable collector of European art, WR Hearst (1863-1951) had the means to build a great estate. He kept workers busy for 28 years, constantly building and rebuilding to his unique and ever-changing tastes. Entire sections of palaces and castles were purchased, shipped from Europe, and incorporated into the design. Flemish tapestries, French fireplaces, Italian statues and Persian carpets pack the complex. The estate has 165 rooms, a 104-foot outdoor swimming pool, and a garage for limousines. The surrounding grounds extended for 250,000 square miles - one-third the size of Rhode Island - and included 50 miles of coastline. Roaming the hills were 70 species of exotic animals, the largest private zoo in the world. He called it *La Custra Encantada - "The Enchanted Hill"*.

Hearst Castle™ is a sight designed to be seen. In the golden age of Hollywood, Hearst hosted weekend parties with the biggest names in movies and politics. Today, you can explore the well-preserved estate and wonder what you might have done with such an overwhelming fortune.

Tripods and flash are not allowed so bring fast film for indoor shots. Most shots use a 35mm or 28mm lens.

"This is probably the way God would have done it, if He had the money." Attributed to playwright George Bernard Shaw.

◀ Roman Pool   Neptune Pool ▶

Where

Hearst Castle™ is on a hill, on the northern edge of San Simeon, a remote coastal town half way between San Francisco and Los Angeles.

San Francisco: 6 hrs
via Monterey: 3 hrs

Hearst Castle™

San Simeon

Yosemite: 6 hrs
via Fresno: 3hrs.

Cambria

Los Angeles: 6 hrs
Santa Barbara: 3hrs

It's a long drive from anywhere so plan to stop overnight in one of San Simeon Acre's motels or campsites, 3 miles south. The non-descript parking area is at the base of the hill - buses take you to the top.

When ⏱

A nice blue sky is best. The house is deliberately built above fog level, but the weather can vary. Despite its remote location, there are over 800,000 visitors a year. Aim for the first tour of the day, at 8:20am. The last tour leaves at 3:20pm in Winter, later in Summer. Summer can be busy so reserve ahead on 800-444-4445.

Tours

The only way to visit is on a guided tour, but there are four to choose from (plus one in the evening) and they provide ample time. Tour 1 is the best introduction but all include both pools which give you the best shots. Each daytime tour lasts 1:45 hrs and costs $14 adults, $8 ages 6-12. The tour leaders are refreshingly enthusiastic and well-informed, so plan some good questions.

Evening tours (Fri & Sat, Spring and Fall only) cost $25/$13, last 2:10hrs, and include a Living History program.

Nearby

Cambria (8mi S) is a very pleasant, gold-rush style town with restaurants, shops and inns. Sea lions can be seen on the nearby beaches (best in Jan). The enormous **Morro Rock** (volcanic in origin) in Morro Bay (30mi S) is a sight to behold but not necessarily to photograph. One mile north is **Arroyo Laguna**, a popular spot for windsurfers.

South

Neptune Pool

Previous page main shot, and last page of this section.

The outdoor **Neptune Pool** ☺ is the most beautiful feature of the estate. The blue is natural: the lining of the pool is white. The 345,000 gallon pool is flanked with 30-foot cypress trees and a Greco-Roman temple facade containing 400-year old Italian marble statues of Neptune and his mermaids. This is the third version Hearst had built and 6,000 trees were planted to hide its water tower on a nearby hill.

When ⏱ Most times are good, although try to avoid noon - the lower sun in the early morning or late afternoon gives relief to the statues. This shot is taken at 9am; dusk is also good.

Fog can be a problem in the Summer and is erratic throughout the year. Sometimes the fog rises only to 500' and the pool, at 1,600', can be clear.

How The Neptune Pool is one of the first stops on Tour 1 so be prepared with a 35 or 28mm lens and polarizer (for that great blue). Get close to the small statue by the stairs for a bold foreground.

Roman Pool

Previous page, top left: The indoor **Roman Pool** ☺ is completely lined with hammered gold and venetian tiles, each about an inch square.

Map of Hearst Castle: Tour 1

Neptune Pool   Roman Pool

Finish

Tour Bus

Start

Walking Tour 1

Assembly Room

Refectory

Casa Grande

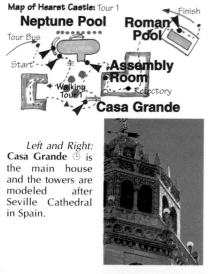

Left and Right: **Casa Grande** ☺ is the main house and the towers are modeled after Seville Cathedral in Spain.

"It was almost as if Hearst subconsciously realized that his newspapers were trashy, his political life a failure, even his motion pictures not entirely successful and he was determined that in San Simeon, if nothing else, he would leave an enduring monument to his greatness." Biographer WA Swanberg.

William **Randolph Hearst** created the largest publishing empire the world had ever known. At it's peak, in 1935 he controlled 26 newspapers, 13 magazines, 8 radio stations, 2 news services, and a film company. In a race for readership he unhesitatingly ruined the careers of people in his path, created news ("yellow journalism"), and even helped start the Spanish-American War. At one time 1 in 5 Americans read a Hearst newspaper. He used his influence to run for the highest political offices and help promote the career of his companion, Marion Davies. Today the San Francisco Examiner and Cosmopolitan magazine are still Hearst publications.

Hearst's wealth came from his father, George Hearst. Born in Missouri, George Hearst was a miner who became rich with the Ophir mine, the first great silver discovery in Nevada's Comstock Lode. Tireless and lucky, he came to own copper, gold, lead, silver and tin mines in South Dakota, Utah, Mexico and Peru, as well as thousands of acres in California and Arizona.

William Randolph Hearst was George and his wife Phoebe's only son. Born in 1863 in San Francisco, Hearst spent his childhood touring Europe with Phoebe and acquiring her taste for buying art and antiques. Hearst had no interest in his father's mines, but was drawn to the *San Francisco Daily Examiner*. Hearst took over the money-loosing paper in 1887, at the age of 23.

Using his taste for vaudeville theatre, Hearst replaced the drab oceans of small type with bold, 'banner' headlines, dramatic illustrations, and dynamic, lurid, and even invented, tales. He exposed corruption and entertained the masses. Circulation doubled. His father died in 1891, leaving Phoebe with $18M, and Hearst used the money to play on a larger stage - New York. With wads of cash, Hearst bought the editors of his main rival, Joseph Pulitzer, and the newspaper wars began.

Troubles were brewing in Cuba and Hearst seized the opportunity, sensationalizing every detail, true or not. When his artist/correspondent in Cuba said that there was really little action, Hearst reportedly cabled back: *"You supply the pictures, I'll supply the war!",* and he did.

According to biographer Swanberg, when war broke out, Hearst sailed to Cuba and captured 26 Spanish soldiers, bought an ocean liner to sink in the Suez Canal to delay the Spanish Navy, and even sent an envoy to Spain with his conditions for cease-fire. It was Hearst's war, and his newspaper won.

Hearst became god and tyrant of the newspaper business. He bought papers in Atlanta, Boston, Chicago and LA, creating the first nationwide chain, and reportedly funded thugs to remove rival papers from the newstands. Championing the poor and the immigrants, Hearst ran for public office. He won two terms as a US Senator, but rarely attended sessions. His newspapers openly called for someone to shoot President McKinley, and when someone did, public opinion turned. He lost bids for mayor, State Governor, and the Democratic Presidential nomination. By 1912, he was known as *William Also-Ran-dolph Hearst.*

In 1919, his beloved mother Phoebe died. Hearst retreated to the 'Ranch' at San Simeon that he had known as a boy and decided to build it into his own estate.

Inspired by San Francisco's 1915 Panama-Pacific International Exposition, Hearst commissioned architect Julia Morgan, a student of Bernard Maybeck at Berkeley and the first woman to graduate from Ecole des Beaux Arts in Paris. She had a passion for detail and quality and designed the main house in a Mediterranean Revival Style.

A pier and roads were built (Highway 1 wasn't completed until 1937), and entire sections of European houses arrived by ship. Anything Hearst saw and liked, Morgan had to incorporate into the design. Whenever a new inspiration took hold, Hearst had sections or buildings torn down and work started anew.

At age 54, Hearst met a pretty and vivacious showgirl, Marion Davies, age 19. Hearst's wife, Millicent Wilson, refused a divorce, so Hearst and Davies became lifelong companions. He put her in movies, using his money to fund the films and his contacts and papers to promote Davies.

'The Ranch' became a fun retreat for the stars. Every major movie and political celebrity of the day attended - those who refused were never mentioned again in Hearst's papers. Charlie Chaplin, Winston Churchill, President Coolridge, Clark Gable, Amelia Earheart, Douglas Fairbanks, Greta Garbo, J Paul Getty, Cary Grant, and Bob Hope all partied here.

Marion Davies was the life of the party - Jean Harlow said: *"All the men used to flock around her. She was very attractive in an evening dress because she never wore anything under it."*

The celebrities were brought 210 miles by train (with a jazz band and open bar) from Glendale, and each given a personal maid or valet. After exploring the grounds, with it's bears, elephants, leopards, llama, lions, ostriches, and reindeer (today sheep, elk and zebras still roam the hills), they attended dinner in the Refectory, presided by Hearst.

Hearst was an unstoppable buyer, acquiring a $50M art collection. A 12th Century monastery was dismantled in Spain, and a road and railtrack built to transport the stones to a port. Besides San Simeon, he had six other homes, including St. Donats castle in Wales, plus several five-story warehouses in New York and San Francisco filled with crated works.

The Depression found Hearst unprepared and by 1934 his empire was $126M in debt. Financial control passed to the banks who sold 40% of the corporations. Marion Davies sold all her gifts and gave the proceeds to Hearst, saying: *"I started out a gold digger but I fell in love with him".*

In 1941, at the height of the Golden Age of Hollywood, the 25-year-old boy-genius Orson Welles filmed *Citizen Kane* - a fictional story loosely based on Hearst's life. Hearst was enraged by the deliberately cruel and inaccurate portrayal of the Marion Davis character and used his media dominance to block distribution. The film showed on only a few screens, then was shelved for ten years. Welles became an outcast and never directed another film.

In 1947, ill-health forced Hearst to leave San Simeon for medical care in Beverly Hills. He never returned and died in 1951. The estate was never completed, and never has been.

Hearst Castle™ was donated to the people of the State of California in 1957 and tours began the following year. Today it is a State Historic Monument, its richness and beauty preserved by California State Parks.

Right: The **Assembly Room** ☉.
Next page: **Neptune Pool** ☉.

One good shot that isn't pictured here is of the **Refectory**. Stand at the long end of the table (away from the fireplace) and use a wide angle to include the medieval flags.

✍ Photography for publication requires written permission. ☎805-927-2020.

The Neptune Pool at Hearst Castle™.

Caples Lake (el. 7,953 ft.) in the
Sierra Nevada mountains along
Route 88, and (inset) windmills
on Altamont Pass.

PhotoSecrets Northern California

Going East

East

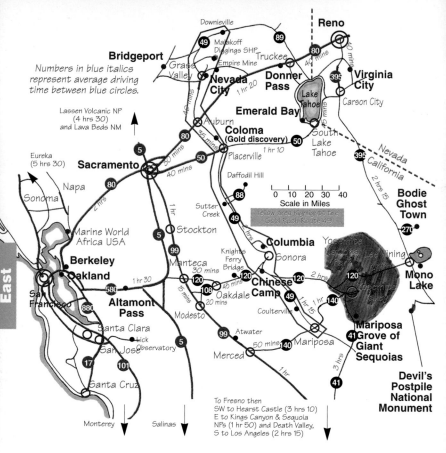

Numbers in blue italics represent average driving time between blue circles.

Reno

Downieville

Bridgeport

Malakoff Diggings SHP

Truckee

Donner Pass

Virginia City

Grass Valley

Empire Mine

Nevada City

Lake Tahoe

Carson City

Lassen Volcanic NP (4 hrs 30) and Lava Beds NM

Emerald Bay

Auburn

Coloma (Gold discovery)

South Lake Tahoe

Nevada

Eureka (5 hrs 30)

Sacramento

Placerville

California

Napa

Daffodil Hill

Bodie Ghost Town

Sonoma

Sutter Creek

0 10 20 30 40
Scale in Miles

Marine World Africa USA

Stockton

Columbia

Yosemite National Lee Mining

Mono Lake

Berkeley

Oakland

Manteca

Knights Ferry Bridge

Sonora

Chinese Camp

Yosemite

Altamont Pass

Oakdale

San Francisco

Modesto

Coulterville

Mariposa Grove of Giant Sequoias

Santa Clara

Lick Observatory

Atwater

Mariposa

San Jose

Merced

Devil's Postpile National Monument

Santa Cruz

To Fresno then SW to Hearst Castle (3 hrs 10) E to Kings Canyon & Sequoia NPs (1 hr 50) and Death Valley, S to Los Angeles (2 hrs 15)

Monterey   Salinas

Going East of San Francisco is to step back in time. 160 years ago, a steady procession of wagons was crossing the soaring Sierra Nevada range, just north of present-day **Reno**. Their story is told at **Donner Pass**, where the ill-fated Donner Party made their final camp. The settler's headed for the oasis of John Sutter's Fort in **Sacramento**. In 1848, one of Sutter's employees, James Marshall, found gold in a stream near **Coloma**. Aptly named **Route 49** follows the old stagecoach trail and winds between most of the colorful mining towns.

As the riches were spent, silver and gold was discovered in the Comstock Lode in Nevada. **Virginia City** became the largest city in the west. The lode's wealth built much of San Francisco, changed the course of the civil war, and helped establish

Sacramento as the new state's capital. Meanwhile, **Yosemite** quietly remained one of the most beautiful places in the new state of California.

Right: The 1855 St. Francis Xavier Catholic Church, in **Chinese Camp**. This dusk shot was taken with a compact camera utilizing the flash to highlight the gravestone.

Suggested Routes

Area	Time fm SF	Highlight
Yosemite NP	5hrs	Valley floor
Northern mines	3:15	Nevada City
Southern mines	2:30	Columbia
Sacramento	2:00	Riverfront
Tahoe	5:20	Virginia City

Oakland is the first city east of San Francisco. Industrial and suburban, it was the western terminus of the transcontinental railroad (1869) and is now one of the largest container ports in the country.

Jack London spent his early years on the Oakland waterfront, Gertrude Stein (b.1874), famous mainly for her inherited wealth and damning insult, was schooled here, and the Black Panthers campaigned against 'white America' here. from 1966-72

Oakland has many Victorian houses (try Preservation Park at 12th St and Martin Luther King Jr Way) and a small but authentic Chinatown. In October 1991, fire swept through the prized Oakland Hills, killing 25 people and destroying 2,810 homes.

"There is no there there."
Gertrude Stein.
(Oakland has since rectified this situation with a statue in the center of town - Broadway/13th - called 'There').

Tourist central in Oakland is **Jack London Square** ①, a modern complex with large shops and restaurants, named after the famous novelist. The square (and this statue of London, 24mm) is at the foot of Broadway, overlooking the Inner Harbor. Two blocks southeast of the statue is the **First & Last Chance Saloon**, a favorite watering hole of London's now displaying a fine set of old photographs inside, and his turf-roofed log cabin relocated from Alaska.

Jack London was born in San Francisco in 1876 and originally worked on the Oakland waterfront. After a brief spell at UC Berkeley, he moved to Alaska's Yukon seeking fortune and adventure in the 1897 Klondike Gold Rush. A year later he returned penniless, with scurvy instead of gold, and turned to writing. Between 1900 and his death in 1916, he wrote over 30 books including *Call of the Wild* and became the most famous and highest paid writer of the day. London moved to Sonoma Valley in 1910 and built Wolf House, now a ruin near the Glen Ellen winery.

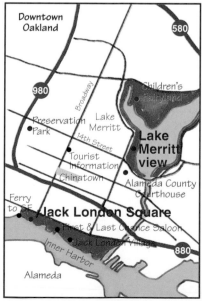

Downtown Oakland

580

980

Broadway

Children's Fairyland

Preservation Park

Lake Merritt

14th Street

Lake Merritt view

Tourist Information

Chinatown

Alameda County Courthouse

Ferry to SF

Jack London Square

First & Last Chance Saloon

Jack London Village

Inner Harbor

880

Alameda

Above: Oakland is one of the few cities to be based around a lake. Hidden amongst the urban city center is **Lake Merritt** ☉, a 155-acre saltwater lake popular for sailing, fishing and ferry rides. It was the first wildlife refuge in the country. Created in the 1870's by damming a tidal basin, the lake is named after its proponent, Mayor Samuel Merritt.

A good foreground is the ***Merritt Queen***, a paddle-wheeler which sails around the lake on weekends (11-3pm, 510-444-3807). On the southwest bank is the elegant 1935 **Alameda County Courthouse**, best photographed across the lake at dawn from Lakeside Avenue, or at late afternoon from the rooftop garden of the Oakland Museum at Oak/11th (Wed-Sat 10-5, Sun 12-7, $4/2). On the north bank is Lakeside Park and **Children's Fairyland**, best photographed in the late afternoon.

Right: The magnificent **Mormon Temple** ☉, built in 1963, has a colorful flower-garden entryway. The interior is closed to non-Mormons but free tours are given of the outer temple (9-9pm, ☎510-531-1475).

Mormons were significant pioneers of the West. The Church Of The Later Day Saints, founded by Joseph Smith, was the first American religion.

The temple is in the Oakland hills at 4770 Lincoln Ave near Freeway 13 and is best in the late afternoon. A good dusk shot of the temple, with the south part of San Francisco Bay in the background, can be taken from **Joaquin Miller Park** (named after a local poet) at a turnout on the way to Woodminster Memorial.

Nearby, the winding **Skyline Blvd** has good views (but those from Lawrence Hall and Grizzly Peak Blvd are better; see *Berkeley*). Just down the road, at 4700 Lincoln Avenue, is the Byzantine, gold-domed **Greek Orthodox Church**. Flower lovers should check out the eight-acre **Morcom Rose Garden** at 700 Jean Street (off Grand, near I-580 and Piedmont, free, best in Spring).

Photographing the East Bay

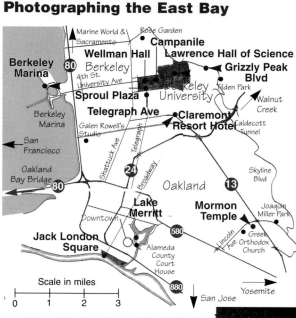

Mr. Jacuzzi
The Jacuzzi was invented in Berkeley. Candido Jacuzzi designed it as a portable hydrotherapy for his son's rheumatoid arthritis. His grandson Roy Jacuzzi turned it into a marketable product in 1968.

Galen Rowell, the famous wilderness photographer and author, has a museum-style studio near the Marina, at 1466 66th Street (by Hollis St.) in Emeryville. ☎510-601-9000.

Coffee and conversation in Berkeley.

Below: The view from **Grizzly Peak Boulevard** ⊕. You can see the Oakland Bay Bridge, the city of San Francisco, the Golden Gate Bridge, San Francisco Bay and Berkeley Marina.

Left: The 1915 **Claremont Resort, Spa and Tennis Club** ☾ (☎510-843-3000) is off Route 13 (Tunnel Road) at Ashby and Domingo Aves. This magnificent complex originally had no bar since a local law forbade the sale of alcohol within a mile of the university campus. However, a student proved that only half the hotel was within the radius and a bar was opened on the terrace (which has great views of the bay).

Below: This stunning view of San Francisco Bay and the Golden Gate Bridge was taken at 1,600' above sea level, from **Grizzly Peak Blvd** ☾, above the Berkeley campus. The easiest route is to take Freeway 24 northeast towards Walnut Creek. Immediately after the Caldecot Tunnel exit on Fish Ranch Road. Turn right over the tunnel then, after one mile, right again at the stop sign. There are many pullouts to choose from and the view is best in the early morning and at sunset. Nearby **Tilden Park** has an antique carousel, petting farm, and miniature steam train.

Almost identical shots can be taken from the **Lawrence Hall of Science** or the **Botanical Gardens**. **Skyline Blvd** (south in Oakland) has similar views (though not as good). The **Berkeley Marina** and Pier has the same view but from sea-level.

UC BERKELEY CAMPUS

Famous for its radical liberal politics, the prestigious University of California at Berkeley is the most attractive college campus in California. Of the nine campuses in the UC system, Berkeley is the oldest and, with 30,000 students, the second largest, after UCLA. There are so many Nobel laureates that some parking spaces are *Nobel-Only*.

The college was founded in 1863 as the *"Athens of the Pacific"*. It was started by Protestants eager to contain Catholicism, and named after an irish Anglican Bishop, George Berkeley, who wrote a poem about a new golden age of learning in America. The state of California took over the college in 1873, and additional support came from Phoebe Apperson Hearst, the mother of W.R. Hearst of Hearst Castle fame. In the 1960's, Sproul Plaza (by the Student Union) was the epicenter for Free Speech and anti-Vietnam protests, with student activists battling the UC Regents (college administrators) and even the National Guard, called in by California's Governor, Ronald Reagan.

Free guided walking tours start at Visitors Center by the west entrance, at Oxford and University (M,W,F, 10 & 1pm, 1-1/2 hours, ☎510-642-5215).

Top: **Wellman Hall** ☉.

Center: The **Lawrence Hall of Science** ☉ is an engaging 'hands-on' science museum, popular with children. Outside are two climbing frames, a life-sized whale and this 60' model of the DNA double-helix molecule. The plaza has a great view of the Bay and the Golden Gate Bridge, stunning at sunset on a clear day. The Hall of Science is on a steep hill along Centennial Drive. Ernest Lawrence won Berkeley's first Nobel Prize for developing the particle accelerator. He patented the color TV tube and, along with fellow Berkeley physics professor Robert Oppenheimer, helped develop the atomic bomb.

Below: **Bowles Hall** ☉ near the California Memorial Stadium.

Nearby, the **Botanical Garden** (☎510-642-3343) also has a great Bay view, as well as 13,000 species of plants, primarily used for research. Flower lovers will also like the **Municipal Rose Garden**, 1/2-mile north of campus, with over 4,000 varieties of roses (best in Spring).

Sproul Plaza and the Student's Union building is the main gathering place on campus. **Telegraph Avenue**, particularly between Bancroft and Channing, is great for people shots and at weekends has a street market replete with vibrant tie-dye shirts and hand-made jewelry. The area has the highest density of bookstores and coffeehouses in California. Shattuck Avenue is another great people area and is home to **Chez Panisse** (1517 Shattuck), the birthplace of 'California Cuisine' (where 'the bill is larger than the portions').

A 1/4 mile north of the campus, on La Loma Ave at Buena Vista Way, is the **house of Bernard Maybeck**, designer of the Palace of Fine Arts and Berkeley's first professor of architecture.

East

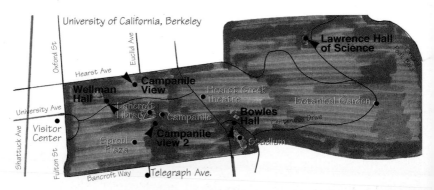

University of California, Berkeley

Oxford St · Euclid Ave · Hearst Ave · **Lawrence Hall of Science** · **Campanile View** · **Wellman Hall** · Bancroft Library · Hearst Creek theatre · Botanical Garden · University Ave · Campanile · **Bowles Hall** · Centennial Drive · Shattuck Ave · Visitor Center · Fulton St · **Campanile view 2** · Sproul Plaza · Stadium · Bancroft Way · **Telegraph Ave.**

The most distinctive building on Berkeley's campus is '**The Campanile**' (an Italian derivation of 'bell tower'). Its official name is Sather Tower. Built in 1914, the 307 ft. Campanile houses a 61 bell carillon, rung at noon and 6pm, and is modeled after St. Mark's Basilica in Venice.

To the right of the tower is the Bancroft Library, which houses the brass plate thought to be left by Sir Francis Drake at Point Reyes. Drake claimed the region for Queen Elizabeth I as 'Nova Albion', New England. Also at the Library is the nugget of gold that James Marshall found in Columa in 1848, triggering the California Gold Rush.

ALTAMONT PASS

Altamont Pass is home to the world's largest wind-fueled power plant. On your drive east towards Yosemite, you'll pass through this surreal landscape of modern windmills. Use a slow shutter speed to capture the motion of the blade.

Altamont Landfill

Altamont Pass Road

Windmills

580

Greenville Road exit

Mountain House Road exit

California's **capital city** is a relaxed, tree-lined suburban town with a rich heritage. Home of pioneers, miners and railroad barons, Sacramento has the largest collection of gold-rush era buildings and the country's most spectacular State Capitol.

John Sutter, a swiss adventurer, founded the town in 1839 as 'New Helvetica', a trading post at the confluence of the American and Sacramento rivers. He was granted 50,000 acres by the Mexican Governor. Sutter's Fort quickly became the destination for wagon trains on the California Trail and it was from here that the first rescue team for the Donner Party was dispatched. In 1848, one of Sutter's foremen discovered gold in the American River and triggered the California Gold Rush. The massive migration overwhelmed the fort and ironically ruined Sutter.

As a supply base for the rich Northern Mines, Sacramento became wealthy enough to offer the State a million dollars for the honor of being the capital, beating out Berkeley, San Jose and Monterey in 1854. In 1863, after completion of the West's first railway (from Sacramento to Folsom), four local grocers won grants from the US Congress to build the eastern half of the Transcontinental Railroad. Completed in six years with Chinese and Irish laborers, the associated landgrants and influence made the four storekeepers some of the richest and most-hated men in America.

Today, Sacramento is an agricultural center (from the fertile Sacramento Valley) and a major port (with the 1963 deepwater channel linking it to San Francisco Bay, 43 miles away).

"An edifice should be constructed ... with a beauty and luxuriousness that no other capital can boast."
Governor Leland Stanford, 1863.

Right: The magnificent white 210' rotunda of the **State Capitol building** turns a beautiful shade of gold with its clear view of the setting sun. Greek democracy and Roman republicanism were the passions of the young nation, inspiring this classical-revival design by MF Butler. Built from 1860-74, the Capitol is surrounded by 40 acres of beautiful parkland and plants from around the world. The trees are Italian Stone Pine. Surrounding structures are limited to six stories or 75 feet.

The dome is best photographed from the fountain on Capitol Mall. Use a 35mm for the wide shot (left) and 300mm and tripod for this detail (right). The white dome turns gold around one hour before sunset on a clear day.

Where Sacramento is two hours NE of San Francisco along I-80. It's enroute to the northern mines (Nevada City, Columa) and Reno/Tahoe. The Capitol is at 10th and Capitol Mall. Free guided tours 9-5 (Room B27). ☎916-324-0333.

When 🕐 The Capitol and Governor's Mansion look best in the late afternoon, and Old Sacramento at dusk.

Anytime of year is fine. The Central Valley gets hot in the summer so keep your film in a cooler packed with ice.

Nearby **Safetyville USA** is a miniature town where children can practice the rules of the road. The **Sacramento Delta** ('Everglades of the West') is a series of waterways and islands lined with historic towns and inns, popular for houseboating. **Folsom** has many restored Gold Rush buildings on Sutter St, including a Pony Express office. **Modesto** is the birthplace of Steven Spielberg and where he filmed *American Graffiti*. Stockton has the unusual **Wonderful World of Windmills**, a collection of six 6'-high metal windmills, at 6553 Waterloo Road.

Sutter's Fort

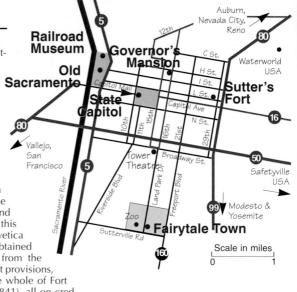

utter's Fort was once the only European outpost in the California interior. The restored adobe fort, built from 1839 to 1846, is now a fascinating museum with period artifacts. 27th and L Streets (10-5, $2, (☎916-324-0539 or 916-445-4422).

Fleeing his native Switzerland to avoid massive debts, Swiss-born John Sutter traveled the world as a cook, clerk and trader, before founding this settlement as New Helvetica (New Switzerland). He obtained a grant of 50,000 acres from the Mexican Governor, bought provisions, seeds, tools, guns and the whole of Fort Ross from the Russians (1841), all on credit. The first pioneer wagons reached California in 1843 and Sutter, ruling like a generous king, was in business.

Sutter's goal was to promote agriculture but the 1849 gold rush destroyed all that. His workers deserted for the mines and squatters overran his land. *"Miners would not buy from me what they could more easily steal."* The new American Government refused his claim to the goldfield land - he had bought it from the Indians but they weren't recognized as landowners - it was now federal land. Creditors called in his $100,000 debt, the precarious empire crumbled and Sutter's Fort was auctioned off in 1849.

Sutter fled, leaving his son to sort out the mess, and died almost penniless.

Above: The **Governor's Mansion** 🕐 was the residence of California's Governor, from Leland Stanford in the 1860's to Ronald Reagan the 1960's. The Victorian mansion is at 16th and H Street and is best photographed in mid-afternoon.

Tours $2, 10-4, ☎916-323-3047.

Below: Next to the zoo is **Fairytale Town**, a 2.5 acre park where nursery rhymes become climbing frames. (Sutterville Road, 10-5 $2.75, ☎916-264-5233).

Old Sacramento

Above: The **Pony Express Monument** ⏱ in Old Sacramento. Bordering the river, Old Sacramento is the restored commercial center with 130 shops and restaurants and the country's largest collection of Gold Rush buildings.

The Pony Express started here in April 1860. 121 riders and 500 ponies shuttled between Sacramento and St Joseph, Missouri. They delivered the mail over a distance of 1,966 miles in only ten days and, despite mountains, Indians and harsh weather, only lost one pouch. The romantic venture lasted 18 months, ending four days after completion of the first transcontinental telegraph line in 1862.

This dusk shot requires a long exposure (about one second) and thus a tripod or other platform. A 50mm lens was used.

Below: The **Spirit of Sacramento** ⏱ is an historic 100-foot paddlewheeler. There are one-hour sightseeing tours and murder-mystery dinners. (☎800-433-0263).

Right The **California State Railroad Museum** ⏱. At the north end of Old Sacramento, where the 'Big Four' planned track routes and located the western terminus of the Transcontinental Railroad, is the

largest railroad museum in North America. A three-story building contains 21 restored trains and carriages (between 2nd and 1st, $5). The best photographs however are outside (free) at the adjacent Central Pacific Passenger Station and railyard.

The Railroad Barons

"Some people praised 'em, some people cursed 'em, but everybody respected 'em. They gambled and won."

In the mid-1800's, it took five months to reach California by land, or six months by sea. A railroad could reduce this time to five days. One man had such a vision - Theodores Dehone Juddah.

Juddah had engineered California's first railroad (a 22-mile route to linking Sacramento and Folsom in 1856) and needed financial support. He turned to four Sacramento shopkeepers (Charles Crocker, Mark Hopkins, Collis P Huntington and Leland Stanford - *The Big Four*) and together they formed the Central Pacific Railroad Company. But the Big Four's vision was less about engineering and more about greed - whoever controlled the railroad would control California.

In 1862 the Pacific Railroad Act was passed, bringing untold wealth to the Big Four. For every mile of track laid, they would be given $16,000 to $48,000, plus 20 miles of land on either side. The Central Pacific was to build east from Sacramento, and meet the Union Pacific (building west from Nebraska) in Promontory, Utah. Cities in between vied in a life-or-death struggle to be included in the route. Cunning and greedy, the four 'Barons' exploited their influence and exclusive land grants and their 'Octopus' soon had its tentacles in every part of California's politics and economy.

As soon as the route was designed, Juddah was ousted. He died accidentally, days before ground was broken. For the hard mountain work, 3,000 Irish and 12,000 Chinese were brought in. The railroad was supposed to bring prosperity but when it opened in 1869 there was a depression, into which the thousands of laborers were discharged.

But the Big Four were now rich men and moved to Nob Hill in San Francisco. Leland Stanford founded Stanford University and became a State Senator and later State Governor. The railway was extended to Oakland and Monterey and the owners sponsored travel photography to attract visitors.

"I reached my hand down and picked it up, it made my heart thump for I was certain it was gold." James Marshall, 1848.

The Indians had known of the gold for centuries but had no use for it. The Spanish Padres had been shown it in the 1700's but, wary of the unmanageable traders it would bring, advised silence. It wasn't until poor calculations forced construction workers to dig into the Sierra foothills that Americans learned of the free wealth in their newly acquired land. In 1849, after a 195-pound nugget was found near Carson Hill, the California Gold Rush was on, becoming one of the largest and most frenetic migrations in history.

'Gold Fever' spread and mainly men swarmed to the hills of eastern California. The old Mexican capital of Monterey lost most of its population (as did San Jose, Oregon and Utah), ships docked in San Francisco disgorging hopeful Europeans, and sailors and farmers deserted their employers. Bret Harte, the storywriter, described the settlements as: *"Hard, ugly, unwashed, vulgar, and lawless."*

Perhaps this was the Spaniard's famed *El Dorado*. California's population swelled from 13,000 to over 100,000 between 1849 and 1852. Prices soared (an egg cost $1) and speculation, gambling and violence were rampant. But most miners went bust. The money was in supplying not digging, and Sacramento was the main supply base.

California became a US State in 1850. The gold peaked in 1852, with $80M coming out of the hills, and died out by the 1860's. Towns were abandoned almost as quickly as they had been built. Gold was later found in the eastern Sierras in 1859 at Bodie, California and Comstock, Nevada (which turned out to be mainly silver), then in Yukon, Alaska in 1897. But the 49-ers had changed California's status and future.

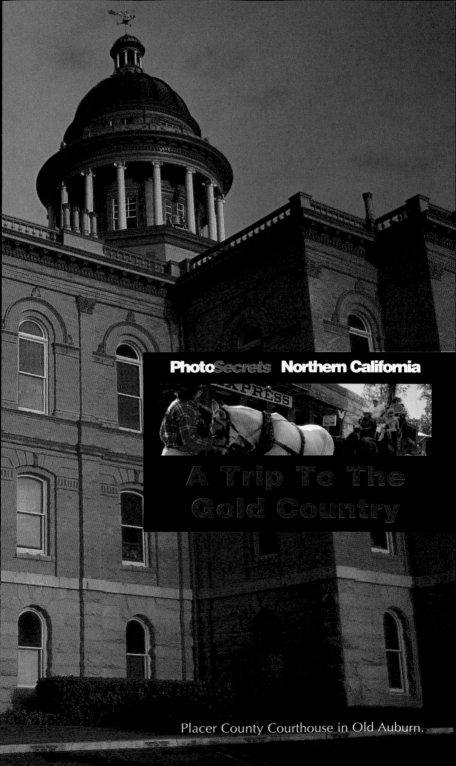

PhotoSecrets **Northern California**

A Trip To The
Gold Country

Placer County Courthouse in Old Auburn.

The Gold Country is a 320-mile-long chain of picturesque Victorian towns set amongst the rolling Sierra Nevada hills. The area is known for its Bed & Breakfast Inns, gold panning, antique shopping, wineries, whitewater rafting, caving, and of course, great photo opportunities.

The deliberately-named Route 49, the *"Golden Chain Highway"*, follows the 49-ers trail and winds through most of the historic towns. Within four years of discovering gold in the American River near **Coloma**, 550 mining towns had sprung up and about half remain today.

The towns are distinguished by the different mining methods used. The gold, lacing the foothills, lay in a thin vein which the Mexican miners called "La Veta Madre" - the Mother Lode. The easy pickings were in the eight rivers draining the eastern Sierra Nevada where gold flakes had naturally eroded out of the hills and settled in sand bars. You can still find gold in the rivers today. Individuals staked small claims, limited to the ground a man could actually work, and used pans, then sluice boxes, to separate the heavy gold from the lighter sand. This 'placer' mining was mainly in the south, the *Southern Mines*, and is best illustrated at **Coloma** and **Columbia**.

Placer gold was exhausted in a few years, forcing people to dig deep into the ground (see the **Empire Mine** near Grass Valley) or simply blast the hillside away with pressurized water (hydraulic mining, best illustrated at **Malakoff Diggins**). Significant capital was required and the *Northern Mines* are characterized by a small number of large corporations.

'There's gold in the Sierra foothills!'
Sam Brannan in his San Francisco newspaper, 1849

Right: The porch of 'Victorian Closett' in Amador City.

When 🕐   Anytime of year is fine. Most sights are best in the appropriately golden light of late afternoon. This is too much mileage for one day: spend a weekend concentrating on the Northern or Southern Mines. **Columbia** is the best place for children and **Nevada City** is the most attractive town to spend a weekend in.

Where   Approach Nevada City and Coloma from San Francisco via Sacramento and I-80. Sonora and surroundings are a good detour en route to Yosemite via Modesto.

East

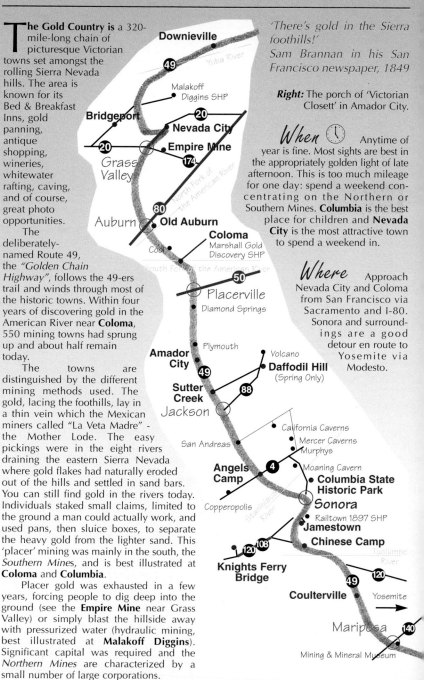

Downieville

49

Yuba River

Malakoff Diggins SHP

Bridgeport   20

Nevada City

20   **Empire Mine**

174

Grass Valley

North Fork of the American River

80

Auburn   **Old Auburn**

Coloma
Marshall Gold Discovery SHP

Cool

South Fork of the American River

50

Placerville
Diamond Springs

Plymouth

Volcano

Amador City   49   **Daffodil Hill**
(Spring Only)

Sutter Creek   88

Jackson

California Caverns
Mercer Caverns
Murphys

San Andreas

Angels Camp   4   Moaning Cavern
● **Columbia State Historic Park**

Copperopolis

Stanislaus River

● *Sonora*
Railtown 1897 SHP
Jamestown
Chinese Camp

120   108

Knights Ferry Bridge

Tuolumne River

49   120
Coulterville   Yosemite →

Mariposa   140

Mining & Mineral Museum

Downieville, in the rain.

Above and previous page: **Downieville** ⏱ is one of the most northern and smallest towns of the Mother Lode. It straddles the Yuba River with two single-lane bridges and is the only town displaying a gallows. They were used only once in 1885 when 20 year old James O'Neil was hanged for murder. California ended hanging as a punishment in 1941. The 73-mile drive from Nevada City is long but has many scenic views of the Yuba River.

13 miles north of Downieville is **Sierra City**, a photogenic town burned by fires in the 1940's.

Below: A pleasant drive west of Grass Valley is **Bridgeport Covered Bridge** ⏱, the longest existing single-span covered bridge in the world. The 232' span crosses the Yuba River and was built in 1862 by David Wood. It was part of a 14-mile toll road and from 1862-9, a third of all Gold Rush freight passed through this bridge. The Turnpike was the main route to the Northern Mines and the Comstock Lode but was displaced by the Transcontinental Railroad.

The bridge has been lovingly restored and is best photographed from today's parallel concrete road.

Surrounded by pine-clad hills, **Nevada City** ☺ is one of the most attractive towns in the Gold Country. *'Queen of the Northern Mines'*, its elegant restaurants, theatre, and delightful coffee houses make Nevada City a romantic weekend destination. The heart of town, Main Street, is best photographed from the top looking down with mist-graced pine trees in the distance, or the bottom looking up from the historic National Hotel.

20 miles north is **Malakoff Diggins State Historic Park**. This is an alien landscape created by hydraulic mining (1850-80) that tore away at the hillsides.

The Cornish Influence

Most of the mine's laborers were experienced tin miners from Cornwall, England. Almost a third of the Cornish population emigrated to this region in the 1840's. They brought with them the famous Cornish Pasty - meat, potatoes and onion wrapped in a pastry turnover - heated over a candle while they worked. Nevada City has good pasty shops.

The **Empire State Mine** 🕐 is an immense complex of over 367 miles of mining shafts. It was one of the first shaft mines in California and is the best preserved of such operations. There are several mining buildings (made of waste rock), a good museum, and the small house and grounds of the owning Bourn family. An underground train is planned to take visitors deep into the mine shafts.

Inheriting his father's mine in 1878, William Bowers Bourn Jr. invested heavily in the mine, making it one of the richest and longest-running operations in California. From 1850-1956, his company sank shafts almost a mile into the ground and removed over $2B of gold. They built 49 separate mines within a five square mile surface area. They tracked gold veins, and their neighbors' operations, using a detailed scale model kept in a secret room. This stunning model is now on display in the Visitors Center and shows the labrynthian-warren below your feet.

The most photogenic area is the Bourn's English Manor house, designed by San Francisco architect Willis Polk. The front of the house is best photographed in the morning and has an English Rose Garden, while the rear, containing two fountains and a lilly waterfall, is best in the afternoon.

The Bourns also built Greystone Winery in St Helena (now the Culinary Institute) and Filoli, an extensive mansion and gardens 15 miles south of San Francisco. Filoli was the family's motto, a contraction of *Fight, Love, Live*.

Empire Mine State Historic Park is a few miles east of Grass Valley on Route 174 at 10791 E Empire Street. ☎916-273-8522.

Far Right: Stand over the pool and overflow the bottom of your frame for a punchy shot. Use a slow shutter speed to stream the fountain.

Nearby A few miles west is **Grass Valley** which, thanks mainly to the Empire Mine, is the largest and longest-lasting mining town in California. In the 1860's, Grass Valley had a greater population than Los Angeles. Despite this, there's little to photograph.

Auburn, with its convenient location on I-80, is the most-visited Gold Rush town. **Old Auburn** is a fun restored area with Awful Annies (a popular restaurant) and a large statue of a panning miner. The best sight however is **Placer County Courthouse** (below), built in 1894. Apparently one of the punishments of the 19th Century was to strip a man naked, tie him to a tree, and leave him there in the middle of mosquito season. The courthouse faces north but makes a good photograph from many angles and at all times of day.

COLOMA

*"Mr Marshall arrived from the mountains on very important business."
John Sutter in his diary, four days after Marshall found gold.*

Left: The reconstructed mill is built from the original plans and actually saws timber. The classic view is taken as you approach from the east parking area. Open up a stop or two (overexpose) to get detail in the dark wood.

Right: Just north is a bridge over the South Fork of the American River, a great place to photograph Summer river rafters at the end of a day's paddling. Use a long lens (210mm) to contract the image and wait for a fun boat to form your foreground.

Where Coloma is 48 miles from Sacramento, via Auburn and I-80 or Placerville and Rt 50.

When ⏲ The main sight is the reconstructed mill, which faces northwest, so afternoon is best.

Coloma, at the **James Marshall Gold Discovery State Historic Park**, is where gold was first discovered. There is a reconstruction of Marshall's mill, a small museum and park, and informative presentations by park rangers. You can walk to the actual spot where Marshall made the discovery, and, with a little patience, still find gold in the river.

In 1847, Captain John Sutter needed timber for his trading fort in present-day Sacramento. He commissioned the construction of a sawmill, 30 miles upstream on the South Fork of the American River, and his foreman James Marshall and a team of Mormon laborers set to work.

A miscalculation forced them to increase the size of the millrace, thereby digging a deep hole in the riverbank. While inspecting the work, Marshall saw yellow flakes glistening in the sand. The Mormons vowed to keep the secret while Marshall rode to see Sutter. After testing the gold and discovering more, Sutter bought the land from the local Indians and tried to register it with the new American authorities. But they didn't recognize Indians as landowners and declared the land federal property. Word leaked out and by May Sam Brannan had published the news in San Francisco. Within a year, 6,000 people flocked to Coloma and beyond.

Sutter's farmland was ruined, Marshall's claim was ignored, even the mill proved uncompetitive. Marshall never found gold again and was cast out of towns when he claimed that all the gold was his. He died penniless (like Sutter) in 1885, a nugget's throw from the mill.

"And I found a nugget THIS big!"

North on Rt 49 is this 'Cool' sign.

The Gold Country is famed for its Victorian Bed and Breakfast Inns, and the **Amador Gate House Inn** in Jackson is one of the most photogenic.

Kennedy Wheel Park was the first major environmental project in the Gold Country. In 1912, legislation was introduced to prevent hydraulic mines from dumping their huge amounts of residue (finely ground rock and water called 'tailings') into rivers. At Kennedy Mine, an ingenious method was devised that lifted 850 tons of watery waste a day to an impound dam a mile away. Four huge wooden wheels, 58' in diameter, were used to ascend two hills. The wheels were housed in buildings and kept secret. Most of the locals never knew of their existence until the buildings were torn down in 1942. Two wheels remain. From the hill to the north of the parking area you can photograph a wheel with the Kennedy Mine head in the distance. From the south hill you can see south to the impound dam. From Jackson, drive two miles northeast on Main Street.

Nearby is **Daffodil Hill** where, for a brief few weeks in March you can visit and photograph a field of 300,000 daffodils. Closed for the rest of the year. The small town of **Volcano** is considered the 'most complete, unrestored mining town in the Gold Country' but there's little to photograph. **Murphy's** is a quaint town worth exploring with a camera. There are several deep caves in the area (use a fast film and a tripod - a flash won't help). By the way, **San Andreas** has nothing to do with the San Andreas fault (the 650-mile fault is best seen in the Carrizo Plain, a wasteland east of Taft, 200 miles south near Bakersfield).

Angels Camp is famous as the source of Mark Twain's Jumping Frog story. They have a small statue of Twain hidden in Utica Park (best around noon). Across the street is St. Vasilize, a rare Serbian Orthodox Church, built in 1910.

Brady's Store is in Columbia State Historic Park (see next page).

Sonora was named after Sonora in Mexico. On Route 49 heading north out of town (Washington & Snell) is the strikingly red **St James Episcopal Church**. It faces south so anytime is fine (this shot is taken in the late afternoon). There are other red churches in Santa Rosa and Mendocino. In the center of town (on Yaney Ave) is the 1898 **Tuolumne County Courthouse** (not pictured).

East

Amador Gate House Inn, Jackson.

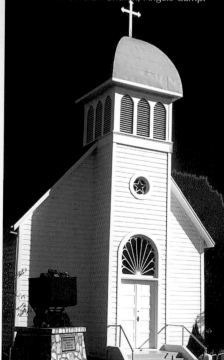

St. Vasilize Serbian Church, Angels Camp.

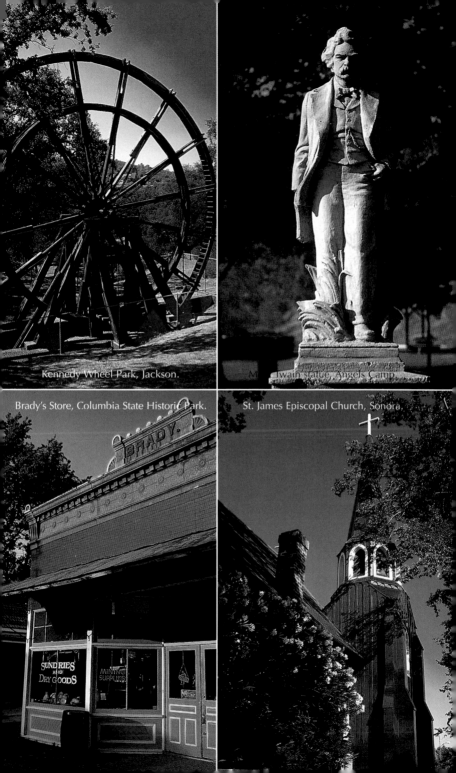

Kennedy Wheel Park, Jackson.

Mark Twain statue, Angels Camp.

Brady's Store, Columbia State Historic Park.

St. James Episcopal Church, Sonora.

COLUMBIA

The best family place in the Gold Country is **Columbia State Historic Park**. Here you can pan for gold, ride the stagecoach and visit the saloon. Storekeepers wear period costume. There are four blocks of 1850's buildings, many of brick with iron doors to protect against fire.

At one time this was California's second-largest city with 5,000 people and 150 businesses. Over $1.5B at today's prices was mined at the 'Gem of the Southern Mines'.

The late afternoon sun is quiet magical here making for good photography of the hotel and Brady's Store.

Columbia is 3 miles north of Sonora.

Just south is **Jamestown**, another interesting town. It was named after Col. George James because he gave away free champagne. When James ran away to avoid mining debts, his creditors tried to rename the town but failed. There's nothing obvious to photograph but adjacent is **Railtown 1897**, a steamtrain station and turning yard.

Below: Towards Oakdale is **Knight's Ferry Covered Bridge**.

The adobe Chinatown Grocery (1851) in **Coulterville** is one of the earliest Gold Rush buildings remaining. Made of sun-dried clay rather than wood it survived the fires that often destroyed towns. It still contains the original shelves and counters. The store was owned by Mow Da Sun and his son, Sun Kow, calling themselves the SunSun Wo Company. It was run by Chinese up until 1926 and is thought to have been a popular opium den.

Coulterville is a small one-street town great for photography. It was named for George Coutter after he opened a tent store here in 1850. Facing Rt. 49 is 'Whistling Billy', a tiny steam engine.

The grocery is east of Rt. 49 on Chinatown Main Street and faces the setting sun, giving this golden glow.

DONNER PASS

The most stirring and haunting place in California is a small area off I-80 called **Donner Memorial State Park** ○. It was here in 1846-7 that George Donner and his wagontrain of 84 people (most of them children) were trapped in the worst snow storm ever recorded in the Sierra Nevada. It is a bewitching tale of family ambition, erroneous shortcuts, unfortunate timing, terrible endurance and daring rescues.

There is a good museum (☎916-582-7892) about overland pioneers and you can visit the sites of the Party's four shacks around what is now called Donner Lake. The most photogenic sight is the Donner Memorial (above), near the museum. In that fateful winter, the snow was as deep as the memorial's shaft - twenty feet - and the Party lived subterranean lives, buried under the snow.

"When we stopped at night we would take off our shoes, which by this time were so badly rotted by constant wetting in snow that there was very little left of them. In the morning we would push our shoes on, bruising and numbing the feet so badly that they would ache and ache with walking and the cold, until night would come again. Oh! the pain! It seemed to make the pangs of hunger more excruciating."

"Half-crazed people living in absolute filth, with naked, half-eaten bodies strewn about the cabines."

From the journal of a rescuer.

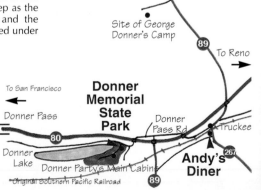

Site of George Donner's Camp

To Reno

To San Francisco

Donner Memorial State Park

Donner Pass

Donner Pass Rd

Truckee

Donner Lake

Donner Party's Main Cabins

Original Southern Pacific Railroad

Andy's Diner

Truckee is where the Transcontinental Railroad crossed the 7,000' Sierra Nevada mountains. The West's first train robbery occurred here in 1870. There is a small gold rush area on Commercial Row and the retro **Andy's Diner** ① is by the train depot.

Reader Recommendation:

Bob Lichty from Ohio writes:

*"On the way to Truckee on I-80 you go over **Immigrant Pass**, about 7-10 miles west of Donner Pass. Stop at the turn-out overlook on the west bound lane. You can see one of the largest panoramic views in all of California from this turn out. I would guess you can see 60-70 miles west and north. On the right day it is breath taking.*

"The Truckee River is spectacular in late April and early May - it roars!"

RENO

(Next page)

At the base of the eastern Sierras, starting the high-desert of Nevada, is **Reno** ①. It's like visiting a smaller version of Las Vegas before the theme-hotels moved in. There is a great dusk view as you enter on I-80.

The most distinctive area is this sign on Commercial and Virginia Street, next to Fitzgerald's. To capture the bright lights of the big city ("The Biggest Little City in the World"), stand your camera on a tripod or other platform, switch off the flash, and leave the shutter open for a second or two (this shot was one second at f22 and ISO50). You could use a fill-flash to include your friends in the foreground, throwing chips from your casino winnings.

You get a good skyline view of Reno as you enter on I-80, although there's no good place to stop and take a photograph.

Reno was formed when the railroad came through and grew with a connection to the Comstock Lode (Virginia and Truckee Railroad). It was named after Union General Jesse Reno who was killed in the Civil War.

Reno has a pleasant university and there's a rose garden in **Idlewild Park**. Elvis' Pink Cadillac, and 200 other cars, are in the **National Automobile Museum**.

Nearby **Sparks** is a major distribution center and has a waterpark called 'Wild Island'. Nine miles east (exit 23 on I-80) is the 100-bedroom **Mustang Ranch**, (this is one of the few counties in the US where prostitution is legal) where 200,000 men are 'entertained' each year. **Highway 50**, a dull drive towards Salt Lake City, is accurately known as "The Loneliest Road in America".

The Donner Party

WARNING: This is not a pleasant story.

"Never take no cut-offs and hurry along as fast as you can."
Virginia Reed, 1847.

No story of the American west is as tragic or as haunting as that of the Donner Party. Of the 84 people that tried to cross the Sierra Nevada's, only half survived, most resorting to cannibalism.

In the 1840's, many easterners were tempted by the fertile lands and gentle climate of Alta California. Believing that Mexican rule was fading, small groups probed dangerous and uncharted territory, trying to find an overland route passable by wagons. In 1843, the Chiles-Walker Party became the first pioneer wagon train to reach California, and the next year a great migration was underway.

In Illinois, a wealthy 61-year-old farmer called George Donner decided that the future for his family lay out west. With his brother Jacob Donner, friend James Reed, their wives, and sixteen children, they packed most of their possessions into six wagons and set forth on the 2,000 mile journey. They left from Springfield, Illinois in April 1846. The last survivors of their ill-fated party would reach their destination, Sutter's Fort in present-day Sacramento, more than one year later.

The first half of the trip was beautiful and pleasant. Game was bountiful and there was singing and dancing around campfires at night. They traveled with other emigrants and counted 478 other wagons in front and another 20 behind, all destined for Oregon and California.

The troubles started with news of a short cut. In a new guidebook, a famous trapper, Lansford W. Hastings, claimed that his 'Hastings Cut-Off' saved 300-400 miles. In an open letter, he offered to lead the first party. Other men disagreed and most of the emigrants continued on the main route to Fort Hall (Idaho). But the Donners and Reeds, plus other families and 16 single men split off on July 20 and headed South to Fort Bridger (Utah), the entrance to 'Hastings Cut-Off'. George Donner was elected wagonmaster and they became known as the *Donner Party*.

But Hastings had left with an earlier group and his Cut-Off was a folly. What was passable by horse was not by wagon. The Donner Party hacked their way through undergrowth, felled trees, carried the wagons over mountains and almost died crossing the barren 80-mile Salt Lake. They lost most of their animals, possessions, and hope. The Cut-Off was 125 miles longer than the main route and instead of taking two weeks, it had taken eight. By the time the Donner Party rejoined the main trail at the Humboldt River on Sept. 26, all the other emigrants, including Hastings and his group, had already crossed the Sierras.

Tempers frayed. In a petty argument, James Reed accidently killed a man. Reed was banished from the train - forced to leave his family and continue on alone.

On October 19, desperately low on provisions, the party was met by Charles Stanton. He had ridden on ahead to Sutter's Fort and returned with mules loaded with beef and flour, and two indian guides, all donated by the generous Captain Sutter. Stanton told of a difficult mountain crossing but had heard that the high pass would not be blocked by snow for another month. The party decided to rest the cattle for five days, near the present site of Reno. Had they not, they could have crossed the Sierras before the storms began.

As snow began to fall, the party started ascending the mountains, following the Truckee River. In total there were 25 men, 15 women and 41 children. On October 31 an axle broke on George Donner's wagon and he and his family stopped at Alder Creek to fix it - they were never to leave this spot. The other families continued on for six miles to Truckee Lake (now Donner Lake) and made camp. They were only 1,000 ft below the summit but decided to wait for the Donners and cross the following day.

That night a fierce storm blew up and they awoke to find the road buried in snow. Panicking, the party raced for the summit but the snow was too deep and soft for the wagons and they could no longer find the road. They returned to the Lake.

Throughout November more snow fell and several independent ascents failed. They resigned to spend the Winter at the Lake, cramped together in hurriedly-made cabins, with the Donner family - still snow-bound six miles away at Alder Creek - living in a tent. An Irishman, Patrick Breen, kept a haunting diary as they were buried deeper by snow, writing: *No living thing without wings can get about.* They had traveled 2,500 miles in 7 months and had lost the race by one day, 150 miles from Sutters Fort.

East

Fishing and hunting proved unsuccessful, the horses and mules were lost in the snow, and by December the families by the Lake were down to three cattle for food.

In mid-December, Charles Stanton and the Indian guides led an escape group of six other men, five women and a boy of 12, calling themselves 'The Forlorn Hope'. They walked about five miles a day in soft, yielding snow, up to 60' deep, using snowshoes made from ox-bows and hide, and carried only one pound of beef each. The food ran out after five days and Stanton, exhausted and snowblind from the glaring sun, fell behind and died.

The group was so hungry that they decided that one person should be killed in order to feed the others. Straws were passed around to select someone but no-one had the heart to kill the chosen man.

On Christmas Day, 1846, one of the most furious storms ever witnessed on the Sierra raged. The group huddled together under a canvas for three days, trapped with no food or fire, and four men died. One of them, with his dying words, begged his daughters to use his flesh for sustenance. When the storm abated, a fire was started and the survivors of the 'Camp of Death' severed pieces of soft flesh from the bodies and cooked them. The meat was wrapped and labeled so that no one would eat the flesh of their kin.

On New Years day they ate their moccasins and the strings of their snowshoes. That night another man died and his wife consented that his body be eaten.

The two Indian guides refused to eat flesh. They continued to act as guides but camped alone, fearful of their lives. One night they were tracked down and, as they lay dying of starvation, were shot and eaten.

Eventually after 32 days, the seven delirious survivors reached an Indian settlement. The local Indians gave them food and carried them to the nearest white settlement of Johnson's Ranch, on the Sacramento plains. After they told their terrible tale, the alarm was raised.

Within a week, Capt. Sutter had assembled provisions and a relief party of 13 men. Half of them back along the way, but seven men reached Truckee Lake on February 19. They saw no sign of life but, after shouting loudly, emaciated, ghoul-like people began appearing from holes in the snow. One woman said: *"Are you men from California or do you come from Heaven?"*

The cabins had been buried in snow and steps had been cut in the icy snow leading from the doorways to the surface. The inmates lived subterranean lives and the dead lay all around. All were reduced to mere skeletons. No-one had had yet resorted to cannibalism but they had lived on pieces of cow hide, boiled until it resembled glue, or on old bones which were boiled until they could be eaten.

Only 21 of them could be taken back; the others, many of them children, had to be left at the Lake. They crossed the mountains and, just as they ran out of food, were rescued by a second rescue party, led by the once-banished James Reed.

James Reed had made it to Sutter's Fort in October where he raised a rescue team, but failed to recross the Sierras in December. Most Californians were too busy fighting the Mexicans in Los Angeles to help on a second attempt, so he traveled to San Jose and San Francisco to raise money, and to Napa to get men and horses.

After a brief reunion with his wife, James Reed reached his children at the Lake on March 1. There was now evidence of cannibalism in the cabins by the Lake, and at the Donner's tent at Alder Creek. Leaving eleven survivors, Reed returned with the rest. But crossing the summit, they were stranded in another fierce storm and more deaths and cannibalism occurred before they finally reached safety.

A third relief party of four men, including two survivors of *The Forlorn Hope* group, brought out all but three of the survivors. Left in the mountains were George Donner suffering from an infected cut, his wife Tamsen Donner who refused to leave her husband, and Lewis Keseberg, a respected German suffering from a bad foot.

A fourth rescue party arrived in April 1847. Only Keseberg was left alive, having subsisted on the body of Tamsen Donner.

Of the 87 people in the Donner Party, 41 died (including most of the Donner family) and 46 survived. Most survivors settled in California - James Reed and his family in San Jose, Patrick Breen and his family in San Juan Bautista, and Lewis Keseberg in Sacramento where he opened a restaurant. Lansford W. Hastings, blamed for the delays which caused the Donner Party to be stranded, became a lawyer in San Francisco.

Their plight was an often-told story and is recorded in several of their diaries. Occasionally their descendants meet for a weekend at Donner Lake.

LAKE TAHOE

"The Lake in the Sky."

"Noble sheet of blue water lifted 6,300 ft above the level of the sea, and walled in by a rim of snow-clad mountain peaks... I thought it must surely be the fairest picture the whole earth affords."
Mark Twain.

Of the many photogenic lakes in the Sierras, by far the largest and most stunning is **Lake Tahoe**. 22 miles long and 12 miles wide, it is the largest alpine lake in North America and contains enough water to cover all of California to a depth of 14". The water is as pure as distilled water and is great for swimming. The *"lake in the sky"* is encircled by pristine mountains and split between California and Nevada.

The 72-mile shoreline takes three hours to drive around. The best photographs are from the southwest, around Emerald Bay and South Lake Tahoe.

"So singularly clear was the water that where it was only twenty or thirty feet deep the bottom was s o perfectly distinct that the boat seemed floating in the air! ...Every little pebble was distinct, every speckled trout, every hand's-breadth of sand. ... Down through the transparency of these great depths, the water was not merely transparent, but dazzling, brilliantly so. So empty and airy did all spaces seem below us, and so strong was the sense of floating high aloft in mid-nothingness that we called these boat excursions balloon-voyages."
Mark Twain, Roughing It.

Fanette Island and Emerald Bay.

East

Eagle Falls in Spring, with a 24mm lens.

Previous page:
Emerald Bay ⊕ is the most recogniz-able view of Lake Tahoe. The steep pine-clad hills surround the lake's only island, Fannette Island. A very small turnout on Rt 89 provides this symmetrical shot.

Below right: Further south is a side-on view from **Inspiration Point** ⊕ (above).

Above: On the west end of Emerald Bay is Eagle Park where a short walk towards the lake brings you to **Eagle Falls** ⊕. The Falls are most impressive during the Spring runoff but often last throughout the year. Dawn is a hypnotic time as you can capture the sun rising over the distant mountains. Crouch low over the water so that the falls overflow the bottom of the frame.

Nearby From Eagle Park you can hike down one mile to the lake and discover an unusual house. **Vikingsholm** is a 38-room mansion modeled after an eighth-century Scandinavian medieval castle. Tours in June-Sept ($2, 10-4, ☎916-525-7277). It was owned by Laura Knight who made a tea house on Fannette Island.

One mile north on Rt 89 is the most attractive beach, the small **DL Bliss Beach** ($5, ☎916-525-7277), and **Rubicon Point**. Other good views are from **Meeks Bay** and **Kings Beach**.

Detail of Emerald Bay

Rt 89 closes in winter storms.

Rubicon Point

Bliss Beach

Lake Tahoe

Border of D.L. Bliss State Park

Vikingsholm

89

Eagle Falls

Eagle Lake

Fanette Island

Emerald Point

Emerald Bay

Eagle Point

Eagle Point

Classic view of Emerald Bay

Inspiration Point

Cascade Lake

Map of the Lake Tahoe area.

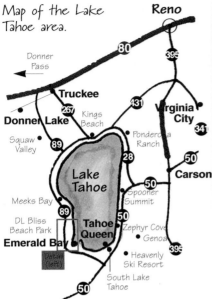

These two shots are taken from **South Lake Tahoe**, and both face west (best in early morning).

Above: The **Tahoe Queen** ⏰, a real Mississippi paddle wheeler, is at the end of Ski Run Blvd, off Hwy 50. ($14/$5. ☎916-541-3364.). There is another ship, the **MS Dixie II** (☎702-588-3508), four miles east at Zephyr Cove Resort. Both steam around the lake in the Summer.

Below: "God Beams" (technically known as crepuscular rays) make this moody shot of Lake Tahoe in the rain. From the boating pier at the end of Lakeview Ave and Harrison, off Hwy 50.

There are 15 ski areas around the lake but the best photographs are taken from **Heavenly** (3,500 vertical feet, 23 lifts). A gondola ($12, open year round) takes you 2,000' above the lake for a great winter shot of skiers flying off the slopes and the lake in the distance.

From South Lake Tahoe, with a 100mm lens.

East

The Comstock Lode

The California Gold Rush was just dying out when, in 1859, two miners discovered gold in the eastern Sierra. Another miner, Henry Comstock, fooled them into thinking it was his land and won the claim. But when the gold was assayed in Grass Valley it was found to be wrapped in a much more plentiful material - silver.

The silver was buried deep in the rocky hills and substantial capital was needed, bringing stock ownership and rampant speculation. Seven major mines grew up, digging tunnels throughout the 2.5 mile-long vein. Two booms and two busts occurred before the Consolidated Virginia Mine struck the 'Big Bonanza' in 1873, disgorging over $2B in today's figures. The four Irish owners (miners John Mackay and James Fair, and saloonkeepers/financiers James Flood and William O'Brien) suddenly had wealth rivaling the kings of europe and were called *"The Silver Kings"*.

For 19 years, the Comstock Lode became the largest silver source ever mined. It financed Union interests in the Civil War and won statehood for Nevada, as Lincoln needed an extra vote to abolish slavery. Nevada is now known as *"The Silver State"*.

The Richest Railroad in the World

The Virginia and Truckee Railroad was completed in 1869 and was called the *"Richest Railroad in the World"* for the silver it carried. For 70 years the 'V&T' brought water and timber 30 miles from Lake Tahoe (flumes brought pine logs down from Spooner Summit), and took the silver down to Carson City for processing. A later extension met the transcontinental railroad at Reno.

A small section is still in operation. In the Summer, a 30-minute trip takes you to Gold Hill and back. (10:30-5:45, $4.50, ☎702-847-0380). The Gold Hill Hotel has a great bookstore (and French restaurant with 22 Champagnes) and there's a V&T museum in Carson City.

Virginia City (elevation 6,200') is a fascinating high-desert mining town and America's largest national monument. The main street and several mines are well preserved and there is a short steam train ride. Most of the buildings date from 1874, after the city's last fire. For four miles around, the earth is riddled with 750 miles of tunnels, the entire length of which can be traversed underground.

Virginia City (named after a drunk from Virginia) was once the largest population center west of the Mississippi. From 1859 to 1878 over $400m in silver and gold was extracted here. It was the starting place for George Hearst (father of William Randolph of Hearst Castle), Mark Twain (who, with Bret Harte, was a reporter at the **Territorial Enterprise**), Adolph Sutro (SF's Lands' End), James Fair (Fairmont Hotel) and William Ralston (Bank of California). At it's height, Virginia City had 30,000 residents, 110 saloons, seven major mines, six churches, five newspapers, five police precincts, four banks, competing fire companies, millionaire clubs, an internationally-known opera house and the West's first elevator.

Visitor Information is in the Railroad car on C Street, ☎702-.847-0311.

The **Chollar Mine** (opposite, bottom-left) was the fifth highest producer in the Comstock, disgorging $17m of silver. Built in 1861, it is the last of the old original mines. At the Ward School, take the truck route down the hill to F Street and the first gateway on the right. There is an infrequent 30-minute tour ($4, ☎702-847-0155).

In town on the main street (C at Taylor), the **Ponderosa Saloon** offers mine tours every 20 minutes for $3.50. They don't have mines but the **Delta Saloon** and the **Bucket of Blood Saloon** have marvelous bars.

Saint Mary's in the Mountains is a rebuilt brick church and the distant boot hill **cemetery** has interesting tombstones.

Right: *Clockwise, from top-left:* The C Street boardwalk; the Ward School house on C St.; a disused V&T car at the railyard; the entrance to the Chollar Mine.

East

"Goodbye God, I'm going to Bodie."
A 19th century schoolgirl.

Nearby A few miles north is **Bridgeport** with its 1880 **County Courthouse**. The Texaco gas station has a scenic view of red barns, green pastures and white mountains. Four miles north of Bridgeport, on Reservoir Road, is Masonic Ghost Town, with a smaller number of cabins and mine heads.

Bodie is the best-preserved and most photogenic ghost town in the country. About 170 mostly dark, wooden buildings (only 5% of the original town) stand in a remote area of high-desert, uncommercialized and preserved in a state of "arrested decay".

Schoolbooks and desks lie in the one-room schoolhouse, grocery tins line a store's shelves, and original tools sit in the Mine Union building.

There are many photography subjects and this is a fun place to explore. Try Green Street, Prospect Street, and Standard Mill. The lack of color favors black & white film.

Summer in Bodie is fiercely hot and the park closes during winter snowstorms.

Where Bodie is on Hwy 270, 7 miles south of Bridgeport, and 18 miles north of Lee Vining.

In 1859, gold was discovered here by Waterman S Body. A town grew up (his name was spelled incorrectly on the signpost) and became one of the busiest in the Gold Country, mining $100M. Between 1878 and 1882, Bodie was home to 10,000 settlers, 30 mines and its own narrow gauge railroad. It also had the worst reputation: it was rumored that a murder was committed in the town every day before sunrise. As the gold died out, many residents moved to the Comstock Lode and the town has been desolate ever since. Only park rangers live here now.

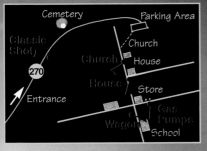

East

The **alien-like** landscape of **Mono Lake Tufa State Reserve**, with its strange tufa and sand towers and mountainous backdrop, is a popular destination for photographers. In 1941, the City of Los Angeles Department of Water and Power started draining the 60-square-mile lake. Four of the five tributaries were diverted to the water-starved city. The lake shrank to half its size and the water level dropped by 40 feet. This exposed natural limestone stalagmites called 'tufa' (pronounced 'too-fa') towers that had been growing for 200-900 years. The number and variety of towers is unique in the world. In 1994, the lake became protected. Rivers are no longer diverted and the water level is planned to rise by 17 feet over 15 years. This will re-cover most of the tufa so photograph it while you can.

Tufa is rock, in this case hardened calcium carbonate, formed around mineral springs. The towers formed when natural springs of calcium-rich water percolated through the carbonate-rich lake water. The towers only grow in the water and, now exposed, have stopped growing. Most of the tufa is on the south shore at **South Tufa Grove** ☉. There is a one-mile self-guided trail. Nearby, on **Navy Beach**, are delicate Sand Towers, created as the springs bubbled through briny sand.

The lake itself is more than 700,000 years old, the oldest continuously existing

> *"Half a dozen little mountain brooks flow into Mono Lake, but no stream of any kind flows out of it. It neither rises nor falls, apparently, yet what it does with its surplus water is a dark and bloody mystery."*
> Mark Twain, 'Roughing It', 1872.

body of water in North America. Although fed by rivers and springs, it has no outlet and depends on evaporation to loose the water. It is almost three times as salty and eighty times as alkaline as seawater. In the Summer you can swim and float high in the water.

In the center are two volcanic islands, one of which, Paoha Island, was created only 200 years ago. On the north shore at **Black Point** are deep volcanic fissures. This is a popular area for bird watching.

Mono Lake, called the *"Dead Sea of the West"* by Mark Twain, has a unique ecosystem. 90% of California Gulls breed here, feeding on a unique species of shrimp and brine flies. The flies lay their eggs on the tufa and the local Yukat Indians used to eat the pupa (developing insect). *"Mono"* is the indian word for the flies.

The informative **Visitor Center** is on the west shore, off Hwy. 395, north of Lee Vining. Open year round ☎760-647-6331.

Dawn is the best time for photography.

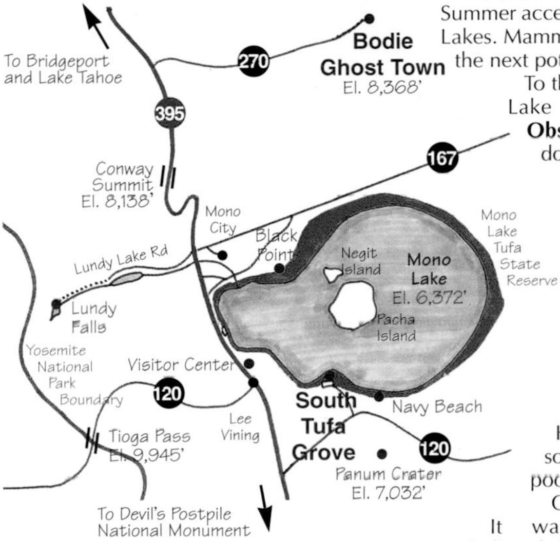

flowed down the San Joaquin valley. As it cooled into rock, it shrank and vertically fractured into geometric columns. A glacier (a slowly moving river of ice) then crept through the valley, carving away the andesite to a sheer cliff and polishing its top down from 400 ft. The Postpile faces west and is best in the afternoon.

Three miles downstream is south-facing Rainbow Falls. Misty rainbows envelop the water as it cascades 101' into a box canyon.

Devil's Postpile is closed in Winter. Summer access is by shuttle from Mammoth Lakes. Mammoth Mountain is thought to be the next potential 'Mt. St.Helens' volcano. To the north (3 miles south of June Lake on Glass Flow Road) is **Obsidian Dome**, a 300' high dome of black volcanic glass.

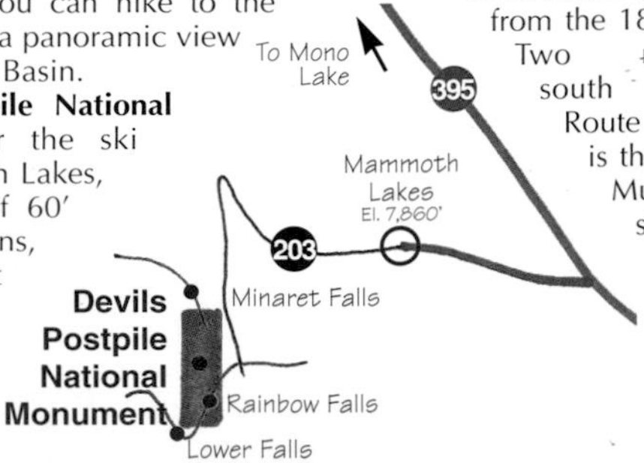

Elsewhere

Genoa, an 1851 trading post, is the oldest permanent settlement within the present borders of the state of Nevada. It's mountain backdrop, and one of the most attractive little villages anywhere in the American West. Nearby (1mi N) is Walley's Hot Springs where you can soak in the natural hot spring-fed pools.

Carson City is Nevada's capital. It was named (indirectly), after Kit Carson a scout for surveyor John Fremont. The **Capitol** (1870) is made of sandstone and has a silver dome. Free tours (8-5 ☎702-687-4810). Ten miles north on Hwy 395 is Bowers Mansion, a millionaire's house dating from the 1870's.

Two miles south on Route 395 is the Nevada State Railroad Museum with three V&T steam locomotives.

Visitor Information is at 1900S Carson St Suite 100, ☎702-882-1565.

Nearby

Mill Creek, a tributary in the northeast corner of Mono Lake, has a beautiful **waterfall** near Lundy Lake. Further north on Hwy 395 is a scenic overlook. North and east is the sage-brush covered **Great Basin Desert**, over 11 million years old. To the south is **Panum Crater**, the remains of a volcano which erupted only 600 years ago. You can hike to the dome and rim for a panoramic view of the Mono Lake Basin.

Devil's Postpile National Monument, near the ski town of Mammoth Lakes, is a sheer cliff of 60' high basalt columns, likened to a giant pipe organ. 900,000 years ago, hot lava

Map labels (upper)

To Bridgeport and Lake Tahoe
270
Bodie Ghost Town El. 8,368'
395
167
Conway Summit El. 8,138'
Mono City
Black Point
Negit Island
Mono Lake El. 6,372'
Mono Lake Tufa State Reserve
Pacha Island
Lundy Lake Rd
Lundy Falls
Yosemite National Park Boundary
Visitor Center
120
Lee Vining
South Tufa Grove
Navy Beach
120
Tioga Pass El. 9,945'
Panum Crater El. 7,032'
To Devil's Postpile National Monument

Map labels (lower)

To Mono Lake
395
Mammoth Lakes El. 7,860'
203
Devils Postpile National Monument
Minaret Falls
Rainbow Falls
Lower Falls

Mono Lake at sunset, from the South Tufa Reserve.

Photo © George D. Lepp/BIO-TEC IMAGES

Mono Lake is one of my favorite places to photograph. I've been visiting the area for 17 years and lead several photo tours around the lake. The photographic subjects are endless and always changing while the location has very few visitors, making it uncrowded.

"The best time to photograph Mono Lake is just before sunrise as the glow in the sky reflects in the lake, giving the shapes of the tufa formations an ethereal backdrop. Sunset is another magic time if clouds are over the lake and the setting sun lights the bottoms of the clouds. A tripod is important, as are a pair of rubber boots."

-- George Lepp, Field Editor of *Outdoor Photographer* magazine, for *PhotoSecrets*.

"**A** **country of** wonderful contrasts, hot deserts bounded by snow-laden mountains, cinders and ashes scattered on glacier-polished pavement, frost and fire working together in the making of beauty."
-- John Muir, describing the Mono Lake region.

Lower Yosemite Fall and Yosemite Creek Bridge. Inset: Bridalveil Fall from Tunnel View.

PhotoSecrets **Northern California**

YOSEMITE

INTRODUCTION

By Galen Rowell

By Greg Heisler for Mountain Light

Galen Rowell is an internationally renowned wilderness photographer and author. His writings and photographs appear in *Life*, *National Geographic*, *Sports Illustrated*, and *Outdoor Photographer*.

Galen was scaling Sierra peaks by the age of ten, and had made over 100 first ascents by thirty. In 1984 he received the Ansel Adams Award for his contributions to the art of wilderness photography. Galen's latest of 13 books is called *Bay Area Wild*.

Yosemite

After photographing for three decades on all seven continents, Yosemite remains as enticing as ever to photograph, and just as unique as when I first saw it as a child. People have told me about a lot of places that are supposed to look like Yosemite, but none have come close. Sure, I've seen higher cliffs, deeper valleys, and countless big waterfalls in the course of my travels, but, like the words of a poem, it's not the individual elements that are poignant, but the way they come together into a meaningful whole.

My mother first arrived in the Valley by open touring car in 1916, during the first year that automobiles were allowed. She fell in love with the park, and in the 1920s performed classical music on summer nights at Camp Curry and the old Glacier Point Hotel. When she introduced me to Yosemite in 1943 at the tender age of three, traffic in the valley wasn't a problem. War time gas rationing was in effect, and no new tires could be purchased. My father saved gas coupons for months, then glued strips of inner tube around his tires to save the treads, taking two full days to make the journey at less than twenty miles per hour.

Regardless of the recent floods of people and water, the essential Yosemite is still 100 percent there for me. I experience it when I'm photographing Half Dome from Ahwahnee Meadow at sunset, when I'm hiking up the Yosemite Falls Trail at dawn, or any time I'm away from the roads in the 96 percent of the park that is designated Wilderness.

The rare times that I've been caught in summer traffic jams in the Valley, I've deserved it. I should have planned to have driven there earlier, or to have been out on a remote trail, or to have ridden around the Valley on my bike with my camera pack. There are any number of options to avoid self-imprisonment by seatbelt inside the same mechanized world of vehicles and crowded roads that most visitors seek to leave behind, but never really escape. One survey found average visits to Yosemite lasted two hours with only minutes spent out of a motor vehicle.

Despite the many thousands of photographs I've made in Yosemite over the years, I know I'll never say I've seen it all and put down my camera. I have not put *"done"* Yosemite yet, as tourists who collect park stickers are prone to say, because the landscape means more to me than a visual scene to be passively ingested and recorded in snapshots. The Yosemite experience becomes more powerful with each return visit because it is self-renewing, quite unlike the one-time visual exploitation of our senses that happens when we watch an action movie or even a real-life event, such as the Olympic Games, where it's basically all over once the outcome is known. The more you know about the natural world, the more you want to see.

Yosemite has a long history of great interpreters - from John Muir, to Ansel Adams, to the photographers and writers doing the best work today - who have found it necessary to spend long periods of time witnessing the cyclic, but never directly repeated movements of the clouds, the light, the rising mists, and the flowing waters in order to communicate their essential meaning to the public. Thus a guidebook like this should not be shelved after the first flush of familiarity with Yosemite. It needs to be kept handy to savor for new ideas. I'll have my copy of PhotoSecrets beside me on each repeat visit to help me discover ever more moments of serendipity, when the images in my mind and before my eyes can be brought together into inspirational photographs.

Right: *El Capitan and Merced River.*

The Incomparable Valley

Sheer, granite walls, laced with some of the world's tallest waterfalls, tower over verdant fields and the meandering Merced River. The valley is named after it's original indian inhabitants, who white discoverers called the 'Yosemites' after the Miwok name for grizzly bear, 'uzumati'. The indians called the valley 'Ahwahnee' and themselves the 'Ahwahneechees'. Classic 'Ansel Adams' views abound - at every turn there seems something spectacular to photograph. It's an unforgettable sight and justly known as *"The Incomparable Valley"*.

PhotoSecrets Top Ten sights of

Yosemite Valley

Map on following page

Tunnel View
page 264

The most famous 'Ansel Adam's view of Yosemite. From this grandstand vista you can see El Capitan (left), Half Dome (center), and Bridalveil Falls (right). Great at sunset.

Yosemite Falls
page 268

Over a dozen major waterfalls flow into the valley, but none are taller or more renowned than Yosemite Falls. At 2,425 ft. they are taller than any building. Best viewed in the morning light.

Half Dome
page 272

The highest point in the valley, graceful Half Dome is the symbol of Yosemite. It is best viewed in the early morning and late afternoon.

Bridalveil Fall
page 276

This sheer waterfall changes constantly as it wavers in the wind. Creates wonderful rainbows in the late afternoon.

El Capitan
page 278

Guarding the entrance to the valley, 'El Cap' is the largest known exposed block of granite in the world.

Valley View
page 280

An alternate view to Tunnel View, lesser known but almost as spectacular.

Vernal Fall Trails
page 282

A beautiful hike takes you past Vernal Falls, the popular Mist Trail, Nevada Falls, and, if you're energetic, to the top of Half Dome.

Glacier Point
page 290

A magnificent sky-high view of Half Dome, and the Giant's Staircase of Vernal and Nevada Falls. Only accessible in Summer and Autumn.

Taft Point & Sentinel Dome
page 292

Taft Point is a little-known overlook with stunning views of Half Dome and El Capitan. On the top of Sentinel Dome stands a wind-twisted Jeffrey Pine.

Mirror Lake
page 294

Gradually shrinking Mirror Lake provides calming reflections of Mt. Watkins and Half Dome.

YOSEMITE VALLEY MAP

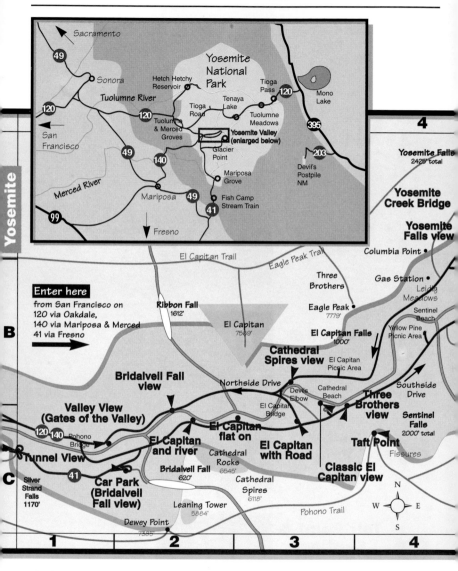

Yosemite

Orientation

The only road entrance is from the west. As the trees clear you'll be treated to amazing views of Bridalveil Falls on your right, and Yosemite Falls on your left. Head first to the Visitor Center by turning left at Sentinel Bridge, or go straight on to the day-use parking at Curry Village and use the shuttle bus.

The campgrounds and the most popular trailheads are in the eastern third of the valley. This area is serviced by a free shuttle bus. There is a mostly one-way road system around the valley. You can drive this 14-mile loop, or use the Valley Floor Tram (fee) for a guided tour.

For more information, pick up a copy of the *Yosemite Guide* (free on entry). Information: ☎209-372-0264.

Legend

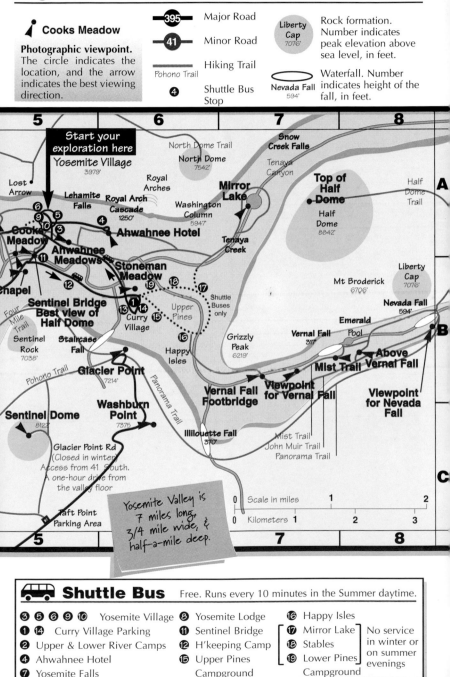

Cooks Meadow

Photographic viewpoint. The circle indicates the location, and the arrow indicates the best viewing direction.

🚌**395** Major Road

🚌**41** Minor Road

Pohono Trail Hiking Trail

④ Shuttle Bus Stop

Liberty Cap *7076'* Rock formation. Number indicates peak elevation above sea level, in feet.

Nevada Fall *594'* Waterfall. Number indicates height of the fall, in feet.

Start your exploration here
Yosemite Village 3979'

Lost Arrow

North Dome Trail
North Dome 7542'

Snow Creek Falls
Tenaya Canyon

Top of Half Dome

Half Dome Trail

A

Lehamite Falls
Royal Arches
Royal Arch Cascade 1250'

Washington Column 5947'

Mirror Lake

Half Dome 8842'

⑥ ⑨ ⑤ ⑩ ③
Cooks Meadow
④ Ahwahnee Hotel

Tenaya Creek

Liberty Cap 7076'

⑪ Ahwahnee Meadows

Mt Broderick 6706'

⑫ Stoneman Meadow

⑱ ⑰
Shuttle Buses only

Nevada Fall 594'

B

Chapel

Sentinel Bridge Best view of Half Dome

⑬ ⑭ ①
Curry Village ⑮

Upper Pines

⑯

Grizzly Peak 6219'

Emerald Pool

Vernal Fall 317'

Above Vernal Fall
Mist Trail

Four Mile Trail

Sentinel Rock 7038'

Staircase Fall

Happy Isles

Glacier Point 7214'

Pohono Trail

Panorama Trail

Vernal Fall Footbridge

Viewpoint for Vernal Fall

Viewpoint for Nevada Fall

Sentinel Dome 8122'

Washburn Point 7375'

Illilouette Fall 370'

Mist Trail
John Muir Trail
Panorama Trail

C

Glacier Point Rd (Closed in winter) Access from 41 South. A one-hour drive from the valley floor

Taft Point Parking Area

Yosemite Valley is 7 miles long, 3/4 mile wide, & half-a-mile deep.

0 — Scale in miles — 1 — 2
0 — Kilometers — 1 — 2 — 3

Tunnel View is the classic view of Yosemite Valley. From this magnificent vista looking east, up the valley, the main features are spread out in front of you. El Capitan and Bridalveil Falls frame the entrance, with Half Dome standing silently in the distance. It was from near here that in 1944 Ansel Adam's composed his famous photograph,"Clearing Winter Storm". There are many opportunities for you to do the same.

Tunnel view is named after the adjacent Wawona Tunnel (knicknamed the "Whiskey Tunnel" because it is 4/5 of a mile long). The view is also known as **Discovery View** since it greeted the first european visitors, **Best General View**, by 19th century photographers, and **Inspiration Point**, after the nearby peak.

Clearing Winter Storm

// I had visualized for many years an image of Yosemite Valley from Inspiration Point and exposed many sheets of film in an effort to achieve that visualization. Finally, in 1944, a sudden heavy rain storm hit, which at midday changed to wet snow.

"I drove to my chosen site and quickly set up my 8x10 camera to capture the marvelous vista spread before me. The clouds were moving rapidly and I waited until the valley was revealed under a mixture of snow and clouds with a silver light, gilding Bridal Veil Fall, realizing the photograph Clearing Winter Storm."

Ansel Adams, in his autobiography.

Where Tunnel View is at the eastern end of the valley, on the road to Fresno and Glacier Point. The Valley Floor Tour bus stops here. If you're driving, take the 'Route 41 Fresno' exit near Bridalveil Falls and drive up the hill. At the entrance to Wawona Tunnel is a large parking area, made of the landfill from the tunnel. You're about 600 feet above the valley floor.

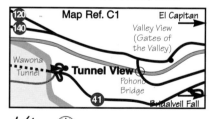

Map Ref. C1

When Afternoon is the best time, as the western sun lights the rocks. This is also the best place to watch the sunset.

Watch the rocks change complexion as the sun moves across the sky. At noon, only the southern edge of El Capitan is lit, highlighting it's stark, vertical form. In the late afternoon, with the sun behind you, a rainbow forms at the base of Bridalveil Falls. Around sunset, the golden light graces each feature in turn - El Capitan, then Bridalveil Falls, and finally Half Dome.

The best time of year is Spring and early Summer when cascading Bridalveil Falls is most prominent. In the Winter, the view takes on an otherworldly appearance as clouds hover in the valley.

El Capitan |

| Clouds Rest   Half Dome |

Bridalveil Falls| Cathedral |
Rocks

Washington Column   Sentinel Rock (Sentinel Dome is just visible)

Ansel Adams images from Tunnel View:

- Bridal Veil Fall and Cathedral Rocks, Thunderstorm, c. 1942
- Clearing Winter Storm, 1944
- Yosemite Valley, Moonrise, 1944
- Thunderstorm, Yosemite Valley, 1945

Watching the Sunset

Arrive about two hours before sunset. If you have a tripod, pick a good spot and get set up. At this time, the entire face of El Capitan is nicely lit.

Zoom into El Capitan and capture a nice shot as the sun recedes half way up the face. About 1 hour before sunset, zoom in to Bridalveil Falls, and then to the rocks to your right, as they are warmed by the golden light.

Now zoom in to Half Dome and Cloud's Rest. Just as the sun sets, the sun's final rays create a magical picture (next page). If you're lucky enough to be here a few days before a full moon, just after sunset you could capture the moon rising behind Half Dome.

Above: The unforgettable view from **Tunnel View** ◐ shows most of the main valley features. You can include your companions in the foreground for that *'we are here!'* shot.

Notice how sheer the walls of the valley are. The granite rocks were carved by glaciers - slowly moving rivers of ice - flowing towards this viewpoint.

Far left, below, and following page: Try isolating individual features with a zoom lens. This is a great place to photograph El Capitan (left) and Bridalveil Fall (below).

Cloud's Rest and Half Dome
at sunset from Tunnel View.

"No temple made with hands can compare with Yosemite. Every rock in its walls seems to glow with life. Some lean back in majestic repose; others, absolutely sheer or nearly so for thousands of feet, advance beyond their companions in thoughtful attitudes, giving welcome to storms and calms alike, seemingly aware, yet heedless, of everything going on about them."
John Muir

"The richest, as well as the most powerful, voice of all the falls in the valley."
John Muir, conservationist.

Right: *Yosemite Falls plunges almost half a mile from the rim above to meet the flat, verdant valley floor below.*
Left: *By the Fall season, Yosemite Falls dries to a whispy thread.*

Ansel Adams images of Yosemite Falls:
• Lower Yosemite Fall, c. 1946 *(from the Yosemite Creek Bridge viewpoint)*
• Yosemite Falls and Meadow, 1953 *(from across Cook's Meadow)*

When 🕐 The Falls face east so the best time to view them is in the morning. At around 9am the sun lights the plunging water, and is low enough to give relief to the sheer granite walls.

Spring is the best season. Most of the watershed feeding the falls is smooth, bare granite. Unable to store water above, the stream is a torrential storm drain during the snowmelt of April-May, but dries to a whispy thread by August.

In the summer, before 8:30am, hang gliders occasionally glide over from Glacier Point. In the winter, a fascinating cone develops at the base of the Upper, and sometimes Lower, falls as the water freezes on it's descent through the cold air.

In the Spring, white Apple blossoms can provide an interesting foreground during the day, and on a full-moon night, ethereal "moon bows" appear in the lower fall.

Right: This shot is taken across Cook's Meadow from the **Sentinel Bridge** parking area. Painting and drawing classes come here in the morning, making for an artistic foreground. You can use the reflections in the river as a foreground by standing on the south side of the Merced.

Out of the thirteen waterfalls that feed the valley, none is as awe-inspiring as Yosemite Falls. Plunging a total of 2,425 feet in three sections, Yosemite Falls is taller than any building, and fifteen times the height of Niagara Falls.

Yosemite Falls is composed of three sections, Upper Yosemite Fall (1,430 feet), a middle cascade, and Lower Yosemite Fall. Combined, they form the highest waterfall in North America and the fifth highest in the world.

Yosemite Falls can be seen from many places around the east end of the valley. A good distant view welcomes you from the South Drive as you enter the park.

Where Yosemite Falls makes a pleasant walk west from the Visitor's Center (see next page). By car, drive west on the Northside Drive towards "Yosemite Exits" to the **parking area** The Shuttle Bus stops here (stop #7), as does the Valley Floor Tour.

From the parking area, a 1/4-mile path leads to the base of the Falls where there is a viewpoint and a **bridge** over Yosemite Creek.

The classic view is taken from the parking area at **Sentinel Bridge** (which also offers a great view of Half Dome). Afterwards follow the **river** west for a great shot over **Cook's Meadow**, then north along Yosemite Creek towards the Falls.

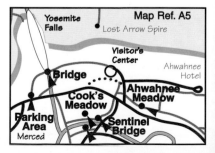

*The view from the path on **Ahwahnee Meadows*** ☺

"The water seems to fall out of the very sky itself." Joseph LeConte, Chief of the US Geological Survey in the west.

Focus On
- Use a slow shutter speed (1/8s) to blur the falling water.

Left: The pathway from the **parking area** leads straight to the falls. It seems designed for your camera. You can create a nicely symmetrical shot, framing the tall, slender falls with the tall, slender trees.

Opposite:

Far Right: Following the path (an easy 10 minute walk) brings you to Yosemite Creek **Bridge**, at the base of the falls. There is a viewpoint here (lower left). The bridge itself makes a delightful foreground, contrasting it's horizontal span with the vertical falls. From the approach side of the bridge, walk gingerly over the rapids to the central section. Be careful of the wet, slippery rocks. It's too rocky for a tripod.

Hiking Up The Falls

Many people's favorite hike takes you up the sheer 2,700 ft. north wall. Start one mile west of the Falls at Sunnyside Campground, behind the gas station near Yosemite Lodge.

One-third of the way up the hike is Columbia Point which has a good view of the top of Lower Yosemite Fall. At the top is a lookout over the entire Yosemite Falls.

Three miles west along the rim is Eagle Point, on top of the Three Brothers rocks. There are spectacular views of the entire Yosemite park, Sierra foothills, and, on a clear day, the Coastal Range far west. If you're camping overnight (permit required) you can hike to the top of El Capitan and return the next day.

3/4 mile east of the falls is Yosemite Point with a view of Lost Arrow Spire, a free-standing shaft of granite.

6-8 hours round trip, very strenuous

Strolling Around The Falls

The best walk in the Valley is around Cook's Meadow to the base of the falls. Start at the Visitor Center and walk south to the river and Sentinel Bridge. Follow the Merced west, then cross the meadow to the base of the falls. Here you can cross the bridge and head back to the Visitor's Center, or return to the parking area and take the Shuttle Bus elsewhere.

1-2 hours roundtrip, easy

Yosemite

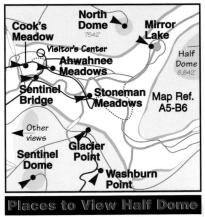

Ansel Adams images of Half Dome:
- Half Dome, Merced River, Winter, 1938 *(from Sentinel Bridge)*
- Half Dome, Autumn, 1938 *(across Cook's Meadow)*
- Moon and Half Dome, 1960 *(from Stoneman Meadow)*
- Half Dome and Clouds, c. 1968 *(from Glacier Point)*

Left: A popular foreground is the Elm Tree in **Cook's Meadow** 🕐. This is particularly attractive in the winter snow.

Right: The most classic view is from **Sentinel Bridge** 🕐. The pathway provides a great place to set up a tripod and watch the afternoon light affect the view.

Stop here for good photographs

In the Summer you can watch rafters cooling off in the meandering Merced River (next page). In the Fall and Winter, the river becomes placid enough to provide a calming reflection of Half Dome (right).

Half Dome is the symbol of Yosemite. Standing at the eastern end of the valley, like a father silently guarding his children, Half Dome is the tallest and most recognized rock in Yosemite.

Half Dome is so tall that the glaciers that formed the valley didn't reach the upper 900 feet. Instead, they undermined it's northwest side. Later, when the glacier receded, the rock expanded due to the reduced pressure and then cracked, shearing off the vertically jointed rock layers. This process, called exfoliation, created the Royal Arches and other valley features.

Half Dome is the second sheerest rock wall in the world (the first being in Pakistan). Occasionally climbers can be seen making the five day ascent. A quicker and marginally less strenuous route to the top of Half Dome is a hike up the northeast side, a continuation of the Vernal Fall/ Nevada Fall hike. The 8-mile hike takes 12-14 hours roundtrip and cables allow you to climb the 60° final leg. But the view of the valley floor, 5,000 ft. below, is spectacular.

Where The classic view (right) is taken from **Sentinel Bridge** and is another Ansel Adams classic. The bridge is a 10 minute walk south from Yosemite Village.

When 🕐 Anytime is great. At sunrise and sunset, just the tip of Half Dome is lit in a golden light.

Noon to mid-afternoon is best to capture reflections in the Merced River from Sentinel Bridge. The lowest light on the full scene occurs around 2 hours before sunset.

The river changes with the seasons. In the Spring, it is a fiery torrent. In the Summer, it's host to children and inflatable rafts. In the Autumn and Winter, the calm river offers beautiful reflections.

Places to View Half Dome

1	Sentinel Bridge	Classic view
2	Ahwahnee Mdws	Bike path
3	Cook's Meadow	With Elm tree
4	Stoneman Mdws	Natural setting
5	Yosemite Chapel	Good foreground
6	Mirror Lake	Sunrise & sunset
7	Glacier Point	30-mile drive
8	Washburn Point	Profile
9	Tunnel View	With Cloud's Rest
10	Sentinel Dome	Little-known view
11	North Dome	Long hike
12	Highway 120	With El Capitan

The Miwok Indians called Half Dome 'Tis-sa-ock', after a woman whose tear-stained face they saw in the granite.

Above: With Summer rafters, from **Sentinel Bridge** ⊕.

Left: Capture the last light of sunset on the sheer face from **Stoneman Meadow** ⊕.

Below: The **Chapel** ⊕ is a good foreground. This shot is from the center of the meadow, north of Southside Drive.

Above: With El Capitan close to sunset, from a turnout on **Highway 120** ⊕ (Big Oak Flat Road).

Below: At **Ahwahnee Meadows** ⊕ you can include cyclists in the foreground. Stand on the bike path and wait for people to cycle past. Don't get run over!

Yosemite

Bridalveil Fall is considered by many to be the most beautiful of Yosemite's waterfalls. The wind gently sways the whispy waters back and forth as it free-leaps down 620 feet. This motion, called the "Pohono effect", is a delight to watch.

Like Yosemite Falls, Bridalveil is a "hanging valley". It was created when the glaciers widened the main valley, leaving the tributary rivers to flow over a sheer precipice. However, Bridalveil Fall has a larger and more absorbent watershed than Yosemite Falls and remains strong through the Summer.

To the right is Leaning Tower and The Acorn. Behind is Cathedral Rocks.

Ansel Adams images of Bridalveil Fall:
- Bridal Veil Fall, 1927
  (from Tunnel View)
- Bridal Veil Fall and Cathedral Rocks, Thunderstorm, c. 1942
  (from the parking area)

Above: Bridalveil Fall and Leaning Tower from the **Northside Drive Pullout** ☾.
Below: The view from the **parking area** ☾.

Right: A long lens helps you isolate the top of the Fall, with the swirling 'Pohono' effect. Taken from **Northside Drive Pullout**.

Where Bridalveil Falls is at the west end of the valley. The best view is from across the river, at a pullout on the **Northside Drive** ☾, near Gates of the Valley.

To reach the falls, head for 'Route 41 Fresno'. Just after the turnoff, turn left into the Bridalveil parking area. A 10-minute trail winds up **Bridalveil Creek** . The creek is the best place in the valley to photograph water flowing gently over mossy rocks. Morning sunlight streams through gaps between the maple trees. Set your camera low, near the ferns and logs, and use a long exposure to 'blend' the moving water.

At the top of the trail is a **viewing platform**. The mist is pleasantly cooling in the Summer, but you'll need waterproof clothing in the Spring.

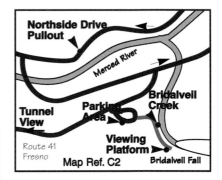

Map Ref. C2

When ☾ The real magic of Bridalveil is watching how the changing light affects the Fall's appearance. In the mid-morning, when sunlight first strikes the Fall, it highlights just the water cresting the rim. Get set up beforehand, zoom-in (200mm with tripod), and wait for the right moment to capture the golden sliver of spray. In the late-afternoon, the swirling mist and the light from the low sun create thick, dramatic rainbows at the base. Both shots are best taken from the west end of the **parking area** ☾. Shortly before sunset, the granite rock face turns golden with the light of the setting sun.

In Spring, the heavy mist makes it almost impossible to photograph from the base. In Winter, various cones and shapes are formed by the frozen water.

"The great rocks of Yosemite, expressing qualities of timeless, yet intimate grandeur... are the very heart of the earth speaking to us." Ansel Adams

Ansel Adams images of El Capitan:
- El Capitan from Taft Point, c. 1936
  (from Taft Point)
- El Capitan, 1952
  (from Devil's Elbow)
- El Capitan, Winter, Sunrise, 1968
  (from Devil's Elbow)

Left: Ansel Adams' favorite view of El Capitan was from **Devil's Elbow** 🕐, near Cathedral Beach. The east face is fully lit by the morning sun, but by late afternoon the distinctive profile is highlighted and more prominent. Winter is particularly attractive as clouds drift across the 3,245 ft. monolith.

There is a small turnout on the Southside Drive with a sign describing the seven different types of granite prevalent in the valley. Walk down to the banks of the Merced and follow the river east for about 50 yards so that the river completely fills the bottom of the frame.

In the Summer canoeists occasionally paddle by, adding human interest and an important sense of scale.

Below: Sunset on El Capitan. This classic shot is taken from **Tunnel View** 🕐.

El **Capitan,** spanish for "the chief", guards the entrance to Yosemite Valley. This giant monolith, rising 3,593 ft. above the meandering Merced River, is thought to be the largest single block of exposed granite in the world.

On the west side is **Ribbon Fall**, the highest single waterfall in Yosemite National Park. With a descent of 1,612 ft. it is also one of the highest in the world. On the east side, during late winter and early spring, is **Horsetail Fall**. This photographs well in the late-afternoon as the sun shines through the whispy spray.

When 🕐 Anytime is fine although the late afternoon turns the granite face a burning orange color. A good shot from **Valley View** 🕐 *(Gates of the Valley)* occurs 1-2 hours before sunset when the sun lights just the top half of the rock face.

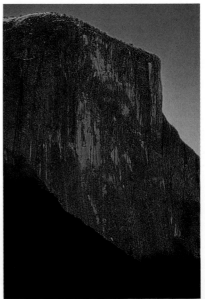

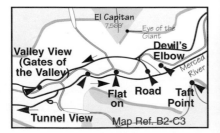

Above: The leading lines of the **road** draw your eye into the deep, immense background. ***Below:*** Facing El Capitan **flat on** ☼, from south of the river, shows you how incredibly sheer and perpendicular it's walls are. From a tiny pullout on Southside Drive, walk north to the river's edge.

Above: The most popular view of El Capitan is from **Valley View** ☼ (also called *Gates of the Valley*). You can use reflections in the river (placid in Fall and Winter) for a foreground. This is a popular view in the winter as snow clumps on the river's rocks, and access is easy.

There's a great temptation to use a wide-angle lens and include Bridalveil Fall, but fight it and isolate El Capitan. Crouch down low at the edge of the water to bring the river through the bottom of the frame.

Below: El Capitan is a haven for climbers. Bring a pair of binoculars to go climber-spotting. Popular routes are the *North American Wall* and the *Wall of the Early Morning Light* which can be best seen at *Eye of the Giant.* You can watch from the base although a more scenic viewpoint is from Taft Point.

The view from Valley View (also known as **Gates of the Valley**) rivals the power of that from Tunnel View, but is far less photographed. It's also a more tranquil spot to watch the last rays of the setting sun move from left to right, as if being covered by a slowly drawn curtain. You can clearly see El Capitan (left), Cathedral Rocks and Bridalveil Fall (to the right).

The river here flows across the shot, forming a unifying foreground. Crouch low to bring the water almost to eye level.

Ansel Adams images from Valley View:
• Gates of the Valley, Winter, c. 1938

Tip This view makes an excellent panoramic shot. If you don't have a panoramic camera, don't worry. Take a normal shot then, when you get the photographs developed, ask for a 8"x10" enlargement. Crop off the top and bottom 2.5 inches, and you'll be left with a 10" x 3" panorama.

When 🕐 The west facing rocks look best in the afternoon light. Bridalveil Fall is most prominent in the Spring. In the Winter, clumps of snow form on the boulders in the river making this one of the best views in the Valley.

"We finally emerged at Valley View - the splendor of Yosemite burst upon us and it was glorious."
Ansel Adams

Where Valley View is a turnout from the north exit road at the end of the valley. The Valley Floor Tram stops here but if you're driving you'll need a quick eye as the turnout is almost hidden by a bend in the road. Take the Northside Drive. 4.2 miles from the gas station. Just after you see the sign for 41 Wawona/Fresno, by Marker V-11, the pullout is on your left.

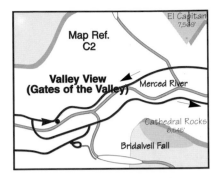

"As I looked, a peculiar exalted sensation seemed to fill my whole being, and I found my eyes in tears with emotion."
Lafayette Bunnell, on first 'discovering' Yosemite.

The Merced River was named in 1806 by Sergeant Gabriel Moraga, a Spanish explorer. His party had traveled over forty miles with no water and were overjoyed to find the river. They called it "The River of Our Lady of Mercy" - *"El Rio de Nuestra Senora de la Merced"*.

Yosemite

"The Vernal Fall I so named because of the cool, vernal spray in contrast at midday with summer heat, reminding me of an April shower, and because of the blue grass curiously growing among dark rocks and gay, dripping flowers, making it an eternal April to the ground."
Lafayette Bunnell, 1851.

Ansel Adams images along the Vernal Fall trails.
• Nevada Fall, Rainbow, 1946
  (from north trail)
• Nevada Fall, Profile, c. 1946
  (from north trail)
• Vernal Fall, c. 1948 *(from viewpoint)*

Left: Vernal Fall is 317 ft. high and 80-100 ft. wide at it's Spring peak. The classic view is from a signposted area, the **Vernal Fall viewpoint** ☺, along the Mist trail. A granite outcrop provides a stable platform.

Right: The most impressive view of Vernal Fall is from the **trail cutoff** ☺ above Emerald Pool. This short trail connects the Mist Trail to the John Muir Trail. Here the full power of the cascading Merced river is apparent.

O f the **840 miles** of hiking paths in Yosemite National Park, the most scenic are those up Little Yosemite Valley to Vernal Fall and Nevada Fall. You can make a short hike to the base of Vernal Fall (which offers the most photo opportunities), spend an afternoon continuing on to Nevada Fall, or spend a 1-2 day trip hiking to the top of Half Dome.

When ⏰ Afternoon is the best time for light as both Falls face west. Because the Merced River drains the large absorbent Tuolumne Meadows above, the Falls remain active throughout the dry summer months. In the Spring, parts of the trail are wet, and in Winter watch for slippery ice.

Where The trails start at Shuttle Stop 16. This area is called Happy Isles for the two small islands in the Merced River where it enters Yosemite Valley. Note that the bus doesn't run during the winter, or in the summer evenings - you'll need to walk to/from Curry Village.

The path starts on the east bank of the river and is signposted to Vernal Falls and the John Muir Trail'. From Nov-May, the higher elevations may be impassable due to snow.

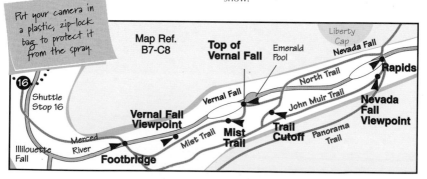

Put your camera in a plastic, zip-lock bag to protect it from the spray.

Yosemite

Above: The view from the **footbridge** 🕐 below Vernal Fall. The fresh spring foliage of white alder, black cottonwood, bigleaf maple, and western azalea, decorate the banks of the Merced River. Overcast, cloudy weather will reduce the contrast of the scene and bring out the verdant greens.

Preparation

In Spring and early Summer it's steep and wet up there. Bring a rainproof jacket and wrap your camera, batteries, and film in a plastic bag. Bring a small towel and cloths to wipe spray from the lens. A backpack is better than a shoulder bag as it balances your upper body and keeps your hands free for walking.

Left: A hundred yards from the bridge is the **Vernal Fall viewpoint** 🕐 (signposted) A large granite boulder provides a sturdy support for your tripod. Bring a lens-cleaning tissue or cloth to keep the lens free of water droplets.

Tip The glorious rapids which pass by will tempt you to use a wide-angle lens to include everything. But this will detract from your main subject. Instead, try a 70mm lens and emphasize the Fall.

Focus On

- Watch for rainbows in the afternoon
- Include hikers for a sense of scale

"Nature's peace will flow into you as sunshine flows into trees." John Muir

Hiking

Base of Vernal Fall. *Roundtrip: 1-2 hours*
A reasonably strenuous 30 minute hike takes you past Illilouette Fall to Vernal Fall. A bridge over the river makes a good viewpoint, but the classic view is 100 yards further on (go left at the trail junction to the signposted "View"). This exposed rock makes a good platform for tripods.

Top of Vernal Fall. *Roundtrip: 2-4 hours*
Continue on the aptly named 'Mist Trail'. Hiker's in the Spring get soaked as they walk past the base of the Fall but it's fun, and the lush vegetation and outstanding view from the top are worth it. The alternative 'John Muir Trail' is a dryer but longer route.

Nevada Fall. *Roundtrip: 4-6 hours*
Follow the river uphill. Just before the bridge the path splits. The path crossing the bridge is shorter and steeper but not as scenic. Instead go right, uphill, and rejoin the John Muir Trail. There are several views of Nevada Fall but the best is where the path straightens out along an overhang. There's a small wall here.

Half Dome. *Roundtrip 10-12 hours*
Continue along the river around to the east side of Half Dome. The last 200 yards are so steep that a steel cable handrails are provided for assistance. You'll need gloves and good shoes on this section. In the Summer, about 600 people a day make the ascent. A one day trip provides little time to enjoy the view, if you can, stay overnight by camping about a mile above Nevada Fall. A permit and bear-proof food storage is required.

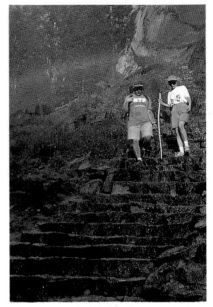

The popular **Mist Trail** is a 1-mile long slippery route through the spray of Vernal Fall. In the Spring, intrepid (or foolhardy) hikers are drenched as they race through the luxuriant vegetation and descending spray.

Above: It's a brave person who snaps this shot as the spray can ruin a camera (*mine stopped afterward and I had to return back to get a replacement!*). Use a waterproof camera, or a clear plastic bag stretched over, or cut around, the lens.

Next page: The Miwoks called Vernal Fall *'Yan-o-pah'*, meaning *'little cloud'*, after the enormous spray it generated. In 1897, a 300-foot granite staircase, called the Mist Trail, was carved into the rock, winding it's way through the *little cloud.*

A quote by the Vernal Fall Viewpoint.

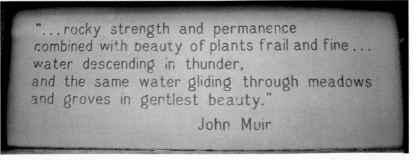

"...rocky strength and permanence combined with beauty of plants frail and fine... water descending in thunder, and the same water gliding through meadows and groves in gentlest beauty."

John Muir

The luscious **Mist Trail** glows like an exotic land in the Spring. This shot is best in the late afternoon, facing west into the setting sun.

Twelve Highest Waterfalls

		Height in feet
1	Yosemite Falls	2,425
2	Sentinel Falls	2,000
3	Ribbon Fall	1,612
4	Staircase Falls	1,300
5	Royal Arch Cascade	1,250
6	Silver Strand Falls	1,170
7	El Capitan Falls	1,000
8	Lehamite Falls	800
9	Bridalveil Fall	620
10	Nevada Fall	594
11	Illilouette Fall	370
12	Vernal Fall	317

Left: At the **top of Vernal Fall** is a viewpoint only inches from the edge. Use a wide-angle lens (24mm) to include a peron in the foreground to complement the far background.

Lower Left: From the **Mist Trail** ☉ you can catch rainbows at the base of the fall. Rainbows occur when the sun is directly behind you.

Right: Where the famous John Muir Trail runs under an overhanging rock, a small safety wall provides a good **Nevada Fall viewpoint** ☉. Here you can see the 594 ft. Nevada Fall with the 7,076 ft. Liberty Cap behind.

Below: At the brink of the fall, you can see the raw, tempestuous power of the Merced River as is is forced through a narrow chute. A small bridge has good views of the **rapids** ☉ before the chute.

The Giant's Staircase

As opposed to the "hanging valleys" of Yosemite and Bridalveil Falls where the glaciers sliced across the river, Vernal and Nevada Falls were formed when glaciers moved down the river. The huge pressures cracked the rock along natural fault lines, dislodging large blocks of granite, and creating two major steps. This effect earns Little Yosemite Valley the nickname of "The Giants' Staircase". It is most apparent from Glacier Point.

"With Yosemite, we have one of the most extraordinary places on earth, but Yosemite possesses a "Fatal beauty" which invites self-destruction unless we make a strenuous effort to control visitation and use."

Ansel Adams in a radio address, 1968.

"I long for the high places - they are so clean and pure and untouched."
Ansel Adams in a letter to Virginia Best, March 30, 1923.

Ansel Adams images from Glacier Point.
• Half Dome and Clouds, c. 1968

Left: From **Glacier Point** ☯ you have a great view of Half Dome. In 1973, the entertainment company MCA planned to put a gondola from the valley floor up to Glacier Point.

When ⏱ The afternoon offers the best light, but be sure to come here at sunset for the last light on Half Dome.

Winter Only: Snow closes the road between November and May, when it becomes a popular destination for cross-country skiers.

Summer Only: On weekend mornings (before 8am), hang gliders occasionally leap from Glacier Point and swoop to the valley below. There is a large telescope on Glacier Point and rangers provide evening astronomy programs.

Glacier Point offers the most dramatic overlook in the Sierra Nevada. From here you have a commanding view of Yosemite Valley, Half Dome, and the High Sierra with its rugged ridges, glaciated canyons and serrated summits. Mt. Lyell, the highest point in the park, is behind Nevada Fall. On the valley floor, 3,214 ft.below, cars look like toys and people look like ants.

Afterwards, head to Sentinel Dome and Taft Point, Mariposa Grove, or hike along the rim.

Where Glacier Point is a 32-mile, 1-hour drive from the Valley floor. Take the 'Route 41 Fresno' exit through Wawona Tunnel, then left on Glacier Point Road. The Valley Floor Tour does not go here but the Glacier Point Tour does. In the Summer there is an evening Kodak Photo Tour.

The adventurous can take a 3-4 hour hike from the valley floor up Four Mile Trail (actually 4.8 miles). The trail starts on Southside Drive, one mile west of Yosemite Village by Sentinel Rock. An alternate route is the Panorama Cliffs Trail (6-8 hours, 8.5 miles), past Vernal and Nevada Falls.

The adventurous-but-wise can take the Hiker's Bus to Glacier Point and hike down instead of up the trails.

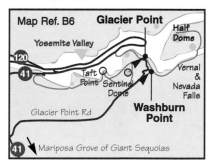

Map Ref. B6 **Glacier Point**
Yosemite Valley — Half Dome
120
41 — Taft Point Sentinel Dome — Vernal & Nevada Falls
Glacier Point Rd — **Washburn Point**
41 Mariposa Grove of Giant Sequoias

"If you were to give me the pleasure of showing you Yosemite Valley for the first time, I know just how I would want to do it. I would take you by night from the San Joaquin Valley up through the forested mountains and out to the Valley's rim, so that when sunrise came you would be standing on Glacier Point. Up before dawn, you would lean against the railing, trying to see down into the shadows for the first sight of something whose descriptions you never quite believed."
Ansel Adams, in 'Travel and Camera', October, 1946.

Above: Glacier Point offers aerial views of most of the valley features. You can see Mount Lyell, the tallest peak in the park, at 13,114'. Mt. Lyell is home to one of the two glaciers which still remains in the park.

Below left: Use a telephoto lens to isolate the 'Giants Staircase' of Nevada Falls (top) and Vernal Falls (below).

Below right: This is an excellent place to watch the sunset. In the fleeting last minutes of sun, the granite glows a golden brown. You'll need 210mm lens and a tripod to get a sharp photograph. This shot was taken from nearby **Washburn Point** ©.

Yosemite

Half way along **Glacier Point Road** are two notable hikes that share the same trailhead. One mile east brings you to the summit of Sentinel Dome with it's famous Jeffrey Pine, and a similar distance west takes you to the overhanging viewpoint of Taft Point.

Where Start at the parking area on Glacier Point Road, marked by a sign and some bathrooms.

When ⏱ Anytime is fine. A low light is preferred to bring out the depth of the valley (at midday the scene looks flat).

Glacier Point Road is closed in the Winter (Nov-Mar).

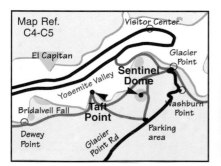

Map Ref. C4-C5

[Map showing: Visitor Center, El Capitan, Glacier Point, Sentinel Dome, Yosemite Valley, Bridalveil Fall, Taft Point, Washburn Point, Dewey Point, Glacier Point Rd, Parking area]

Ansel Adams images from Taft Point:
• El Capitan from Taft Point, c. 1936

from Sentinel Dome:
• Jeffrey Pine, Sentinel Dome, 1940

Taft Point   Map Ref. C4
1-2 hours

This little-visited area is one of the 'Secrets' of Yosemite. A mostly flat 1.1 mile trail leads through delightful woods. In the Spring, a carpet of colorful wild flowers surrounds you. Near Taft Point are huge fissures - gaps in the rock which are a few feet wide and hundreds of feet deep. But this is just a teaser for the main event. At Taft Point, the granite abruptly stops in an almost sheer vertical drop. Standing on the overhang, there's nothing between you and the valley floor, over 3,000 ft. below.

Bring a pair of binoculars. Across the valley is El Capitan and this is a great place to have lunch and spot the miniscule climbers creeping up it's face.

Tip Fortunately there are actually two overlooks at Taft Point. Stand at the railings and look west (left) to the second overlook. Include your companions standing on the edge - if they're brave enough!

Below: For a sense of scale, that's me in orange on the overhang!

"A sturdy storm-enduring mountaineer of a tree, living on sunshine and snow, maintain tough health on this diet for perhaps more than a thousand years."
John Muir

Above: The wind-twisted Jeffrey Pine on Sentinel Dome is considered one of the most photographed trees in the world.

Sentinel Dome   Map Ref. C5
1-2 hours

After Half Dome, Sentinel Dome is the highest point in Yosemite Valley. From the 8,122 ft. high peak you have a glorious 360-degree view across the park. This is a great panorama at any time, but sunrise, sunset, and full moon nights offer artistic opportunities.

Most of the elevation is covered by car leaving only a 30 minute moderate walk from the parking area to the peak. This is a relief for anyone with a heavy tripod or large-format camera.

The most fascinating feature of Sentinel Dome is a lone **Jeffrey Pine**, poised on the summit. For several hundred years this tree grew from the cracks of seemingly barren rock, but it died in the drought of 1979. Now a stark, eerie form, it provides a unique subject.

Sentinel Dome is almost 1,000 feet higher than Glacier Point but unfortunately doesn't offer a view of Yosemite Valley.

Top Ten Highest Peaks

		Height in feet
1	Mt Lyell	13,114
2	Mt Dana	13,053
3	Rodgers Peak	12,978
4	Mt Maclure	12,764
5	Mt Gibbs	12,764
6	Mt Conness	12,590
7	Mt Florence	12,561
8	Simmons Peak	12,503
9	Excelsior Mountain	12,446
10	Electra Peak	12,442

"The entire Yosemite Valley is the supreme concentration of grandeur and beauty."
Ansel Adams, Architectural Record, February, 1957.

Nearby
Dewey Point

Dewey Point (7,385 ft.) offers interesting views of El Capitan and Bridalveil Fall. The trail head is also on Glacier Point Road, just west of the Bridalveil Campground. This is an easy hike with little elevation change but a roundtrip distance of 7 miles make it a 4-6 hour hike.

Mirror Lake was once a large body of water with a mirror-like surface. Some terrific photographs were taken here, particularly in Winter, with reflections of Half Dome. However, the lake is naturally filling with silt and has all but disappeared. Many a hiker asks *'Is this it?'* and leaves disillusioned. So catch it while you can!

From this soon-to-be meadow there are good views of Half Dome, Mount Watkins and Basket Dome. It's a pleasant hike up Tenaya Creek.

Where

Start at Shuttle Bus stop #17. In winter this stop is not accessible so you have to walk from the Pines Campground, stop #19. The lake is a pleasant easy half-mile walk up Tenaya Creek. This is a popular destination by bike.

When ⏰

Early morning or sunset is the best time.

Winter and Spring are the best seasons as the lake can dry up by Summer. The most romantic view is probably sunset in Winter.

In the Spring, Tenaya Creek is lined with dogwood, making for beautiful nature photographs.

"Yosemite is one of the great gestures of the earth. It isn't that it is merely big - it is also beautiful, with a beauty that is as solid and apparent as the granite rock in which it is carved."
Ansel Adams in a letter to Alfred Stieglitz, November, 1937.

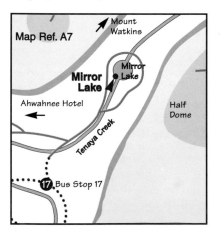

"Yosemite Valley, to me, is always a sunrise, a glitter of green and golden wonder in a vast edifice of stone and space."
Ansel Adams

Right: Idyllic Mirror Lake reflects the distant Mount Watkins.

Ansel Adams images of Mirror Lake:
• Mirror Lake, Mount Watkins, Spring, 1935
(from the west bank of the lake, facing Mount Watkins)

Making the Valley

Mirror Lake is a living example of how the flat Yosemite Valley floor was formed.

Millions of years ago, the Tenaya Creek and Merced River carved a deep 'V'-shaped valley. Later, one-and-a-half million years ago, the rivers turned to ice, forming glaciers (slowly moving rivers of ice) and gouged the lower levels of the valley into a distinctive 'U' shape. (Two glaciers still exist in the park). Waterfalls were created as the widening valley became lower than the tributary rivers, leaving "Hanging Valleys".

Near El Capitan, large rocks formed a dam and turned the valley into a lake. Gradually silt accumulated, filling up the lake, just as Mirror Lake is now. Sediment collected to a depth of 2,000 feet in 6,000 years. Eventually the lake disappeared altogether, replaced with a flat, fertile valley floor.

Mirror Lake is following the same process. Soon, the lake will disappear altogether and the area will become a meadow.

"The silver light turned every blade of grass and every particle of sand into a luminous metallic splendor; there was nothing, however small, that did not clash in the bright wind, that did not send arrows of light through the glassy air. I was suddenly arrested in the long crunching path up the ridge by an exceedingly pointed awareness of the light... I saw more clearly than I have ever seen before or since."
Ansel Adams in Yosemite and the High Sierra.

OTHER SIGHTS

Yosemite

Ahwahnee Hotel Map Ref.A6

Left: Opened in 1927, The Ahwahnee is one of the most beautiful hotels in America. Built from native stone and wood, it blends with the sheer granite rocks behind. Even the concrete beams are stained to look like redwood. The Ahwahnee has housed Presidents, royalty and celebrities, and has been designated a National Historic Landmark.

The elegant dining room is flooded with sunlight through the massive 34-foot high floor-to-ceiling windows. Some have called it the most beautiful restaurant in America. To eat dinner here, jackets are required, as are reservations (☎209-372-1489 or, from your room, ext. 1304).

Ahwahnee is the Miwok name for the Yosemite Valley. It means "place of the gaping mouth". This shot is taken from the gardens behind the hotel.

Ansel Adams images:
- Sentinel Rock and Clouds, Winter, c. 1937
- North Dome, Royal Arches, Washington Column, Winter, c. 1940

- Cathedral Rocks, c. 1949
- Eagle Peak and Middle Brother, Winter, c. 1960
- Fern Spring, Dusk, c. 1960

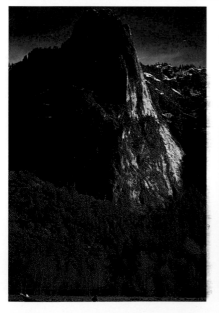

Sentinel Rock   Map Ref.B5

Far left: Jagged Sentinel ("guarding soldier") Rock is 7,038 feet high and anchors the south side of the valley. This shot is taken from a meadow near Northside Drive.

Chapel   Map Ref.B5

Near left: Built in 1879, this Chapel was originally part of a small town built on the valley floor. The other structures have since been demolished and the area restored, but the Chapel was relocated in 1901 and still hosts worship services and weddings. It is a short walk from Sentinel Bridge on the south road.

The Chapel makes a good foreground to Half Dome, but it's a challenge to fit the two together. This shot is taken from center of the meadow, north of Southside Drive.

Royal Arches   Map Ref.A6

Above: Behind and to the east of the Ahwahnee Hotel is this unusual rock pattern. Leaves of rock fell away (a process called 'exfoliation') leaving these Royal Arches. To the right stands Washington Column and behind is North Dome.

This shot is taken from Stoneman Meadow and benefits from the late afternoon sun.

Three Brothers   Map Ref.B3

Right: Just east of El Capitan are the distinctive slopes of Three Brothers. The apex, Eagle Peak, can be reached from the top of the Yosemite Falls trail. The three peaks are named after the three sons of Tenaya, the last chief of the Ahwahneechee.

This shot is from Cathedral Beach, near Devil's Elbow. There is a small parking area on Southside Drive (with an information board about granite in the valley), just after the cutoff to El Capitan. Walking west allows you to include the reflecting Merced River in the foreground. A little further west is the classic view of El Capitan.

Yosemite

M ariposa Grove of Giant Sequoias is the finest strand of giant sequoias outside of Sequoia National Park (5 hours south). Giant Sequoias are the world's largest trees, in fact the world's largest lifeform, and are only found in a small belt of the Sierra Nevada.

Inside the park there are several interesting specimens. Grizzly Giant is thought to be the oldest living sequoia at 2,700 years. The 232' California Tree has a pedestrian tunnel through it's trunk, cut in the 1800's. You can stand inside Telescope Tree and see the sky through the top. There was a tree that you could drive a car through, the Wawona Tree, but this collapsed from a weakened base.

Clothespin Tree has an open trunk, caused by fire.

Sequoias and Redwoods

The Coast Redwood and the Giant Sequoia (Sierra Redwood) are relatives with slight differences. The Sequoia has a spongier, cinnamon-colored bark while the Redwood has a thinner, orange/gray bark. The Redwood is thinner and taller since, once a Sequoia has reached a certain height, its growth is *outward*. Both trees were once widespread throughout the world but, for some reason, have retreated to grow only on opposite sides of California's Great Valley, one tree as the largest living thing and the other as the tallest.

Where   **Mariposa Grove** is 36 miles (1 hr 15) south of Yosemite Valley via Rt. 41. It is popular in the Summer so visit before 10am or after 3pm. Overflow parking is located in Wawona with a free shuttle service. The grove can be closed in Winter.

There are two other groves in the park (both near Crane Flat) but they are not as large and accessible. **Tuolumne Grove** has more trees including the **Dead Giant**, a 40' stump with an automobile tunnel (but cars are no longer allowed through it) and the **Siamese Twins** (two trees which grew close together and unite to be 114' in circumference). **Merced Grove** has 20 trees and requires a two-mile strenuous hike. There are only 75 Sequioa groves in California.

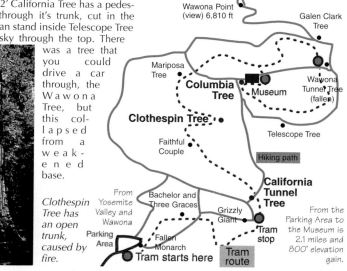

Yosemite Valley occupies only 5% of Yosemite National Park. Most of the remainder is reached by Tioga Road. Originally built in 1883 as a wagon road for a silver mining company, Tioga Road (Highway 120) passes forests, wide open meadows and sparkling blue lakes. There are frequent turnouts offering broad, beautiful panoramas. In the summer the wildflowers bloom and the resident climbers relocate here from Yosemite Valley.

At 9,945 feet, Tioga (pronounced 'Tie-o-ga') Pass is the highest automobile pass in California and the drive up, carved out of a nearly vertical cliff, can be demanding.

Because of the elevation, the road closes with the first major snowstorm, and doesn't open again until most of the snow has thawed. The road is usually open from June to October although chains may be required in June, September and October. A hiker's bus operates from July 1 to Labor Day (☎209-372-1240).

Wawona

The Pioneer History Center transports you back to the late 1800's. There is a New England-style covered bridge and a collection of stage coaches and in the Summer, the staff wear Victorian costumes.

The elegant Wawona Hotel, built in 1875, is a magnificent white building with neatly mown grass, deck chairs and a golf course. A fountain in front provides a good foreground.

Hetch Hetchy Reservoir

Once-upon-a-time this was a beautiful waterfall-graced valley similar to Yosemite Valley. From 1919 to 1923 a large concrete dam was built, turning the area into a large reservoir. Hetch Hetchy now provides most of the water and power for San Francisco. The water flows 200 miles from here to the city purely by gravity.

You can photograph O'Shaughnessy Dam with Tueeulala and Wapama waterfalls in the distance. Hetch Hetchy is fed by the Tuolumne River, from Tuolumne Meadows, and is named after the Miwok word for an edible grass.

Olmstead Point

Olmstead Point has a great, although distant, view of Half Dome. Several round boulders provide a popular foreground. They were deposited here by the glaciers and are called "Glacial Erratics".

The point was named after Frederick Law Olmstead who designed New York's Central Park and was appointed Chairman of the Yosemite Valley Commissioners.

Tenaya Lake

Tenaya (pronounced 'ten-eye-a') Lake is a beautiful and large alpine lake. It was named in 1851 by the Mariposa Battalion to honor the Chief of the Yosemite Miwoks, Tenaya. The Miwoks called the lake "Py-wi-ock" or "Lake of the Glistening Rocks".

Tuolumne Meadows

"The Tuolumne Meadow is a beautiful grassy plain of great extent, thickly enameled with flowers, and surrounded with the most magnificent scenery."
Joseph LeConte.

Tuolumne (pronounced 't-wolo-me') Meadow is the largest sub-alpine meadow in the Sierra Nevada. Wide, verdant meadows are laced with mountain springs and surrounded by stark, snow-topped peaks. At an elevation of 8,575' above sea level, it can be buried in 20' drifts of snow in the winter but, in the summer, it is a peaceful haven from the busy valley. The mountain air is fresh and wildflowers abound. Fed by the winding Tuolumne River, this is a beautiful area for hiking and photography.

Tuolumne Meadows is 55 miles from Yosemite Valley. From the Visitor Center, trailheads lead to the major sights.

Lakes and Peaks

From behind Tuolumne Meadows Campground, a 2.3 mile trail takes you to Unicorn Peak and Elizabeth Lake. With elegant Unicorn Peak in the background, the lake makes one of the most attractive photos in the area. Another popular hike is 3.5 miles to Cathedral Lake. The trail starts from the parking area west of the Visitor Center.

Waterwheel Falls

A long hike (8-10 hours roundtrip) is rewarded by Waterwheel Falls, one of a series of cascades. The river smashes into granite shelves, sending enormous arcs of water skyward, and down the 5,000 foot-deep chasm.

The best time for viewing is mid-June through mid-July. Waterwheel Falls is 6 miles NW of the Tuolumne Meadows Ranger Station along the Pacific Coast Trail.

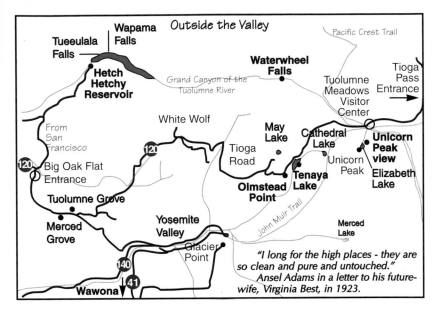

Outside the Valley

Tueeulala Falls
Wapama Falls
Pacific Crest Trail
Hetch Hetchy Reservoir
Waterwheel Falls
Tioga Pass Entrance
Grand Canyon of the Tuolumne River
Tuolumne Meadows Visitor Center
White Wolf
From San Francisco
120
Big Oak Flat Entrance
120
Tuolumne Grove
Merced Grove
Tioga Road
May Lake
Cathedral Lake
Unicorn Peak view
Unicorn Peak
Elizabeth Lake
Tenaya Lake
Olmstead Point
Yosemite Valley
John Muir Trail
Merced Lake
Glacier Point
140
41
Wawona

"I long for the high places - they are so clean and pure and untouched."
Ansel Adams in a letter to his future-wife, Virginia Best, in 1923.

Further Information:

Yosemite National Park *(for Road & Weather Information, Lodging and Campground Information, Ranger-Led Activities, Trails, Permits)* 209-372-0200
TTY 209-372-4726 or 0294

Reservations
Camping/Lodging 800-436-7275
Outside-US 619-452-8787
TTY 209-255-8345
Lodging 209-252-4848
Tours & Hikers Bus 209-372-1240
Wilderness Permits 209-372-0740
Bike Rentals 209-372-1208
Gray Line Buses 209-384-1315
Mountaineering School:
Summer:209-372-8435; Winter:-8444
Other Services:
Emergency (Fire, Med., Police) 911
Medical Clinic 209-372-4637
Dental Clinic 209-372-4200
Ansel Adams Gallery 209-372-4413
Lost and Found 209-379-1002
Visitors Center 209-372-0299
Bookstore 209-379-2648
Public Information 209-372-0265
Press Information 209-372-0248 & 0529
Yosemite Association 209-379-2646
Yosemite Field Seminars 209-379-2321
Yosemite Institute 209-372-9300
Yos. Mountaineering Sch'l 209-372-8435
Friends of Yosemite 415-434-1782

Further Reading:

Yosemite Visitor's Kit - includes The Complete Guidebook to Yosemite National Park, The Yosemite Road Guide, and maps $14.95 ☎209-379-2648.

About Ansel Adams:
Ansel Adams, An Autobiography
Ansel Adams: A Biography
Ansel Adams and the American Landscape
Yosemite

By Galen Rowell:
The Yosemite; The Vertical World of Yosemite; Bay Area Wild

Internet Addresses
For a current jumplist to related web sites, as well as weather, photographs, and updates to this book, visit:
http://www.photosecrets.com

My Mumb and Dad visiting Yosemite!

Yosemite

The Whistlestop Tour

Yosemite Valley requires at least three days but if one is all you have, here's a suggested itinerary.

When you first arrive, head for **Yosemite Village** which has information, restaurants, and reservations. Find the **Visitor's Center** (open 9-5pm/8-6pm, Shuttle Stops 6 & 9) for a good orientation. There are displays showing the formation of the valley, lots of guide books, and enthusiastic rangers to offer advice.

The best overview is on the **Valley Floor Tour** ($14, from Yosemite Village), a guided, two-hour trip to the main sights on an open-air tram. It stops at most of the main sights including **Yosemite Falls**, **El Capitan**, Sentinel Bridge (for a view of **Half Dome**), **Gates of the Valley**, and **Tunnel View**. Alternatively you can drive this 8.5 mile loop. There probably won't be time but Glacier Point (1-2 hours) has spectacular aerial views of almost the entire valley.

In the afternoon hike to either Yosemite Fall (1-2 hrs) or Vernal Fall (2-4 hrs).

Yosemite Fall makes for a very relaxing walk. Start at the Visitor Center and head south to Sentinel Bridge. Follow the river east, then head north to the Fall. From the base of the Fall, a path leads back to the Visitor Center.

A more strenuous but equally spectacular hike is to **Vernal Fall**. Take the Shuttle to Happy Isles at stop 16. Budget 3 hours total for a moderate hike to the base of the falls. If you enjoy getting wet, hike to the top of the falls on the popular **Mist Trail** (4 hours total). Extending on to **Nevada Fall** (go up the southern John Muir Trail and return down the north trail) adds two more hours which is just possible for the quick of feet in the long days of Summer.

The best place to watch the sunset is **Tunnel View**. Also try **Glacier Point**, **Stoneman Meadow** and **Gates of the Valley**.

Getting There

By Car: The quickest route from San Francisco (4-5hrs, 195 miles) is on Route 120 via I-580 and Oakdale. Route 140 via Mariposa follows the Merced River and is a more scenic and gentler climb (may be closed due to Jan '97 floods). Southerners can take Route 41 via Fresno and Oakhurst.

By Bus or Train: Get to Merced or Fresno and take the Yosemite Gray Line bus (800-345-4950 in CA, or 209-383-1563) or a private tour bus (☎209-384-2576, 209-443-5240, or 209-372-1240).

Getting Around

As you enter the park, pick up the free **Yosemite Guide** for information on tours, photography walks and other activities. A free shuttle bus operates all year around the Valley floor, and from Wawona to Mariposa Grove (Spring to Fall). Hiker's' buses go to Glacier Point (late spring through fall) and Tuolumne Meadows (late June through Labor Day). Call 209-372-1240, or a hotel tour desk. A wide range of sightseeing tours, with informed guides, are available ($14 - $38.50, ☎209-372-1240).

Staying There

Accommodation in the valley is limited. There are four camp grounds ($3-$14) but reservations are often necessary (☎800-436-7275 or 619-452-8787). The only walk-in camp ground is Sunnyside. The nights get cool in the summer, and downright freezing in winter. For the tentless, there are four lodges (☎209-252-4848) and, if it's someone else's credit card, the $215 a night Ahwahnee Hotel. Additional camp sites are by the south entrance, near Wawona and at the western entrance in Hodgdon Meadow. There are B&B's 30 minutes away at Yosemite West and motels about an hour away in Oakhurst (South), El Portal, Mariposa, Sonora and Oakdale (all West).

Entrance Fees (may change)

• Vehicle (valid for 7 days)	$20
• Individual (e.g. in a bus)	$10
• Over 62 (US resident)	$10
• Blind or disabled (US resident)	Free
• 1-Year Pass to Yosemite	$40
• 1 Year Pass to All National Parks	$50

Note: Due to the Jan 1997 floods and congressional legislation, the information above is subject to change.

Fun Things To Do In (or around) Yosemite Valley

Year Round

- Take a **Photography Class**. Experienced photographers give you tips in Awhahnee or Cook Meadow. Sign up at the Ansel Adams Gallery, Ahwahnee Hotel or Yosemite Lodge. The two-hour classes start around 8:30 or 9am.
- Fed up of photography? Take a free **Painting Class** instead and *create* the picture you want. Sign up at the Art Activity Center.
- Tour the **Ansel Adams Gallery**. An inspiring collection of books and prints will soon get you off that painting kick and back to the real action.
- Go **Hiking**. There are over 800 miles of trails so it'll take you a while to do them all. Favorite routes are up Yosemite Falls (start behind Sunnyside Walk-In) and up Vernal/Nevada/Half Dome.
- **Rent A Bike**. It's easier than hiking. There are 8 miles of rideways along the flat valley floor, and Mirror Lake makes a good destination. Bikes cost $16 a day from Curry Village.
- Go **Horseback Riding**. It's more elitist than biking. Trot around the valley or up to Vernal Fall. ☎209-372-8348.
- Forget traveling altogether and watch a Yosemite-themed play at the **Theater**.

Summer Only

- Go **Rafting.** Terrific fun, especially for children. Rent rafts and paddles at Curry Village ($12.50). You can spend the day floating down the cool river (take pictures with a disposable waterproof camera), then catch the free shuttle bus back.
- Go **Fishing**. A license is required but you might catch a raft.
- If rafting or fishing don't give you a rush, learn to **Rock Climb** at Yosemite Mountaineering School. Call 209-372-8435 for details or ask at the School's store at Curry Village. In the Spring & Autumn classes are held in Yosemite Valley; Summer in Tuolumne Meadows. You'll be climbing the 3,593' sheer face of El Capitan in no time (not!).

- Watch **the rock climbers** from the base of El Capitan or from Taft Point.
- Watch the **Hang Gliders** that leap from Glacier Point. This requires getting up early on weekend mornings as they usually finish by 8am.
- Step back in time at the **Pioneer History Center** where school groups dress in costume and character. Tours start at the Covered Bridge in Wawona.

Summer Evenings

- Take the sunset **Kodak Photo Tour** to Glacier Point and get some practical tips.
- The more romantic can take a two-hour **Moonlit Tour** of the valley.
- Astronomy buffs can watch the night sky from the **Observatory** on Glacier Point. Now there's a good place for an ultra-long exposure shot.
- There are other **Evening Programs** on natural history, outdoor adventure, storytelling, and music. at the LeConte Memorial, Shuttle stop #12.
- Watch the **Ansel Adams Photographer** film (about one hour long) at the Visitor Center's West Auditorium.

Winter Only
A certain 'snow' theme pervades these excursions:

- Take a ranger led **Snowshoe Tour**.
- **Ski Cross-country** to Glacier Point and see what Half Dome looks like in the snow. Bring your own gear and start at the junction of Route 41 and Glacier Point Road.
- Go **Downhill Skiing** at Badger Pass.
- Go **Ice Skating** at the delightful outdoor rink in Curry Village.
- Load up on film and gloves and **photograph** El Capitan from Gates of the Valley and the ice cones on Yosemite Falls.

Book Ahead

- Take a **Field Seminar**. 1-7 day outdoor classes in botany, geology, photography, art, or poetry. ☎209-379-2321.

Photo Walks

An excellent feature of the park is the availability of informative Photo Walks. These walks are offered daily in the summer, less frequently in other seasons, and are all staffed by experienced professional photographers. They are an enjoyable way to meet people of a similar interest, and to get ideas and tips to use during your visit. The Walks last about two hours and are all highly recommended.

The **Morning Lights Photo Walk** (free) leaves 8:30am from the Ahwahnee Hotel or Yosemite Lodge. Sign up at the appropriate hotel tour desk. The **Ansel Adams Camera Walk** (free) meets at 9am at the Gallery porch. Sign up at the Gallery, by the equipment counter. The **Kodak Sunset Tour** ($7, summer only) leaves the Visitor's Center main parking area at 5pm and includes a roundtrip ride to Glacier Point. Sign up at the Tour booth, behind the Village Store. Check the *Yosemite Guide* (free as you enter the park) for actual dates.

Photo Tours

Several companies offer 1-7 day tours:

Yosemite Field Seminars	209-379-2321
Sierra Photo Workshops	916-974-7200
Workshops in the West	512-295-3348
Dramatic Light Nature	800-207-4686

Photography central in Yosemite is the **Ansel Adam's Gallery**. You could spend a morning here browsing the beautiful images of it's namesake artist, believing that Yosemite is not just a park but an entire exotic world. It's only a matter of time before a strange force overcomes you and you dash outside, camera in hand, in search of the next *"Clearing, Winter Storm"*.

Besides an excellent selection of Adams' prints and books, the Gallery sells an eclectic range of artistic photography books. Check out Galen Rowell's books with the Sierra Club. A small equipment department offers film (including high-end slide and medium format film), filters, and cleaning accessories. Cameras can be rented by the day, which is handy when, like me, your camera breaks on the first day. An organized person would stock up with film and equipment before leaving home, but the Gallery is a welcome haven for those of us who aren't so well blessed.

Open 9-5pm, ☎209-372-4413. There is a sister store at the Inn at Spanish Bay, on the Monterey Peninsula.

The **Village Store** also has a good selection of film, picture books, disposable cameras, and polarizer filters.

Annette Walklet gives advice to photographers on the Morning Lights Photo Walk.

WHEN TO VISIT

Yosemite Valley is beautiful all year, though it's beauty changes with the seasons. The marginally best time to visit is late Spring, particularly mid-May, when the waterfalls are at their fullest. In Winter and Spring, the roads across the Sierras (120/Tioga Pass, 108, 4) are closed so don't plan on going farther east. I-80 and 50 usually stay open.

The climate is always mild. For the current weather , call 209-372-0200.

Spring

The melting snowpack floods the waterfalls producing awe-inspiring power. Concentrate on the dramatic waterfalls, particularly Yosemite Falls and Bridalveil Fall which significantly decrease in the Summer. Some transitory Falls appear, such as the whispy Horsetail Fall (east side of El Capitan) and Ribbon Fall (west side of El Capitan).

The Mist Trail is like walking through a heavy rainfall so carry a rain-proof jacket and wrap your camera in a plastic zip-lock bag. The Merced River swells and in some places overflows creating small reflecting lakes. Apple trees and dogwood trees blossom with large white flowers. The higher elevations (Glacier Point, Taft Point, top of Half Dome) are closed so you can't get those shots.

Summer

Unfortunately Yosemite Falls and, to a lesser extent, Bridalveil Fall, dry up by August as their granite watersheds don't hold the spring runoff. Instead, concentrate on Vernal and Nevada Falls which remain active.

The higher elevations open around Memorial Day so explore Glacier Point, Taft Point, or take a strenuous all-day hike to the top of Half Dome. Tioga Pass is now open also so you can drive east to the delightful Tuolumne Meadows, and maybe to Bodie Ghost Town and Mono Lake.

Over 20,000 people visit on Summer weekends and the rangers may delay traffic after 10am. This is not a pleasant result after a four-hour drive, so plan on arriving early. Temperatures can exceed 100°F so keep your film in the ice chest, wrapped in zip-lock bags.

Autumn

The crowds disappear by mid-September. The fall foliage is fabulous so concentrate on views of Half Dome from the meadows near the Ahwahnee Hotel & Curry Village, Sentinel Bridge, the Chapel, and Valley View. The Merced River is now placid and offers a great reflection of Half Dome from Sentinel Bridge.

Winter

Winter is the favorite season for many photographers. Thick snow lines the banks of the Merced River, creating idyllic shots of El Capitan from Valley View, and Half Dome from Mirror Lake. Cones of snow form at the base of waterfalls, particularly Upper Yosemite Falls, as the water freezes on it's descent. Low clouds settle in the valley, adding a primeval mood to your shots. Sunset from Tunnel View before or after a storm can be truly spectacular.

The temperature is down in the mid-20s to mid-50s, but the valley seldom sees severe weather. Winter snow rarely accumulates more than two feet deep. Tire chains may be required between Nov-April and the best access is via Mariposa on Rt. 140. Tioga and Glacier Point Roads are closed although you can still reach Glacier Point on cross country skis. From November to March a large outdoor ice rink opens at Curry Village and there's skiing at Badger Pass.

Temperature	
Min/Max in °F	
Jan	26-49
Feb	28-55
Mar	31-59
Apr	35-65
May	42-73
June	48-82
July	54-90
Aug	53-90
Sept	47-87
Oct	39-74
Nov	31-58
Dec	26-48

Best Time Of Day

The light moves magically over the west-facing valley. To get the best photographs, visit the sights at the following times:

8:30 ish: Take a photography class
Morning: Yosemite Fall, Ahwahnee Hotel, Mirror Lake, Taft Point.
Noon: Tunnel View.
Afternoon: Vernal Fall, Nevada Fall, Glacier Point, and Half Dome from Sentinel Bridge.
Late Afternoon: Mist Trail, Bridalveil Fall, Valley View, Mariposa Grove.
Sunset: Tunnel View, Bridalveil Fall. Half Dome from Glacier Point or Sentinel Dome.

ANSEL ADAMS

One cannot discuss photographing Yosemite without paying homage to the work of Ansel Adams. Most of the classic views of the valley were first popularized by his expertly crafted images. His black and white prints, rich in tones and details, capture moody and heroic landscapes and are almost grander than the scenery itself. Our views of Half Dome, Vernal Falls, or the vista from Tunnel View, are forever influenced by his work.

"The best of his pictures stir our memory of what it was like to be alone in an untouched world." John Szarkowski

Over a 50-year career, Ansel Adams (1902-1984) became America's best-known photographer. His name became almost synonymous with *Yosemite*. He helped establish landscape photography as an artform and inspired many to take a camera and find the beauty in nature.

San Francisco

The Adams family emigrated from Northern Ireland in the 1700's. Lured by the riches of the Gold Rush, Ansel's grandfather, W.J. Adams, moved to California in 1849. He soon saw that the money was not in joining the miners but in supplying them and opened a grocery store in Sacramento. He was neighbors of the future railroad barons (Huntington, Hopkins, and Stanford, who also greatly promoted travel photography). After his store burned down twice, W.J. saw the value of timber and built a chain of sawmills and a fleet of ships - the prosperous Washington Mill Company - inherited by his youngest son, Ansel's father.

Ansel Edward Adams was born in San Francisco in 1902. He was raised in a wealthy household, in a mansion overlooking Baker Beach, just south of today's Golden Gate Bridge. The earthquake and fires of 1906 destroyed most of the city but left the Adams' house untouched, and gave Ansel a broken nose which remained crooked. But a greater disaster was befalling the family. In the space of ten years, three of the sawmills had burnt down and 27 of the ships had been lost at sea or to fire. With no insurance, the fortune was lost. Another business venture failed (undermined by friends) and Ansel's father spent the rest of his life trying to repay the debts.

Despite the financial difficulties, Ansel's father resolved that the freedoms he was now denied would be given to his only son. He encouraged Ansel's gift as a self-taught pianist, and allowed him to visit the 1915 Panama-Pacific Exposition almost every day for a year. It was at this world's fair that Ansel first studied photography as a serious fine art.

Yosemite

Ansel Adams fell in love with Yosemite through a description in a book. In 1916, at his insistence, the family spent their 4-week summer vacation camping in the park. During this trip, his parents bought Ansel his first camera - a Kodak #1 Box Brownie.

Adams was captivated by Yosemite's beauty and visited the park every year for the rest of his life. In 1919, he got a summer job in the park looking after the LeConte Lodge, the headquarters of the Sierra Club. He led hikes, met learned people, and became a keen mountaineer.

Despite Adams' growing interest in photography, he intended to become a concert pianist. During the summers in Yosemite, he used the piano at the studio of Harry Best, who sold paintings, books, and souvenirs. Adams met and fell in love with Best's daughter, Virginia and they were married in the park in 1929. On Harry's death in 1936, the Adams inherited the studio and moved completely from the Bay Area to Yosemite. Best's Studio is still owned by the Adams family and is now operated as the Ansel Adams Gallery.

"Ansel Adams created some of the most influential photographers ever made, contributing more than any other photographer to the public acceptance of the medium as a fine art." Jonathan Spaulding, biographer

Fine Arts Photographer

In the early 1920's, most of Adams' income came from taking publicity shots for the Yosemite Park and Curry Co., but he sold his personal work at Harry Best's studio.

Most of Adams' artistic photographs at this time were not of landscapes but more fine art, deliberately banal subjects, such as a single flower or a doorknob. It was not until Adams reached his late thirties and early forties that he concentrated on the style more familiar to us.

His art soon began to get noticed, and he was asked to work on a fine arts book about Taos, New Mexico - an opportunity which changed the direction of his career.

In Taos, in 1929, Adams met and befriended painter Georgia O'Keefe, whose husband was Alfred Stieglitz, a powerful force in photographic art. Stieglitz ran the influential gallery, *An American Place*, where Adams later exhibited what some consider the height of his fine arts work.

The next year in Taos, Adams met photographer Paul Strand and was moved by his work. Adams then decided to devote himself not to the piano, but to the camera.

Adams' photographs of Taos were published in 1930. He insisted on hand-printing every page and only 108 books were made. The price was a then-exorbitant $75, but every copy was sold in two years.

At that time, the style for fine art photographs was to look like charcoal drawings, with blurry, soft-focus images. But, along with other Bay Area photographers such as Edward Weston and Imogen Cunningham, Adams argued for clear, pure images. In 1932, they formed 'Group f/64', after the smallest aperture setting on a camera (which produces the sharpest, most focused images). They met only a few times but the Group was a seminal influence, turning the tide away from pictorialist images towards simple, straight prints.

Heroic Landscapes

On October 31, 1941, Ansel Adams took what is often considered the best-known image in the art of photography. While driving past the little town of Hernandez, New Mexico, he saw the light of the setting sun on the adobe buildings and church and stopped to take *Moonrise, Hernandez, New Mexico*. The image is famous for its deep velvet black sky, an element which Adams added years later with a different exposure in the darkroom.

"Photography is a way of telling what you feel about what you see."
Ansel Adams

In 1944 Adams took the classic *Clearing Winter Storm*. He had photographed departing snow clouds as they swirled majestically around the sweeping gates of the Valley, but he had captured an epic, delicate portrait, showing the ideal of nature. Adams and other photographers had photographed this vista hundreds of times before, but it is this grand, haunting, glorious vision of unspoiled America that is the most famous.

Much of Ansel's talent was utilized in the darkroom where he would spend days printing one shot. He wrote several technical books and codified his 'Zone System'. Adams allocated one of eleven 'zones' to each potential tone in a photograph -- 0 for deepest black, 5 for middle gray, and 10 for pure white. Techniques were then given for compressing or expanding the tonal range through printing to achieve the desired, 'visualized' image.

Adams continued his commercial work, producing huge transparencies for the Eastman Kodak Company to advertise their new color film. These 18' x 60' images of happy vacationers in front of waterfalls became a popular feature at New York's Grand Central Station.

Environmentalist

Adams became an energetic missionary for the Sierra Club. He raised awareness of the country's fragile land and natural resource and lobbied Congress for the establishment of King's Canyon National Park. The newspapers called him *"America's most influential environmentalist."* In 1942, Adams brought attention to the plight of interned Japanese-Americans at Manzanar with his sensitive photographs.

In 1962, Ansel and Virginia Adams and their two children moved to Carmel. The demand for his prints became so high that he stopped taking orders in 1975, but spent the next three years custom printing the 3,000+ pictures already requested.

Adams remained a keen conservationist and educator, teaching at California schools and leading photography tours of Yosemite in his trademark Stetson hat and gray beard. He continued to love music and enjoyed entertaining friends at his home. Perhaps it is fitting then, that on April 22, 1984, the day Adams died, his good friend pianist Vladimir Ashkenazy, played a recital in his honor at the Adams house.

Today

On Sunday evenings, the Visitor Center shows a 1-hour documentary on the life, spirit, and artistry of Ansel Adams. The Ansel Adams Galleries in Yosemite and on the Monterey Peninsular display his work to millions of visitors each year.

Resources

Sentinel Rock in Yosemite
Valley

PhotoSecrets

Resources

One Day In San Francisco

Everything In A Day:
Take the 49-Mile Scenic Drive to see most of the major sights.

Photography Highlights:
The Golden Gate Bridge at dawn and dusk from Marin; The Palace of Fine Arts; Alamo Square.

Panoramic Overview:
You can see the entire city from Twin Peaks, the Carnelian Room in the Bank of America building, and the top of the Marriott Hotel. The best skyline is from Yerba Buena/Treasure Island.

Tourist Things:
Fisherman's Wharf makes a fun half-day, then visit Alcatraz or ride the cable car to Union Sq. for some shopping.

Atmosphere:
Stroll the fashionable coffee-houses and stylish shops of the Marina District along Chestnut, and North Beach around Washington Square.

Shopping:
The big names are around Union Square and along Market Street, but Chestnut St. in Marina is more eclectic.

Several Days

Divide your days into regions:

Downtown (east):
Start at the Visitor Center on Powell and Market. Visit: the cable car turnarounds at Powell/Market and California/Market; Union Square; Civic Center; Transamerica Pyramid; Ferry Building; walk up Columbus into North Park, or up Grant St into Chinatown.

SoMa (southeast):
San Francisco Museum of Modern Art (SFMOMA); Buena Vista Gardens.

Central San Francisco:
Nob Hill with Grace Cathedral and fancy hotels; Chinatown; North Beach and Coit Tower.

Fisherman's Wharf (north):
Many tourist attractions including Alcatraz, historic ships, restaurants. Walk up Hyde Street to 'crooked' Lombard Street.

Golden Gate Bridge (northwest):
Great views from both sides. You can follow the south coast around to Lincoln Park, Land's End, The Cliff House.

Golden Gate Park (west):
It's so big it takes a day. Haight-Ashbury and Twin Peaks are nearby.

A Grand Day Out

Romantic:
You can't beat the Wine Country.

Kids - Theme Parks:
Great America in Santa Clara and Marine World Africa USA in Vallejo.

Long Drive:
Hwy 1 to Santa Cruz.

Redwoods:
Big Basin, via Palo Alto.

Boutiques:
Sausalito and Tiburon, by car or ferry.

Universities:
Berkeley (east near Oakland) and Stanford (south in Palo Alto).

Two+ Days Out

Photographic:
Yosemite National Park. The valley deserves several days. Make overnight reservations in advance.

Natural Wonders:
Besides Yosemite, photographers love Mono Lake, Bodie Ghost Town, Lake Tahoe, Muir Woods, Point Reyes, Avenue of the Giants, and the Big Sur coastline.

Weird and Wonderful:
Winchester Mystery House, Hearst Castle™.

Romantic:
Bed & Breakfast in the Wine Country, lots of wine tasting, and mud baths in Calistoga.

Quaint Towns/Shopping:
The Monterey Peninsula. Explore Monterey, Carmel, Pacific Grove, The 17-Mile Drive™, Monterey Bay Aquarium and even Big Sur.

History:
The Gold Country. Sacramento is the gateway to historic Route 49 (two days). Further afield is Donner Memorial, Virginia City and Bodie.

Themes:
Visit some of the 21 Spanish Missions, from Sonoma down to San Diego. Check out the many lighthouses all along the coast.

I **f you only have one day** in San Francisco (a crime), a good way to see most of the sights is by driving the 49-Mile Drive. However, many key sights are not on the drive so use it more as a guide.

Developed for the 1939-40 *Treasure Island Exposition* (when the drive finished on the island) the 49-Mile Drive is a loop around the city following city streets. 49 is a good number for San Francisco - the Gold Rush occurred in 1849 (the city's football team is named after the migrating miners - the 49ers) and the city is approximately 7 miles wide and 7 miles long, making it about 49 square miles in area.

The route often changes so get a free map and updates from the Visitor Center.

The 49-Mile Drive

How Long With the obligatory sightseeing stops, the drive will take a whole day.

Where You can start anywhere, as long as you drive counterclockwise. In theory you follow the blue 49-Mile signposts however they are poorly maintained, often leaving you stranded at a junction, so it's better to use the route just as a guide. With roadworks there are frequent diversions, so pick up the latest updated information at the Visitor Information Center at Hallidie Plaza on Market/ Powell, and a good map, before heading out.

Tip The 49-Mile Drive is a little outdated. Skip the long, uninteresting section down to Lake Merced. Instead, go straight from the Cliff House into Golden Gate Park. Also skip the Mission District if you're short of time. Make detours to see Alamo Square's 'Postcard Row', the Haas-Lillienthal house, Nob Hill, and SFMOMA. Cross the Golden Gate Bridge and check out the view from the Marin headlands.

We Recommend

Around the city: Cable Cars and Buses; To Berkeley: BART; Stanford and San Jose: CalTrain; To/from the airports: Super Shuttle; Around California: A rental car, buses, or Southwest Airlines.

Tourist Information

The best source for practical information are the Visitor Information Centers.

San Francisco Visitors Information Center. Market St. and Powell St., in Hallidie Plaza near the Powell St. Cable Car turnaround. ☎415-391-2000. Hours: M-F 9-5:30, Sa 9-3, Su 10-2.

San Francisco Convention and Visitors Bureau. 201 Third St., Suite 900, San Francisco CA 94103-3185. ☎415-974-6900; TDD/TTY 415-227-2619; Fax 415-227-2602.

California Division of Tourism. PO Box 1499, Sacramento CA 94103. ☎800-862-2543 or 916-322-1396.

Nevada Commission on Tourism: ☎702-687-4322.

California State Automobile Association (AAA). 150 Van Ness, San Francisco CA 94102. ☎415-565-2012

Maps

The first thing you need is a good street map. Ours are just for illustration (although they are all to scale and all face north). The *San Francisco Visitor Map* (from SF ConVis) is excellent and free from the Visitor Center. Members of AAA can get excellent maps of all regions for free. Stores sell good maps from HM Gousha ☎800-421-7308, Compass Maps ☎209-529-5017, and others.

Guide Books

We're not even pretending that this is a general travel guide. PhotoSecrets only shows you the most visual places for photography - you will also need a good traditional guide book. There are many to choose from, including Access, Berlitz, Berkeley Guides, Birnbaum's, Compass America, Eyewitness Guides, Fielding's, Fodor's, Frommer's, Insight, Knopf, Let's Go, Lonely Planet, Rough Guide, Time Out, and others. There are many fine bookstores around the region and our website has links to on-line bookstores. In San Francisco, good travel book and map stores are:

Borders: Powell/Post on Union Sq. ☎415-399-1633

City Lights Bookstore: 261 Columbus ☎415-362-8193

Cody's Books: 2454 Telegraph Ave., Berkeley. ☎510-845-7852

The Complete Traveler: 3207 Fillmore St ☎415-923-1511

Rand McNally Map Store: 595 Market St. at 2nd St. ☎415-777-3131.

Sierra Club Bookstore: 730 Polk St. by Eddy, ☎415-923-5600.

Thomas Brothers Maps: 550 Jackson St. at Columbus. ☎415-981-7520.

In The Movies

The Maltese Falcon (1941) - Humphrey Bogart's trail starts at Stockton Tunnel.

East of Eden (1954) - James Dean visits Mendocino.

Vertigo (1958) - James Stewart / Alfred Hitchcock.

The Birds (1962) - Alfred Hitchcock strikes terror at the School House in Bodega.

Bullitt (1968) - Steve McQueen and a car chase around steep city streets.

Dirty Harry (1971) - Clint Eastwood goes to Candlestick Park.

American Graffiti - Local boy George Lucas in films 1950's Modesto.

The Conversation (1974) - Gene Hackman in the St. Francis Hotel on Union Sq. By Francis Ford Coppola.

Murder, She Wrote (1984-88) - Mendocino becomes Cabot Cove for TV. Angela Lansbury.

Basic Instinct (1992) - Michael Douglas, Sharon Stone.

The Joy Luck Club (1993) - Chinatown.

The Rock (1996) - Sean Connery and Nic Cage meet in The Palace of Fine Arts and find tunnels under Alcatraz.

Internet Access

Perhaps you're posting progress reports of your trip to your web page. If so, your laptop will appreciate the growing number of 'data ports' in hotel telephones (just unplugging the telephone usually doesn't work as they lines are not standard analog lines). You can surf the 'net at the new Public Library (Larkin and Grove streets) or at Internet Cafes such as The Icon Byte Bar and Grill at 297 9th St., ☎415-861-2983.

Dates To Be Wary Of

You're asking for traffic jams, expensive airline tickets and fully-booked hotels if you have to travel on these popular weekends:

Memorial Day	May, last Monday
Independence Day	July 4
Labor Day	September, first Monday
Thanksgiving	November, fourth Thursday
Christmas Day	December 25

Driving Times

From San Francisco, excluding stops:

Eureka: 6 hrs via US101
Los Angeles: 6 hrs via dull I-5 or 11 hrs via scenic Rt.1 (but you'll want to stop)
Reno/Lake Tahoe: 5 hrs via I-80
Sacramento: 2:15 hrs via I-80
San Jose: 1 hr, I-280 less crowded than 101
Wine Country: 45 mins. via US101/37/121
Yosemite Village: 5 hrs via I-580/120.

Public Transportation

Besides walking, rental cars, and taxis ($1.70 a mile), the best way to get around San Francisco on its clean and convenient MUNI buses ($1 anywhere, or $15 for a week's pass ☎415-673-6864). Cable Cars are $2 per ride but there are only three limited lines. Between the Financial District, Civic Center and the Mission District, and going east to Berkeley and Walnut Creek, is the underground train system, BART (Bay Area Rapid Transit, max. $3, ☎415-788-2278). Ferries that go across the Bay include: Blue&Gold ☎510-522-3300, Golden Gate ☎415-332-6600, Red&White ☎415-546-2628.

Airports

There are three major airports in the Bay Area, being: **San Francisco International Airport** (SFO) ☎415-876-7809, 30 minutes south of the city, off US 101; **San Jose International Airport**, 1 hour south, also on 101; and **Oakland International Airport** (OAK), ☎415-577-4000, 45 minutes east via I-880 and I-80. Add 30 minutes in rush hour. There are rental cars, buses ($8, ☎415-495-8404), shuttle-buses ($15, ☎415-558-8500) and taxis ($40) at each airport. Flying times are London 8 hrs, New York 5 hrs, Chicago 4 hrs, LA 1 hr.

Money Matters

• **Sales Tax** is added to everything and its amount varies by region. San Francisco has the State's highest at 8.5%. Unlike Europe, tax is not included in the price so an item displayed at $10 will actually cost you $10.85. Hotels have to add an additional 12% occupancy tax.

• **Tipping** is expected for anything brought to you or done for you. In the service industry, income _is_ tips so it's unfair to not leave something. At restaurants add 15% of the bill (about double the tax amount), although take-out is not tipped. Taxi drivers expect 10% of the fare; Porters $1 or $2 per bag; Hairdressers 20%; Delivery (such as a valet car or pizza) $2+; Bar staff $1 for a drink or 15% of the tab.

• **Parking Fines** are an easy way to loose money. Always turn your wheels into the kerb so that the car won't roll down the hill, search for any color paint on the kerb, and look for a sign saying 'Loading Zone' or 'Permit Holders Only'. Even though the signs are often hidden you'll still get socked. 'Street Cleaning' is the trickiest and reliably occurs the day your car is there. If a parking space seems too good to be true it usually is.

• **Other Fines** are also annoying. Don't: drive after drinking, drive without wearing a seatbelt, drive over the speed limit, use drugs or stop on a freeway to take a photograph.

• **Travelers Checks** can prove more hassle than they're worth. The Bay Area is literally the home of VISA® and credit cards are far more accepted, give similar rates and avoid the fees.

• **Theft** is a good way to ruin your trip. You're generally safe unless you make your property temptingly easy to steal. Always close your camera bag, keep wallets and purses out of sight, don't leave hotel rooms and cars unlocked, don't walk in poorly lit, quiet streets or parks at night, and don't leave your camera unattended. If someone offers to take a picture of you, think if they're more interested in running away with your camera.

DIRECTORY

Emergency

Police, Fire, Medical Emergency	911
Local Police	415-553-0123
Doctor Clinic	415-476-4602
Dental Referral	415-421-1435
Pharmacy/Drugstore 24hr	415-861-3136
Travelers Aid	415-255-2252
City Tow	415-621-8605
Police Towed Vehicles Info	415-553-1235

General

Directory Inquiries, local	411
non-local	(area code)-555-1212
Highway Information	800-427-7623
International	011+country code+number
Mail	415-695-8760
Time (Speaking Clock)	415-767-8900
Weather (recorded)	415-364-7974

Accommodation

Referral Services:

Bed & Breakfast SF	800-452-8249
B&B International	800-872-4500
Discount Hotel Rates	800-576-0003
Hotel Reservations Network	800-964-6835
San Francisco Reservations	800-677-1550

Campgrounds:

Destinet (campgrounds)	800-365-2267
KOA campgrounds	406-248-7444
Private Campgrounds Info	916-885-1624
MISTIX	800-444-7275
Nat'l. Forests Campgrounds	800-280-2267

Budget & Mid-Price Accommodation:

Best Western	800-528-1234
Comfort Inn	800-221-2222
Days Inn	800-329-7466
Econo Lodge/Rodeway Inn	800-424-4777
Motel 6	505-891-6161
Super 8 Motel	800-800-8000
Travelodge	800-255-3035
Youth Hostels	415-863-9939

Hotel Chains:

Holiday Inn	800-465-4329
Hyatt	800-233-1234
Marriott	800-228-9290
Radisson	800-333-3333
Sheraton	800-325-3535

Concerts & Theatres

BASS (most tickets)	510-762-2277
TIX (half-price on the day)	415-433-7827

Foreign Exchange

American Express Travel	415-981-5533
Bank of America	415-622-2451
Thomas Cook	415-362-6271

Tours

General Tours

Agentours	415-661-5200
Backroads (bicycles)	800-245-3874
Cable Car Charters	415-922-2425
Escape Artist Tours	415-726-7626
Golden Gate Tours	415-788-5775
Gray Line	415-558-9400
Red&White Fleet	415-546-2628
Tower Tours	415-434-8687

Speciality Tours in SF

Architecture/History/Culture	415-557-4266
Chinatown - Wok Wiz	415-355-9657
Crime Tour - Frisco	415-681-5555
Flower Power	415-221-8442
Gay & Lesbian - CtCastro	415-550-8110
Golden Gate Bridge	415-742-9611
Golden Gate Park	415-221-1311
Helen's Walk Tour	510-524-4544
Helicopter - SF Helicopter	800-400-2404
Light aircraft - Scenic Air	800-354-7887
Murals - Mexican Bus	415-546-3747
Murals - Precita Eyes	415-285-2287
Movie Locations - Frisco	415-681-5555
Rogers Highpoints	415-742-9611
The Strolling Nosh	415-441-4221
Victorians - Heritage Walks	415-441-3004
Victorian Home Walk	415-252-9485

Ferry Tours around SF Bay

Blue & Gold	510-522-3300
Golden Gate	415-332-6600
Red & White	415-546-2628

Tourist Information

State-wide

California Tourism	800-862-2543
Nevada Tourism	800-638-2328
National Forests	415-705-2874
National Parks	415-556-0560
California State Parks	916-653-6995
Nevada State Parks	800-237-0774

Convention and Visitors Bureaus

Berkeley	800-847-4823
Carson City	800-638-2321
Monterey County	408-649-1770
Napa Valley	707-226-7459
Oakland	800-262-5526
Sacramento	916-264-7777
San Francisco	415-391-2000
San Jose	408-283-8833
Sonoma Valley	800-326-7666

Visitor Information

Auburn	916-887-2111
Big Basin	408-338-6132
Bodie	619-647-6445
Coloma	916-622-3470
Columbia SHP	209-532-0150
Eureka	800-400-1849

Mammoth Lakes/Mtn	760-924-5500	Japan Airlines	800-525-3663
Mendocino County	800-946-3636	KLM	800-374-7747
Redwood Empire	415-543-8334	Lufthansa	800-645-3880
Reno/Sparks	800-367-7366	Northwest	800-225-2525
San Juan Bautista	408-623-4881	Qantas	800-227-4500
Santa Cruz County	800-833-3494	Southwest	800-435-9792

Chamber of Commerces   Thai International   800-426-5204

Angels Camp	209-736-0049	TWA	800-221-2000
Arcata	707-822-3619	United	800-241-6522
Big Sur	408-667-2100	USAir	800-428-4322
Calistoga	707-942-6333	Virgin Atlantic	800-862-8621

| | | Carmel Valley | 408-624-2522 | *Airports* |

Carson City	702-882-1565	San Francisco SFO	415-761-0800
crescent City	800-343-8300	Oakland	510-577-4000
Eureka	707-442-3738	San Jose	408-277-4759

Fort Bragg   800-726-2780   *Airport Shuttle Services*

Grass Valley/Nevada Cty	800-655-4667	Airport Connection	415-885-2666
Half Moon Bay	415-726-5202	Airport Express	800-835-6000
Marin County	415-472-7470	American Airporter	415-282-8700
Mariposa County	209-966-2456	SFO Airporter	800-862-8405
Modesto	209-577-5757	Supershuttle	415-558-8500
Monterey Peninsula	408-649-1770	Yellow Airport Shuttle	415-282-7433
Nevada City	916-265-2692		
Pacific Grove	408-373-3304		

Transportation - Ground

Palo Alto	415-324-3121		

Associations

Salinas	408-424-7611	AAA Cal State Auto Assoc	415-565-2012

Public Transport

San Juan Bautista	408-623-2454		
San Rafael	415-454-4163	Buses MUNI	415-673-6864
San Simeon	800-342-5613	BART	415-788-2278

Santa Cruz   408-423-1111   *Regional Transport*

Sausalito	415-332-0505	Amtrack (trains)	800-872-7245
Vallejo	707-644-5551	CalTrain (train to San Jose)	800-660-4287
Virginia City	702-847-0311	Green Tortoise (buses)	800-867-8647

Trade Associations   Greyhound (buses)   800-231-2222

The Wine Institute   415-512-0151   *Taxi Cab Services*

Recreational Areas

Golden Gate NRA	415-556-0560	City Cab	415-468-7200
Lassen Volcanic NP	916-595-4444	De Soto Cab	415-673-1414
Lava Beds NM	916-667-2282	Luxor Cab	415-282-4141
Mono Lake	760-647-6595	Veteran's Cab	415-552-1300
Mono Basin NFSA	760-647-3000	Yellow Cab	415-626-2345

Muir Woods NM   415-388-2595   *Car Rental Agencies*

Pinnacles NM	408-389-4485	Alamo	800-327-9633
Point Reyes NS	415-663-1092	Avis	800-331-1212
Shasta-Trinity NF	916-246-5222	Budget	800-527-0700
Yosemite NP	209-372-0200	Dollar	800-800-4000
		Hertz	800-654-3131

Transportation - Air

		Thrifty	800-367-2277
		Sunbelt (sports cars)	415-771-9191

Airlines   *Bikes and Mopeds*

Air France	800-237-2747	American Scooter&Bicycle	415-931-0234
Air New Zealand	800-262-1234	California Scoot	415-751-4100
Alaska Air	800-426-0333	StoF Bicycles	415-202-9830
American Airlines	800-433-7300	W Escapes - bikes in Marin	415-461-6903

British Airways   800-247-9297

Travel Agents

Canadian Airlines	800-426-7000	STA Travel, 51 Grant Ave	415-391-8407
Cathay Pacific	800-233-2742	Council Travel, 530 Bush	415-421-3473
Continental Airlines	800-525-0280	Council Travel, 919 Irving	415-566-6222
Delta	800-221-1212		

General Services

Permits for commercial photography (including still, motion, and advertising) within San Francisco can be obtained from the **San Francisco Film and Video Commission**, 401 Van Ness Ave, Room 417, San Francisco CA 94102. ☎415-554-6244; fax: 415-554-6503.

A directory of media suppliers and service providers is called **The Reel Directory**, ☎707-584-8083.

For information on local camera clubs, visit the web site of the **Northern California Council of Camera Clubs** (N4C) at: "http://www.atchinson.net/n4c/".

Photography central in San Francisco is **Adolph Gasser** at 181 2nd St. ☎415-494-3852. They have an exhaustive range of equipment, film, books, etc. Another branch does pro rentals (750 Bryant St. ☎415-543-3888). We used **Professional Color Lab** for slide developing.

The following is only a sampler - check a local yellow pages for more listings.

Print Developing

In major towns, there are one-hour print developers in many drugstores, supermarkets, and Price/Costco stores. In malls, look for **Bay Photo Lab** ☎800-428-4322, **Dean's Photo** ☎800-400-3686, **Fox Photo** ☎800-944-1842, **Kits Cameras** ☎206-872-3688, **Moto Photo** ☎800-733-6686, **Photo Drive-Up**, **York Photo** ☎304-424-9675 and many others independents.

E-6/C-41 Processing /B&W/PhotoCD:

San Francisco
   Faulkner Color Lab
   1200 Folsom. ☎800-592-2800
   Professional Color Lab
   96 Jessie (1st/2nd). ☎415-397-5057
   Ziba 591 Howard. ☎415-543-6221
Berkeley
   Custom Process
   1700 5th. ☎800-627-5027.
   Ziba 64 Shattuck Sq. ☎510-849-0776
Incline Village (Tahoe)
   Almost Instant Photo
   930 Tahoe Blvd ☎702-831-8171
Mammoth Lakes
   Speed of Light Photo & Video
   Minaret Village Mall ☎760-934-8415
Mariposa
   Photo Express
   7th & Hwy 140. ☎209-966-2003

Oakland
   Continental Color
   2201 West St. ☎510-834-8194
   East Bay Camera Exchange
   1936 Broadway. ☎510-763-5919
Sacramento
   Carmellia Color
   2010 Alhambra at T. ☎916-454-3801
   CFG Photo Lab
   20th & H St. ☎800-464-6861
   Ferrari Color
   601 Bercut Drive ☎800-533-6333
   Superlab
   733 Arden ☎916-649-2133
South Lake Tahoe
   Mountain Photo
   2494 Hwy 50 , ☎702-541-1310
   Sierra Photo Center
   Hwy 50 at 3rd St., ☎702-544-3680

Repairs

San Francisco
   Advance Camera
   118 Columbus. ☎415-772-9025
   John Hawley Camera Repair
   2225 Union St. ☎415-346-1239.
   Metro Camera Service
   30 Mason St. ☎415-421-3551.
   SF Camera & Repair
   1066 Market (6th/7th) ☎415-431-4461
Emeryville
   Camera Repair Service
   1175 59th St. ☎510-547-4447
Mariposa
   Mariposa Photographic
   Hwy 140 & 8th St. ☎209-966-5211
Merced
   Camerafix
   3528 N G St. ☎209-726-5000
Oakland
   Apollo (Old Japan) Camera Repair
   1411 Webster St. ☎510-891-9486
Sacramento
   California Precision Service
   1714 28th St (Q & R) ☎916-451-1330
   Yong's
   10075 Folsom Blvd. ☎916-362-5441
Santa Cruz
   Santa Cruz Photo Equipment Repair
   232 Seaborg Place. ☎408-425-1611
San Jose
   Camera Repair Center
   1864 W San Carlos. ☎408-292-1912
Scotts Valley (near Santa Cruz)
   California Camera Repair
   3109 Scotts Valley Dr. ☎408-439-9003

PHOTOGRAPHY STORES

Equipment

Various branches of **The Good Guys**, **Kits Cameras** ☎206-872-3688 and **Ritz Camera** ☎800-553-7480.

San Francisco
There are many camera shops on and around Market Street near Union Square.
Action Camera
360 West Portal. ☎415-564-0699
Adolph Gasser (also does rentals)
181 2nd Street. ☎415-495-3852
Cameras Unlimited
15 Kearny St. ☎415-392-2400
Discount Camera
33 Kearny St. ☎415-392-1100
Fireside Camera
2117 Chestnut. ☎415-567-8131
Pro Camera (also does rentals)
2298 Third St. ☎415-431-3313
The Camerabug Store
2560 Ocean Ave. ☎415-585-3099

Auburn
Lee of Auburn Photo
819 Lincoln Way. ☎916-885-4312

Berkeley
Sarler's Camera & Video
1747 Solano Av. ☎510-526-0775
Palmer's Camera (also does rentals)
2480 Shattuck Ave. ☎510-845-4560

Bishop
Phillips Camera House
186 N Main St. ☎760-872-4211

Calistoga
The Photo Shop
1373 Lincoln Ave. ☎707-942-6733

Carmel
Camera International
Carmel Plaza. ☎408-622-0833
Carmel Camera Center
5th and San Carlos. ☎408-624-8880

Eureka
Henderson Photo Center
518 Henderson St. ☎707-442-9293
Swanlunds Camera, Video & Optics
527 F St. ☎707-442-4522

Fort Bragg
Fiddles & Cameras
400 N Main St. ☎707-964-7370

Fresno
Boot's Camera
5587 North Blackstone.
☎209-432-0446

Grass Valley
Elliott Photo
109 W Main St. ☎916-273-4917

Mariposa
Photo Express
7th & Hwy 140. ☎209-966-2003

Monterey
GMR Custom Photographic Lab
700 Cass St. ☎408-373-8021
Myrick Photo
217 O'Farrel St. ☎408-649-1900
Shutterbug Shop
484 Lighthouse Ave. ☎408-649-8290

Napa
Film & Stuff
2564 Jefferson St. ☎707-255-9303
John Stutzman Photo Center
1625 Jefferson St. ☎707-224-2882
Custom Image Photographic Service
812 West Napa St. ☎707-935-3191

Pacific Grove
The Camera Exchange
551 Lighthouse Ave. ☎408-373-0448
Camera World
213 Forest Ave. ☎408-373-3686

Palo Alto
Keeble & Shuchat Photography
290 S California St. ☎415-327-8996

Petaluma
B+B Photo Lab
946 Caulfield Lane. ☎707-763-8634

Reno
Silver State Camera
538 South Virginia. ☎702-323-9018

Sacramento
Action Camera
1000 Sunrise Ave. ☎916-786-2288
Pardee's Cameras
3335 El Camino Ave ☎916-483-3435

Salinas
Green's Camera & Video
350 Main St. ☎408-424-5247

San Rafael
Marin Cameras
894 4th St. ☎415-456-6340

Santa Cruz
Camera Club
1325 Mission St. ☎408-426-8718
Camera World
710 Front St. ☎408-426-9488
Meadows Camera
810 Bay St. ☎408-476-3333

Santa Rosa
Shutterbug Camera
2770 Santa Rosa Ave. ☎707-546-3456

Walnut Creek
Reed's Cameras
1524 Locust St. ☎510-934-7207

Yosemite
Ansel Adams Gallery & **Village Store**

WHEN TO VISIT

"The coldest winter I ever spent was summer in San Francisco."
Mark Twain.

When To Go

Unfortunately the famous Mark Twain phrase is on the mark. Summer is by far the most popular time to visit but, in San Francisco and along the coast, can be cold due to the fog. If you can, plan instead for Spring or Fall, when the weather is still warm, and the fog and crowds have thinned. The sunniest days and warmest days in San Francisco usually occur in September and October.

What To Wear

The climate is generally mild so you don't need anything extreme. California is famously laid back so jeans and cotton shirts, blouses and sweatshirts are fine. Exceptions are the inland valleys in the Summer which can be baking hot, coastal areas which can be cool when blanketed by Summer fog, and the Sierra Nevada mountains in the Winter, which can get deep drifts of snow. Unlike Southern California, the ocean is always cold so don't even think of swimming.

Summer

This is the most popular time to visit, and is often delineated by Memorial Day weekend (last Monday weekend in May) and Labor Day (first Monday in September).

Summer is unfortunately pestered by coastal fog. San Francisco, Big Sur and Mendocino are reliably affected. Often the fog will roll in in the morning, clear after midday, and then return in the late afternoon - the worst times for photographers. Or it may stay for several days. San Francisco gets very cold (55°F/15°C) and damp so bring a sweater and rainproof jacket. The eastern downtown financial district may be beautiful when the western Golden Gate Bridge and Golden Gate Park areas are in thick fog.

The only remedy is to avoid the afflicted areas. If you're in the city, take the ferry or a car over to the sun in Sausalito and Tiburon, which are protected by the Marin hills. Save inside trips (such as museums) and inland trips (such as to the Wine Country and Yosemite) for foggy days.

Whereas the coast may be cold, the inland valleys get surprisingly hot. Salinas, Sacramento, routes 5 and 99, Napa, and even Yosemite Valley can reach 100°F. You'll appreciate cotton shorts, shirts and skirts. Make sure you keep your precious film (unexposed and exposed) cool and dry. Put the canisters in zip-lock bags and keep them in the shade, a fridge, or an ice-chest (upon removal, leave for a few minutes to avoid condensation). If left unprotected in sunlight or a hot car trunk, your pictures will loose color and shift red. Consumer-grade print film is quite tolerant but 'professional-grade' film is more sensitive. Try to buy new film from stores that are enclosed and air-conditioned, or, better still, keep it in refrigerators.

The long days give more time for photography. The longest daylight of the year (Summer Solstice) is on June 21.

Fall/Autumn

A good choice. Yosemite has great fall foliage, and the Wine Country is busy harvesting grapes (the 'Crush', Sept/Oct) which are fullest in August/September.

Winter

You have everywhere to yourself, except for the stores around Christmas. The north coast has considerable rainfall between Nov. and Feb. Except for Route 80 to Reno, all of the Sierra Nevada mountain passes are closed, including Tioga Pass Road (Hwy 120). Mono Lake and Bodie can only be reached via I-80. Also closed are the upper elevations of Yosemite (Glacier Point Road and Mariposa Grove), Devil's Postpile NM and Lava Beds NM. Tourist centers close or have reduced hours, including Great America and Marin World Africa USA, so call ahead. Vineyards in the Wine Country are barren as the vines are clipped back ready for next year. Opera belts forth and skiing traverses Mammoth Mountain and around Lake Tahoe. California Gray Whales migrate south and can be seen off the coast, from Mendocino, Point Reyes, and Big Sur. The days are short (Winter Solstice is around Dec. 21) so there's less time for photography.

Spring

Possibly the best overall time to visit. Colorful wildflowers line the roads and fields and trees blossom. The waterfalls are at their fullest (peaking in April/May) and whitewater rafting is popular around the Gold Country.

Temperature

San Francisco

	°F	°C
Jan	42-56	5-13
Feb	44-59	6-15
Mar	45-61	7-16
Apr	47-63	8-17
May	49-66	9-19
June	52-70	11-21
July	53-71	11-21
Aug	54-72	12-21
Sept	54-73	11-23
Oct	51-70	10-21
Nov	46-63	7-18
Dec	52-56	6-14

Yosemite

	°F	°C
Jan	26-49	-3-9
Feb	28-55	-2-13
Mar	31-59	0-15
Apr	35-65	2-19
May	42-73	6-23
June	48-82	9-27
July	54-90	12-32
Aug	53-90	11-32
Sept	47-87	8-30
Oct	39-74	4-24
Nov	31-58	0-14
Dec	26-48	-3-9

Days with a Full Moon

	1997	1998	1999	2000
Jan	23	12	1 & 31	20
Feb	22	11	-	19
Mar	23	12	2 & 31	19
Apr	22	11	30	18
May	22	11	30	18
June	20	9	28	16
July	19	9	28	16
Aug	18	7	26	15
Sept	16	6	25	13
Oct	15	5	24	13
Nov	14	4	23	11
Dec	13	3	22	11

Numbers represent the day of month when a full moon occurs.

Sunrise & Sunset Times

San Francisco

	Sunrise (am)	Sunset (pm)
Jan	7:24	5:15
Feb	6:59	5:49
Mar	6:21	6:17
Apr	6:35	7:45
May	6:00	8:12
June	5:47	8:33
July	6:00	8:31
Aug	6:25	8:02
Sept	6:51	7:18
Oct	7:18	6:32
Nov	6:49	4:59
Dec	7:17	4:52

Yosemite

	Sunrise	Sunset
Jan	7:20	5:05
Feb	6:54	5:40
Mar	6:14	6:10
Apr	6:27	7:39
May	5:51	8:08
June	5:37	8:29
July	5:50	8:27
Aug	6:16	7:57
Sept	6:44	7:11
Oct	7:12	6:25
Nov	6:45	4:49
Dec	7:14	4:42

Times are for the middle (15th) of each month. For example, sunset in Yosemite for July 31 or Aug 1 would be about 8:15pm (between 8:27 & 7:57). For exact times, ask at a local Visitor's Center.

Time Zone

California and Nevada are in Pacific Standard Time (GMT-8 hours). Daylight Savings Time adds one hour (GMT-7 hours) and lasts from the first weekend in April to the last weekend in October.

Locations

San Francisco:
N 37 deg 37'08"; W 122 deg 22'29".
Yosemite (Tunnel View):
N 38 deg 43'47"; W 120 deg 41'12".

Rain or Shine?

	Jan	April	July	October
Chances of a Sunny Day	39%	70%	97%	81%
Chances of Rain	26%	20%	3%	6%

Where else but Northern California can you attend festivals for asparagus, banana slugs, camels, chocolate, clam chowder, garlic, oysters, pears, squids and prunes?

For a complete, free list, call the California Division of Tourism ☎800-862-2543. For current information, check local newspapers, including: *San Francisco Bay Guardian, SF Weekly,* and Sunday's *San Francisco Examiner-Chronicle.* Hotels and Visitor Centers will also have listings.

January

New Years Day: January 1.
Tex Cushion Memorial Sled Race: Early Jan. Mammoth Lakes.
Santa Cruz Fungus Festival: Mid-Jan. A lot of mushrooms.
Pro-Am Golf Tournament: Pebble Beach. ☎408-649-1533.
Martin Luther King Day: Third Monday.
Chinese New Year: Late Jan and early Feb. Chinatown's two weeks of festivities include the Golden Dragon Parade with a 75-foot long dragon. ☎415-982-3000.

February

Clam Chowder Cook-Off: Santa Cruz. ☎408-423-5590
Crab Race: Crescent City. ☎707-464-3174.
Presidents Day: Third Monday. Bankers get a long weekend.
Pacific Orchid Festival: Late Feb. Flower show in San Francisco.

"Travel is fatal to prejudice, bigotry, and narrow-mindedness, and many of our people need it sorely... Broad, wholesome, charitable views cannot be acquired by vegetating in one's little corner of the earth."
Mark Twain, in The Innocents Abroad, after a trip through Europe in 1869.

March

Snowfest: Early March. A winter fair by Lake Tahoe and Truckee.
Great Train Robberies: Felton. ☎408-335-4484.
Dixieland Jazz Festival: Eureka. ☎707-445-3378.
Whale Festival: Fort Bragg and Mendocino. ☎707-961-6300.
Wine Festival: Monterey. ☎408-656-9463.
Saint Patrick's Day: March 17. Suddenly everyone is Irish and, as real Irish people do, wear green clothes and drink green beer. Parade along Market Street. ☎415- 661-2700.
Carnival Santa Cruz: ☎408-429-1324.
Viva el Mariachi: Late March. Mexican bands parade in Fresno.

What's On in SF

Recorded events information:

English:	415-391-2001
French:	415-391-2003
German:	415-391-2004
Spanish:	415-391-2122
Japanese:	415-391-2101

"I'd rather be a broken lamppost on San Francisco's Battery Street than the Waldorf-Astoria in New York."
Turn-of-the-century boxer.

April

Cherry Blossom Festival: Late April. Japantown comes alive with tea ceremonies and martial arts, hopefully not together. ☎415-563-2313.
Outdoor Antique Fair: Petaluma. ☎707-763-7683.
Catfish Derby: Clearlake Oaks/Glenhaven. ☎707-998-9501.
Spring Wine Adventure: Lake County. ☎800-525-3743.
International Marathon: Big Sur. ☎408-625-6226.
Stockton Asparagus Festival: Third weekend. For asparagus fans everywhere.

"The Bay Area is so beautiful I hesitate to preach about heaven while I'm here."
Billy Graham.

May

Cinco de Mayo: The weekend closest to May 5. Everyone turns Mexican to celebrate their victory over the French at the Battle of Puebla in 1862. Mission district. ☎415-826-1401.

Community Festival and Car Show: Willits. ☎707-459-7910.

Kinetic Sculpture Race: Arcata/Ferndale. ☎707-725-3851.

Calaveras County Fair & Jumping Frog Jubilee: Mid-May. A county fair in Angels Camp in the Gold Country.

Cajun Crawfish Festival: Vallejo. ☎707-427-1060.

Chocolate Festival: Oakdale. ☎209-847-0826.

Squid Festival: Monterey. ☎408-649-6547.

Napa Valley Sunsational: Napa. ☎707-257-0322.

Bay to Breakers: Third Sunday. Everyone becomes a long-distance runner between the Bay (the Embarcadero) and the Breakers (the Pacific Ocean). Wearing a topical and ridiculous costume is a plus. ☎415-808-5000 x2222.

Sacramento Jazz Jubilee: Late May. Major 'trad' and Dixieland jazz festival.

San Jose Blues Festival: ☎408-924-6261.

Carnaval: Memorial Day weekend. Celebrates the end of fasting with a colorful parade and costumes in the Mission district. ☎415-826-1401.

Memorial Day: Third Monday. The unofficial start of summer.

June

Merced West Coast Antique Fly-In: Early June. Old and home-made planes in an air show.

Scottish Highland Games: Early June. The *American Grafitti* town of Modesto tosses the caber and turns Scottish.

Festival at the Lake: Oakland. ☎510-286-1061.

Oyster Festival: Arcata. ☎707-826-9043.

Art & Wine Festival: San Anselmo. ☎415-346-4446.

Tour of Nevada City Bicycle Classic: Mid-June. Bike race in a beautiful setting.

North Beach Street Fair: Mid-June. The Italian district offers paintings, bands and food around Washington Square. ☎415-403-0666.

Reno Rodeo: Mid-June. One of the largest rodeos in the country.

Blues Festival: Monterey. ☎408-395-2652.

Peddler's Fair: San Juan Bautista. ☎408-623-0674.

Lesbian and Gay Pride Day: Last Sunday. With 400,000 people on Market Street, this is the biggest parade in San Francisco and the largest celebration of its kind in the world. The night before is the Pink Saturday Party on Castro Street, and the night of the parade is a party at City Hall.

Mid-Summer Scandinavian Festival: About June 22. Celebrate solstice in Ferndale.

Haight Street Fair: Saturday or Sunday in late June. Hippie music and food along Haight Street. ☎415-661-8025.

Juneteenth: Late June. An African-American celebration with jazz and R&B bands around Oakland's Lake Merritt.

Cable Car Bell-Ringing Championship: Late June or early July. Find out who is the loudest and most tuneful cable car bell ringer. ☎415-923-6202.

"San Francisco has only one drawback - 'tis hard to leave."
Rudyard Kipling, writer.

July

Independence Day: July 4. Fireworks at Crissy Field and Fisherman's Wharf celebrate the US of A. Teddy Bear Parade & Picnic in Oakland.

Handcar Races & Steam Festival: Felton. ☎408-335-4484.

Mountain Folk Festival: Leggett. ☎707-925-6425.

Wine-Tasting Championships: Philo. ☎707-895-2002.

Salmon Barbeque: Fort Bragg. ☎707-964-6598.

Blues & Art On Polk: Mid-July. The title says it all. In San Francisco's Polk Street.

"Though we travel the world over to find the beautiful, we must carry it with us or we find it not."

Ralph Waldo Emerson

San Francisco Flower Show: County Fair Building, Golden Gate Park.

San Francisco Marathon: Watch the Golden Gate Bridge flatten when crossed by the country's third-largest marathon.

Frontier Days: Willits. ☎707-459-6330.

National Worm Races: Clearlake. ☎707-994-3600.

California Rodeo: Late July. Photograph bucking horses in Salinas. ☎408-757-2951.

Bach Festival: Carmel. ☎408-624-2046.

Feast of Lanterns: Pacific Grove. ☎408-373-3304.

Gilroy Garlic Festival: Late July. Everything you can possibly think to do with the 'stinking rose'. Gilroy is near Santa Cruz and Salinas. ☎408-842-1625.

August

Hot August Nights: Early Aug. Reno celebrates the 1950's with cars and music.

Chinatown Street Fest: Oakland. ☎510-893-8979.

Reggae on the River: Garberville. ☎707-923-3368.

Fair on the Square: Oakland. ☎510-814-6000.

Concours d'Elegance: Pebble Beach. ☎408-659-0663.

Steinbeck Festival: Salinas. ☎408-753-6411.

Redwood Empire Fair: Ukiah. ☎707-462-3884.

Blackberry Festival: Lower Lake/Clearlake: ☎800-525-3743.

Old Street Town Fair: Vallejo. ☎707-644-6201.

Banana Slug Derby: Orick. ☎707-488-2171.

Historic Automobile Races: Late August. Classic old cars tear around Monterey.

California State Fair: Mid-Aug to early Sept. Livestock and rides in Sacramento.

Nevada State Fair: Late August. Livestock and rides in Reno.

September

A La Carte, A La Park: First weekend. Golden Gate Park hosts an outdoor fair of San Francisco food and drink.

Labor Day: First Monday. The unofficial end of summer.

Opera in the Park: First Sunday following the start of the opera season. Get to the Golden Gate Park for a free Opera. ☎415-864-3330.

Art Festival: Sausalito. ☎415-332-3555.

Paul Bunyan Days: Fort Bragg. ☎707-961-6300.

Tapestry in Talent Festival of Arts: ☎San Jose. 408-293-9727.

Art & Wine Festival: Santa Clara. ☎408-984-3257.

National Championship Air Races: Mid-Sept. Reno hosts the world's longest-running airshow.

Heritage Weekend: Oakland. ☎510-836-2227.

Camel Races: Mid-Sept. Mark Twain made a fake story about racing camels in Virginia City, and now it's true.

"San Franciscans are the luckiest people on earth; they not only get a vacation with pay, they have San Francisco to come home to."

Herb Caen, columnist.

San Francisco Shakespeare Festival: After Labor Day. Free shows in Golden Gate Park and other parks. ☎415-666-2222.

Monterey Grand Prix: Early Sept. India Car racing in Monterey.

Monterey Jazz Festival: Mid-Sept. 'Trad' and modern jazz in a fine setting. ☎408-373-3366.

Valley of the Moon Wine Festival: Late Sept. Sonoma hosts California's oldest wine festival. ☎707-0996-2109.

Tomato Fest: Los Banos. ☎800-446-5353.

Prune Festival: Yuba City. ☎916-673-3436.

San Francisco Chinatown Moon Festival: End of September. The Autumn Moon is celebrated in Chinatown.

California Indian Days: Covelo. ☎707-983-6126.

San Francisco Blues Festival: Last weekend. For two days, Fort Mason rings with 12-bar riffs. ☎510-762-2277.

Folsom Street Fair: Last Sunday. The city's most outrageous street fair, predominantly gay and lesbian, is between 11th and 17th Streets.

"You can't get bored in San Francisco."
William Saroyan, writer.

October

Oktoberfest: Sept and Oct. Various places become German and drink beer

Castro Street Fair: First Sunday. A large gay & lesbian celebration.

Columbus Day Parade: Sunday nearest Oct 12. Columbus Avenue.

Columbus Day: Second Monday.

Black Cowboys Weekend: Oakland. ☎510-531-7583.

PPG/Indy Car World Series: Monterey. ☎800-327-7322.

Pear Festival: Kelseyville. ☎800-525-3743.

Country Pumpkin Festival: Ukiah. ☎707-462-4705.

Apple Harvest: Sonoma. ☎707-725-2123.

Fleet Week: Early Oct. The US Navy displays its ships and Blue Angels above and below the Golden Gate Bridge.

Halloween Parade: October 31. A major parade down Castro Street and Market St. with outlandish costumes, capped by the Exotic-Erotic Halloween Ball ☎415-567-2255.

Pumpkin Festival: October 31. More pumpkins than you can imagine line Half Moon Bay. ☎415-726-9652.

November

Dia de los Muertos (Day of the Dead): November 2. Various Mexican celebrations with macabre art, including in the Mission district. ☎415-826-8009.

San Francisco Jazz Festival: Late Oct/early Nov. ☎415-788-7353.

The Big Game: Third Saturday. University football between Stanford and Berkeley.

Thanksgiving Day: Fourth Thursday. The biggest travel weekend of the year.

Christmas Tree Lighting Festivals: End of Nov/early Dec. Various towns start the countdown to Christmas by lighting a tree.

December

Lighted Boat Parage: Santa Cruz. ☎408-423-9680.

Victorian Christmas: Nevada City has hay rides and chestnut roasts.

Coastal Christmas: Humboldt. ☎800-346-3482.

Christmas Festival: Mendocino. ☎707-961-6300.

Dunsmuir House Christmas: Oakland. ☎510-562-3232.

Lighted Yacht Parade: Oakland. ☎510-814-6000.

Christmas in the Adobes: Monterey. ☎408-647-6226.

Truckers Christmas Light Convoy: Early Dec. Breaker, breaker, there are large trucks in Eureka, do you copy?

Hometown Christmas & Truck Parade: Fort Bragg. ☎707-961-6300.

Russian Heritage Christmas: Late Dec. Guerneville brings Babushka to the Russian River.

Christmas/Hanukkah/Kwanzaa/New Year: Around Dec 24 - Jan 1.

"I knew my destiny when I first saw Yosemite."
Ansel Adams.

Tip:
On overcast days, create a soft, watercolor-style image by adding a diffusion filter and an 80A blue filter, and by overexposing (slide film only) by 1/2- to one-stop.

PHOTOGRAPHY

Photography is the perfect companion to travel. It encourages us - as travelers - to discover an area; it provides tangible memories of the trip; and it is an enjoyable way to expressive ourselves in art.

A camera is really an excuse to delve deeper into a place than we otherwise would. Looking for a good shot forces us to seek out the unique features and scenic beauty of a location, to explore further, and to interact with our surroundings. When you press the shutter release, you're making a personal connection to the place and it's people. You are *there*.

Photographs preserve the memories of our trip. We can show others the exciting places we've been, the wonderful scenery, and the great people we met. Our minds are triggered by images and reviewing our photographs helps everyone on the trip relive it's adventures and misadventures.

Taking pictures is also a very accessible artform. With a little thought and effort, you can create captivating images of your own creation and interpretation.

The Secret of Photography

Fortunately, taking good photographs has little to do with owning expensive equipment and knowing technical data. The secret is in *seeing*. Ask yourself: *What do I look at, and how do I see it?* A good photograph has qualities that display the skill, art, interests, and personality of the photographer.

What Makes A Good Photograph?

A photograph is a message. It conveys a statement (*"Here we are in ..."*), an impression (*"This is what ... looks like"*), or an emotion. You are an author trying to convey this message in a clear, concise, and effective way. But how?

Like any message, you first need a subject. This may be your traveling companions, a building, a natural vista, or some abstract form. The subject is the central point of interest and is usually placed in the foreground of the shot (towards the viewer). Now we compose the message by including a second element, a context, which is often the background. The context gives the subject relevance,

presence, location, or other interest. It is the combination of the two elements - subject and context, foreground and background - that tells the message.

Just as important as knowing what to include, is knowing what to exclude. Anything that isn't part of the subject or it's context is only a distraction, cluttering up the image and diluting the message. So eliminate extraneous surroundings - usually by moving closer to the subject - and make a clear, tidy shot. A painter creates art by addition - adding more paint - whereas a photographer creates art by subtraction - removing unnecessary elements.

The recipe for a good photograph is:
"A foreground, a background, and nothing else."

What Makes A Great Photograph?

A great photograph is piece of art. It captures the spirit of a subject and evokes emotion. Bob Krist calls it: *'The Spirit of Place'*. You are an artist that can use subtle tricks to appeal to your viewer's senses. Let's see how.

A picture is a playground, with places for our eyes to wander and investigate, plus spaces for them to rest and relax. When we first see something, we are defensive. Our eyes instinctually find light, bright areas, and look for people, particularly their eyes and mouth. Do we know the people in the picture? What are they feeling, and how does this relate to us? Are they drawing attention to something? If so, do we recognize it (a building, a landmark) and what does it look like? What is this picture *about*? What is the main subject or objective? How big is the subject? We determine scale by comparing elements to something of known size, such as a person, animal, or car. Once we've checked for people, we turn our attention to more abstract features.

We first notice the subject's color or tone. Firey red, calming blue, natural green, foreboding black. Then we see shape. Soft curves, hard edges, sweeping lines. How the light strikes the subject gives subtle hints as to it's three-dimensional form. You, as a photographer, can manipulate this by searching for shades and shadows, shifting intensities of tone and hues. How is the eye drawn into the picture?

Form leads us to texture, how the subject might feel to the touch. Is it soft, is it smooth, hard, or rough? Does it have character and warmth? The way the elements are juxtaposed and affected by the same light, makes us consider their qualities and interrelation. Balance draws our eye from one element to another, investigating their unity, contrast, and detail, each item adding pleasure to the next. What is the relevance of everything?

The overall composition, the proportions of layout, denotes importance of the elements. As the artist, you can decide which features appeals to you, and how best to emphasize them.

The recipe for a great photograph is:
"Consider how the parts interrelate with the whole".

How To Get Those Professional 'Stock Image' Quality Shots

If you look at the sort of shots that get printed in fancy travel magazines and expensive coffee-table books, they tend to share similar attributes. Look for pictures that you admire and try to analyze *why* you like them. These are some of the features I like:

Include People

Magazines in particular always like people in the shot. It gives the viewer a human connection, a sense of being there, and a sense of scale. Photographs evoke emotion and empathy comes with someone's face. Avoid crowds and simplify the shot down to one person. The young and old are preferred subjects, with their innocent expressions and weather-worn faces respectively. People make your shots warm, friendly, and personable. Just like you are.

Simple, Clear Layout

A good shot focuses your attention on the subject by using a sparse background and a simple but interesting composition. Always remove clutter for the picture - this is a real skill. Like a musician, it's always difficult to make things look easy. Zoom in, get close, get to eye level, find a simple backdrop, look for balance.

Bold, Solid Colors

'Stock-quality' images make great use of color. Look for solid primary colors: bright 'sports-car' red, emerald green, lightning yellow, and ocean blue. Use a polarizer to bring out the colors. Avoid patterns - keep it simple. Bright afternoon sunlight will add warmth.

Alternatively, look for 'color harmony' - scenes restricted to similar tones and colors, or even a single color. This presents a calm, restful image where the eye plays with the differing shades and intensities. Look for pastels, cream, or delicate shades.

Depth

Always include some pointer about depth. A photograph is two-dimensional but we want it to appear three-dimensional. If you're shooting a background (mountains) include a strong foreground (people). If you're shooting people (foreground), add an out-of-focus blur behind them.

Use a wide-angle lens for exaggerated depth. With a 20mm to 28mm lens, get just a few feet from your subject and, with a small aperture (large f-number), include an in-focus deep background too. This exaggerated 'hyperfocal' perspective is used in a lot of magazine shots. What impact!

Alternatively you can remove all depth by using a long, telephoto lens. This compresses or compacts the image, making your 3-D subject appear flat.

Dramatic Lighting

Photographs that win competitions are often ones that make interesting use of light. Look out for beams of light shining through clouds, trees or windows, long shadows, and the effect of side- and backlighting. Shoot in the warm golden 'magic hours' of early morning and late afternoon.

Preparation

"Chance favors the prepared mind."
Louis Pasteur.

A great shot takes time. Scout out the area, make mental notes of important features, unusual and interesting angles, and changing crowd levels. Take time to prepare the shot. Get there before the best time of day, clean your lenses, set up a tripod or mini-tripod, add a cable release, try out different filters, wait for a good foreground, and talk with people who may be in the shot so that they're comfortable and will pose well.

TEN TIPS

"The [35mm] camera is for life and for people, the swift and intense moments of life." Ansel Adams

1 Hold It Steady

A problem with many photographs is that they're blurry. Avoid 'camera shake' by holding the camera steady. Use both hands, resting your elbows on your chest, or use a wall for support. Relax: don't tense up. You're a marksman/woman holding a gun and it must be steady to shoot.

2 Put The Sun Behind You

A photograph is all about light so always think of how the light is striking your subject. The best bet is to move around so that the sun is behind you and to one side. This front lighting brings out color and shades, and the slight angle (side lighting) produces some shadow to indicate texture and form.

3 Get Closer

The best shots are simple so move closer and remove any clutter from the picture. If you look at most 'people' shots they don't show the whole body so you don't need to either. Move close, fill the frame with just the face, or even overflow it. Give your shot some impact. Use a zoom to crop the image tighter.

4 Choose A Format

Which way you hold the camera affects what is emphasized in your shot. For tall things (Redwoods, Half Dome) a vertical format emphasize height. Use a horizontal format to show the dramatic sweep of the mountains.

5 Include People

Photographs solely of landscape and rocks are enjoyable to take but often dull to look at. Include some of your friends, companions, family, or even people passing by, to add human interest. If there's no one around, include yourself with the self-timer.

Have you ever got your photos back only to discover that something that looked awe-inspiring at the time looks dull on paper? This is because your eye needs some reference point to judge scale. Add a person, car, or something of known size to indicate the magnitude of the scenery.

6 Consider Variety

You may take the greatest shots but if they're all the same type or style, they may be dull to look at. Spice up your collection by adding variety. Include landscapes and people shots, close ups and wide angles, good weather and bad weather. Take personal shots that remember the 'being there' - friends that you meet, your hotel/campsite, transportation, street or hiking signposts.

7 Add Depth

Depth is an important quality of good photographs. We want the viewer to think that they're not looking at a flat picture, but through a window, into a three-dimensional world. Add pointers to assist the eye. If your subject is a distant mountain, add a person or a tree in the foreground. A wide angle lens can exaggerate this perspective.

8 Use Proportion

The beauty of an image is often in it's proportions. A popular technique with artists is called the *rule of thirds*. Imagine the frame divided into thirds, both horizontally and vertically, like a Tic-Tac-Toe board. Now place your subject on one of the lines or intersections.

Always centering your subject can get dull. Use the Rule of Thirds to add variety and interest.

9 Search For Details

It's always tempting to use a wide angle lens and 'get everything in'. However, this can be too much and you may loose the impact. Instead, zoom in with a longer lens and find some representative detail. A shot of an entire Sequoia Tree just looks like a tree. But a shot of just the wide base, with a person for scale, is more powerful.

10 Position The Horizon

Where you place the horizon in your shot affects what is emphasized. To show the land, use a high horizon. To show the sky, use a low horizon. Be creative.

1 Use a Narrow Tonal Range

Photographic film can't handle a wide tonal range. When you photograph very bright things and very dark things together (sunlight in water and shadows in trees) the film will loose all the detail and you'll end up with stark overexposed white and total underexposed black. Instead, look for mid-tones with little difference between the brightest and darkest highlights. Flowers and trees for example are often best photographed on overcast, drizzly days.

Your eye can handle a difference in brightness (a 'dynamic range') of about 2,000:1 (11 camera 'stops'). Print film is limited to no more than 64:1 (5 stops) and slide film is even worse, at 8:1 (3 stops). Ansel Adams' 'Zone System' divided light levels into 11 'zones' and advised using a narrow zone (or tonal) range.

2 Work The Subject, Baby!

As film directors say, film is cheap (although it's not always their money!). Work the subject and take different shots from different angles. The more you take, the more likely you are to get a good one. Don't be afraid to take five shots and throw four away. Find different, unusual viewpoint. Shoot from high and from low. It's often said that the only difference between a professional photographer and an amateur photographer is that the professional throws more shots away. National Geographic magazine uses only 1 out of every 1,000 shots taken. (8/95 issue)

3 Hyperfocal

A popular 'pro' technique is capture great depth by combining a close foreground and deep background. Use a wide angle lens (20-28mm), get a few inches from the foreground (often flowers), put the horizon high in the frame. Using a small aperture (f22) keeps everything in focus ('hyperfocal'). Use a hyperfocal chart to correspond distance with aperture, or just use the smallest (highest f-number) possible.

4 Expose For Highlights

When a scene has a mixture of very bright and very dark areas the light meter in

"Emphasis on technique is justified only so far as it will simplify and clarify the statement of the photographer's concept."
Ansel Adams

How To Get Deep Colors

1. Use a polarizer filter
2. Shoot in the late afternoon
3. Use 'saturated' slide film
4. Use a narrow tonal range
5. Keep your lenses clean
6. Underexpose slightly
   (for slide film - overexpose print film)

your camera will have difficulty finding the right exposure. In such high-contrast shots, try to expose for the highlights. To do this, walk up to, zoom in to, or spot meter on the most important bright area (a face, sky, detail) and half-depress the shutter release button to hold the exposure (exposure lock). Then recompose and take the shot. To be on the safe side, take several 'bracketed' shots.

5 Underexpose for Deeper Colors SLR only

On slide film, a slightly underexposed image (on print film a slightly underexposed image) can give deeper, more saturated colors . The deeper color also makes the subject appear heavier. On a manual SLR camera, select the next shutter speed up (1/250 when 1/125 is recommended by the meter). On automatic camera, set the exposure compensation dial to -1/2 or -1. Similarly you can underexpose for paler, lighter images.

The effect is dependent upon your camera and film so try some test runs to find the best combination. On my camera (a Minolta X-700 with Fuji Velvia film) the recommended exposure worked best and underexposure just lost detail.

6 Bracketing SLR only

Always expose for the most important highlight. When in doubt about the correct exposure, take several 'bracketed' shots. You 'bracket' around a shot by taking one regular shot, then a second shot slightly darker (-1 stop) and a third shot slightly lighter (+1 stop). Some cameras offer this as an automatic feature.

The most important element to many great photographs is the lighting. Warmth, depth, texture, form, contrast, and color are all dramatically affected by the angle of the sunlight, and thus the time of day. Shooting at the optimum time is often the biggest difference between an 'amateur' and a 'professional' shot.

In the early morning and late afternoon, when the sun is low, the light is gold and orange, giving your shot the warmth of a log fire. Professional photographers call these the *'magic hours'* and most movies and magazine shots are made during this brief time. It takes extra planning, but saving your photography for one hour after sunrise, or one to two hours before sunset, will add stunning warmth to your shots.

Assuming a sunrise at 6am and sunset at 7pm, and that your spouse, kids, friends suddenly love you, and the weather and security won't obviously deceive, a good day might be:

5am	**Pre-dawn**: A pink, ethereal light and dreamy mist for lakes, rivers & landscapes.
6-7am	**Dawn**: Crisp, golden light for east-facing subjects.
7am-10am	**Early morning**: The city comes to life, joggers in the park.
10am-2pm	**Midday**: The sun is too harsh for landscapes & people, but perfect for monuments, buildings & streets with tall buildings.
2pm-4pm	**Afternoon**: Deep blue skies with a polarizer.
4pm -6:45pm	**Late Afternoon**: Terrific warm, golden light on west-facing subjects. Best time for landscapes and people, particularly one hour before sunset.
6:45 -7:30pm	**Sunset**: Great skies 10 minutes before and 10 minutes after sunset.
7:30-8pm	**Dusk** is great for skylines, while there's still a purple color to the sky
9pm	**Night** shots, or go to bed - you've got to be up early tomorrow!

Mid-Afternoon. Sacramento Capitol.

Late-Afternoon (two hours later).
Notice how the lower sun has turned the white building gold, and added a feeling of warmth to the shot.

How To Predict A Rainbow

Rainbows are scientific phenomena which can be accurately predicted. A rainbow occurs when sunlight passes through a fine spray, such as at the base of a waterfall, and is refracted into it's component colors - red, orange, yellow, green, blue, indigo and violet.

You can see rainbows at the base of Vernal Fall and Bridalveil Fall in the late afternoon, when you're standing directly between the fall and the sun. A circular halo will form with a 42°radius, around a point exactly opposite the sun.

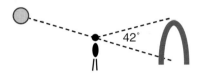

Bridalveil Fall in the afternoon is Yosemite's best place to catch a rainbow. Also try Vernal Fall.

Creative Ideas

Panoramas

Many cameras now have a **panorama mode** which can produce great wide shots. You can have these printed at the standard size or, for an extra cost, at 10"x3".

Another way to capture a panoramic view is to combine several shots. Take a photograph of the left end of the view, then move the camera one frame to the right (use a landmark for reference) and take a second shot. Keep going until you get to the other end of the view.

It's important to keep the horizon in the same height in each shot. Also, try to use the same exposure - meter off the most important or some representative part, then press and hold down the exposure lock button while you take all the shots. Add a little overlap between shots. However, with envelope albums, leave a small gap.

The 'David Hockney'

To make a large print, use the above technique but shoot up and down as well as left to right. When the prints come back, recombine them into a work of art. The modern English artist David Hockney popularized this technique. You can be creative and have the same people in different parts of the scene.

Cartoon

Use a sequence of shots to tell a short story. Get your companions to act out a silly story. Good for jokes.

Reflections

Look out for reflections for interesting shots. Use glass-sided buildings, store windows, puddles, or sunglasses.

Hand Coloring

With black & white film, or infra-red film, you can turn your photographs into art by hand coloring them, perhaps with watercolor paints.

Buildings

To minimize the angular distortions of looking upwards, always look for a high viewpoint. Ascend stairs, stand on top of another building or the crest of a hill. If you can't get high, stand far back.

Use the widest angle you have (24-30mm). Bright blue skies are to offset the gray of the building. A polarizer cuts down on window reflections. Try to include people for scale and human interest.

Look for interesting details, often around the doorway, columns or windows. Zoom in and isolate the detail. Here the diffused light of an overcast day works best.

Interiors

Stand well back or shoot from outside through a window. The low-light dictate a long exposure, so load up with fast film. Bring a tripod if they're allowed or, if not, find a support (a wall, your friends shoulder, or lean against a doorway). Use a cable release, or the self-timer to avoid moving the camera.

Remember to switch off the flash if it is not allowed. If it is, you can bring up dark areas by firing a hand-held flash into them while the shutter is open. Natural lighting casts shadows for a tranquil atmosphere. Expose for the highlights.

Landscapes

Always have something in the foreground. This gives depth and scale - using a person also adds human interest. Look for a high vantage point such as a hotel balcony, roof-top restaurant, or wall. Late afternoon is usually best. Use a polarizer to enhance the sky. Haze increases with distance and this aerial perspective gives a subtle impression of distance and depth. Ansel Adams declared landscape photography to be "the supreme test of the photographer.

Water

With sprayed water, use side- or backlighting for a translucent look. This also works well with smoke, grass and leaves.

Experiment with a slow shutter speed, perhaps 1/30 to 1/4s so that the rushing water creates a soft, romantic blur. I like 1/8s. A tripod or other support is necessary. Be careful with a polarizer - it can enhance the colors but it also removes reflections that you may want.

Sunsets

The best times are when the sun is just about to touch the horizon, and the afterglow 5 minutes after the sun has set. Usually automatic metering works fine, but with high contrast, meter off the brightest part of the sky. Try adding a person in the foreground (they'll appear as a silhouette) for human interest, depth and character. Either include a reflection from the ocean, or eliminate the scenery and keep the horizon low in the frame. A zoom lens is useful and you'll need a tripod or wall for support as the shutter speed will be slow.

Dusk & Night Shots

Dusk shots are best about 30-40 minutes after sunset, when there is still some color in the sky. To add depth, shoot from one end of a bridge or find some other feature coming towards you. A tripod is a necessity. Auto exposure usually works fine but also try manual exposure using a cable release and the 'B' (*bulb* - open) setting. Take several shots with 2, 4, 8, 12 and 16 seconds. Use an FL-D magenta filter to overcome the effect of tungsten lights on daylight film, and to add a pink to the sky.

In Bad Weather

Bad weather doesn't mean bad photographs, it just changes your options.

Overcast skies reduce contrast and are preferred for trees and foliage. Colors may appear cool and blueish so add an 81A, B, or C filter to warm up the image. If the sky is boring, disguise it with an overhanging tree, or exclude it completely by raising the horizon in your frame. When low clouds or rain reduce color saturation, try black and white film to emphasize the range of gray tones. You may need a faster film (ISO 200 or 400) since there's less light.

Storms and heavy **rain** add drama and power to an image. Dusk shots are improved with reflections of neon lights in puddles. **Clouds** create moving patterns of interesting highlights, particularly when a storm is clearing. **Fog** make lakes, rivers and valleys look ethereal and primordial.

Rain or **snow** makes people, kids especially, wear colorful clothing. Cover your camera with a coat, umbrella, or even put it in a plastic bag. In **snow**, give a slight overexposure (slower shutter speed or '+1') to keep the whites free from appearing dirty gray.

There are several factors to consider when photographing people:

Location

The first thing to do is find your location. Choose a spot with a simple, medium-toned background. Tree foliage, grass or the ocean works well. For darker skin, look for a similarly dark background to keep the highlight (and thus the camera's exposure) on the face.

Minimize patterns, shapes and colors. Keep that background simple, or include a famous landmark.

Lighting

Get the sun behind you and to one side. If it's bright, put people in the shade (harsh, direct sunlight washes out the face). If it's dark in the shade, use the fill-flash feature to brighten up the face.

The best time is the late afternoon as it gives a nice, warm, golden glow. At other times, with an SLR camera, you can simulate this glow with an 81B or C filter.

A popular technique is to put your subject in the shade, then use fill-flash to lighten up the face. Bring a small reflector or white card reflect sunlight into the harsh shadow areas.

Occasionally, having the sun shine from behind the subject (backlighting) looks good as it creates a halo through the hair, showing form and drawing the face out of the background.

If you're shooting indoors with an SLR, 'bounce' the flash off a wall or ceiling for more natural lighting. A separate hand-held flash is best and can be positioned far enough away from the lens to avoid red eye.

Lens

If you have an SLR, use a 135mm or similar lens for the most pleasing perspective. Use the widest aperture (lowest f-number) to blur the background and highlight the face for a movie-like look. If the background is important, use a small aperture (high f-number) to get everything in focus.

Positioning

Get close. Don't include their full body but zoom straight in to the face. For close ups, crop out the top of the head and overfill the frame. Being at eye level usually works best, so for children, kneel down.

Proportion

Generally try to keep the eyes, not necessarily the head, in the center of the frame. If the person is looking slightly to one side, add extra space to that side.

If your subject is to one side and there's a lot of contrast in the shot, you might need to control the exposure. To do this, zoom or close in on your subject (perhaps a person's face) then press the exposure lock button. Keep this button pressed down while you recompose and take your shot.

Relax Your Subject

Get your subject relaxed and happy. For friends or family, remind them of a silly event. With children, give them something to play with. For local people, ask them about the location, their job or skill, or complement their clothes. People hate waiting while you adjust your camera so always plan the shot and adjust your camera first, before asking people to pose.

Fun Shots

To add fun and action to a shot, hold the camera at an angle - 30° with the right side up works well. It looks as though the photographer was caught off guard, emphasizing danger and action, and is great for parties! Stage a joke shot by pretending to interact with a statue. Or use a wide angle lens to distort the face.

Action

If your subject is moving (on a cable car or bicycle), deliberately blur the background to emphasize speed, excitement and urgency. Track the subject with your camera and, if you have an SLR, use a medium to slow shutter speed (1/60s). This will blur the background and, optionally, also your subject. Using the flash (particularly a 'rear-curtain sync' feature if your camera has one) helps freeze the subject in a moving background.

Don't Forget You!

The problem with being the photographer is that you end up not being in your own photographs. Remind the viewer what **you** look like and ask someone else to take a shot. You can arrange a photograph by propping the camera on a small tripod or wall (use stones, paper or coins for adjustment) and using the self timer.

Standard

A 'Compact' or 'Point-and-Shoot' automatic camera makes life very easy as it is small and simple to operate. In fact, they're even preferable over more expensive 'SLR' cameras in some circumstances, such as when you need fast response, something less noticeable and intimidating (for photographing people), or something small and light (when walking around town or hiking).

Some models have one fixed lens (usually a 30mm wide angle) which is the lens you'd use most on a more expensive camera. Other model also offer a second, telephoto lens, or a single zoom lens to help you capture details and make good portraits of people.

Look for a model that feels good in your hands and that you can understand how to operate. I like a very wide angle lens (24mm) to capture buildings and make big, punchy shots. A fill-flash feature is very useful to brighten people's faces. Other useful features include lockable autofocus (to focus on subjects which aren't in the center of the frame), a self-timer, and panoramic mode.

Experienced

The 35mm camera of choice for experienced photographers is the SLR - Single-Lens Reflex. This type of camera contains an angled mirror and prism to show you exactly the scene viewed by the lens. This is a benefit over the simple point-and-shoot camera (which has a separate viewfinder lens) as it allows you to better monitor the image.

The greatest benefits of an SLR camera is the ability to change lenses according to the situation, and to have manual control over focus, aperture and shutter-speeds. SLRs are typically more cumbersome, expensive, and technically demanding than a compact camera, but you are rewarded with increased flexibility and control.

Look for a model that feels comfortable and that you understand how to operate. I like a built-in flash, auto-focus capability, and aperture-priority mode (where you set the aperture and the camera determines the corresponding shutter speed). A light-weight design is valuable when you're traveling.

Lenses

Most people start with a medium zoom lens, such as 35-80mm or 80-135mm, then a telephoto 100-210mm. The lens I use the most is a 24-35mm as you can do so much with it. Many professional like a 20mm lens. The exaggerated perspective adds great punch and depth to their shots.

A popular 'long' lens is 80-210mm. I prefer a 100-300mm telephoto as that extra 90mm seems to go a long way. You can use a 2x convertor to double the length but there are drawbacks. It adds two precious f-stops resulting in slower shutter speed, and decreases the optical quality by 10-20%. With such a long focal length you'll need a tripod.

Cases, Caps & Straps

Lenses are fragile and expensive so protect them with front and rear lens caps. Adding a UV or Skylight filter to each lens serves as extra protection. If you're like me and prone to dropping things, it's cheaper to replace a damaged filter than a broken lens.

A strap can be useful for carrying the camera. It keeps your hands free while keeping the camera primed for action. A nice wide strap spreads the load. Personally however I prefer not to use a strap as it just gets in the way. Instead I carry the camera in a padded case.

Choose a camera case that carries all your kit and is well padded. Adjustable compartments and pockets are useful. Shoulder bags are popular but carrying the weight on one side all day can get uncomfortable. I prefer a backpack as it frees up both hands and makes it easier to travel.

Many professionals prefer a bag that also fits around the waist. This way, they have ready access to a range of lenses.

Filters

Your choice of filters, as with everything else, is one of personal preference. I find THE most useful filter (and the only one you need to have) is a polarizer. Rotating the filter gives deep blue skies and strengthens colors by removing glare and reflections. Many of the shots in this book benefit from a polarizer.

In general, don't use a filter unless you require a specific effect.

FILTERS & STUFF

Use	Filter	Effect
Color	**Color Polarizer**	Add blue or yellow to areas (Cokin #173 Blue/Yellow)
	Color Enhancer	Enhances reds, but leaves a cold blue/violet cast and is expensive
	Color Correcting (CC)	Enhances particular colors - green is good to enhance foliage. For example, a CC20G adds 20% green by reducing other colors by 80%.
	FL-D	Used for dusk shots to color balance the green fluorescent light from office buildings.
	Single Color	Add an overall blue, orange or sepia cast to your shot.
Warmth	**81A, 81B or 81C**	Simulates late afternoon light by adding an orange/brown cast. A is light, B medium, and C strong.
Sky	**Haze 1 or Skylight 1A**	Can reduce haze at high altitude. Skylight 1A adds a slight pink 'warming' cast. Used mostly to protect lenses.
Contrast	**Neutral Density or Split-Field Neutral Density**	Reduces the brightness of a scene, for better control of aperture. A Split-Field Neutral Density reduces a bright sky to match a shaded foreground.
B&W	**Red or Yellow**	Increases tonal contrast in black & white photographs.

Extra Film

Always carry extra film as you never when something interesting may happen. I like to carry 2-5 spare rolls. Consider carrying a fast film (1600 ISO) for interiors and night shots, and a good slide film in case you find something suitable to win a competition! Use a sealable 'zip-lock' bag for storage.

Camera Care

Dirty lenses or filters produce low-contrast images and washed-out colors. Keep things clean with a soft lint-free cloth, special dust-free tissues, lens-cleaning fluid, and a blower brush. A pair of tweezers is useful if sand or dirt gets lodged inside the camera. A small screwdriver can tighten up any screws that come loose, particularly on long lenses which don't like the vibrations of traveling.

Flash

A flash is useful for brightening people's faces on overcast days, and for indoor shots. Many cameras today include a built-in flash which is suitable for most purposes. If you're keen on interiors, consider a hand-held flash to brighten dark areas while the shutter remains open. Remember that many museums prohibit flash units as they can damage the exhibits.

Second Camera

If you have it, also take a compact camera, or a disposable camera. This is great for restaurants and quick snaps of unsuspecting friends in embarrassing situations. Many professionals carry a second SLR in case one jams or they're shooting with two different films. But that's a little extreme.

Tripods

A full-size tripod is essential for steady, top-quality shots, but is too cumbersome for most travelers. Instead carry a mono pod, or a mini-tripod - coupled with a wall or table, they're almost as good.

If you have a tripod, you'll also need a cable release to avoid camera movement when you take the shot. Alternatively use the self-timer feature.

Notepad & Pen

Useful for remembering good locations, bus numbers, details about your subjects, and addresses of people you meet. If you're considering submitting shots for competitions, you'll need to note your camera settings.

Batteries

It's easy to avoid buying spare batteries but there's nothing more infuriating than getting somewhere fabulous and finding out your camera won't power up. As Gary Larsen (almost) said, just when you find the Loch Ness Monster, Bigfoot, and Elvis, all sitting together, your batteries die.

There's a **surprisingly large** range of film available. For 35mm alone there are over 120 films. Generally, a good medium speed print film is recommended.

Size

The easiest decision you have is format, as your camera will only accept one size. The most common format is 35mm. This number represents the width of the film (actually 36mmx24mm - a 3:2 aspect ratio). 35mm film gives excellent results and can be enlarged to about 20"x30" before the resolution, or *grain,* becomes too noticeable.

You may have heard of the new APS film ('Advanced Photo System', called *Advantix™* by Kodak). The film is smaller (24mm - 70% the size of 35mm) but yields pictures almost as good as 35mm. APS cameras are generally smaller and lighter than 35mm, and offer additional features such as easier film loading, selectable print formats, and data encoding. However, printing is currently more expensive and few labs do one-hour developing.

Larger formats are available, which produce a high-quality, more detailed images. The cameras (Hasselblad is the choice of many professional studio photographers) are so large and heavy that most professional travel photographers stay with 35mm.

Slide vs Print

Should I use slide or print film? The quick answer is: *Use print film, unless you have a specific reason otherwise* (such as competitions or magazine/book printing).

Print film (also called *negative film* as it records the inverse, complementary colors) is the most popular choice. The resulting prints are easier to store, view, and show to people. They are also cheaper to enlarge, and the film is more forgiving (less picky about it's exposure). Over 90% of the film sold worldwide is for color prints.

If you're looking for the best quality enlargements however (for use in a magazine, to hang on a wall, or to submit in competitions), go for slide film as it captures greater detail, and deeper, truer colors (it's more *'saturated'*). All the shots in this book for example were taken on Fuji Velvia (ISO 50) slide film, famous for it's rich blacks, deep blues and vibrant greens. Kodak Ektachrome Elite and E100S are also popular, and produce more natural, less saturated images. Note that slide film is much more picky about exposure (it has less *'latitude'*) than the more forgiving print film, so correct exposure and the use of a narrow tonal range is more important.

Black and White

With it's emphasis on tonal contrast, this powerful medium can evoke mood and atmosphere, and has a loyal group of supporters. Black and white film is far easier than color to develop and a lot of the appeal is in manipulating the image in a home darkroom, through selective exposure and choice of paper. Much of Ansel Adams' artistry was in the darkroom developing his prints, rather than in the field taking the shots.

Speed

The 'speed' of a film (100, 200, 400, etc) represents how quickly the film reacts to light. 200 is the most popular. If you're pictures come out blurry (you're prone to camera shake), use a 'faster' film such as 400 or 800. Most disposable cameras contain 800 or 1000 film for this reason. If you're looking for quality (entering a competition or enlarging photos), use 100, 64, 50, 32 or even 25 film as the 'grain' or resolution is finer. Pros generally use slow film. Slow films however can end up costing you more as, due to the longer exposure, you're more likely to need a lot of sunlight, faster lenses (ones with low f-numbers - they're expensive), and a tripod. With normal 6"x4" prints you won't notice any grain improvement with films slower than 100.

Generally 'slow' film (100) is suggested for bright days, and 'fast' film (400, 800) for overcast, dim days. 36 exposure is more cost effective than 24.

X-Rays

Old airport X-ray machines used to be so powerful that they could damage your films. But today they are 'film-safe' and you shouldn't have any problems (except for films with speeds greater than 1600 ISO.

Storage

Always keep film out of direct sunlight and heat, and preferably in a moisture-resistant bag in a refrigerator.

As with beer, different brands emphasize different qualities. The choice of dyes results in subtle color variations which are most obvious with slide film as there is no intermediary printing stage. Films are listed in order of increasing cost and quality. Available ISO speeds are given, followed by (in brackets) measures of granularity. For Color Print films (measured in lines per mm), the higher the better. For slide and B&W films (RMS) the lower the better.

Color Print

Kodak
Gold Plus 100(50), 200(50), 400 is the most popular film in the US. Rich colors and fine-grained images.
Royal Gold 25, 100, 200, 400, 1000 is a premium version of Gold Plus with excellent flesh tones. Request a Photofil Index print given with each roll.
Ektar 25(80) is touted as the world's finest-grain color-print film.
Ektapress Plus (100, 200, 1600) doesn't require refrigerated storage. **Pro 100** was designed for commercial glamour, architectural and scenic photography.

Fuji
Super G Plus 100(63), 200(50), 400(50), 800(50), 1600 offers sharp, lifelike colors, wide latitude, good storage.
Reala 100(63) is their premium color film. Grain and color reproduction among the best in class.
Pro 160(163) is a professional film with wide exposure latitude.

Agfa
Ultra 50(50) claims the highest color saturation in it's class. Higher contrast than normal, adding 'snap'.

HDC 100(50), 200(50), 400(50) gives good storage and processing latitude. Ideal amateur film.
Optima, 125(50), 200(45), 400(50). Most accurate color rendition and good for nature and journalism.

Konica
Impresa 50(80)
Excellent colors and a big hit with pros in Japan. **VX** 100, 200, 400 offers good storage, shadow details and wide exposure latitude.**SR-G** 3200 is the fastest color negative film available, great for theater and hand-held night shots.

Color Slide

Kodak
Ektachrome is popular for landscapes and portraits. 64(12) & 400X are warm, 64X(11) neutral, 100(11) cool. 200(13) has finer grain but less color saturation than Elite 200. 1600(17-38) needs push processing.
Ektachrome Elite 50(9), 100(9), 200(19), 400(19) has a subtle warmth. 100 is finest-grained slide film available but 200 is grainy.
Kodachrome 25(9), 64(10)

is among the sharpest, finest-grain slide films available but few labs can process it.
E100S and **E100SW** are high-end saturated films.

Fuji
Velvia 50(9) is the favorite of many travel pro's. It offers rich blacks, neutral grays, deep colors and tremendous sharpness.
Provia 100(10), 400(15), 1600(22-30) is a faster

version of Velvia. 400 is a little red for twilight.
Sensia 100(10), 200(15), 400(15) is a consumer version. Excellent all-rounder with warm, natural colors.

Agfa
RSX 50(10), 100(10), 200(12) has rich colors. **CTX** 100(10), 200(12) has good greens and blues and edge detail.

Black & White

Kodak
Tech Pan 25(3) is the sharpest, finest-grained film available. Little exposure latitude but amazing results.
Plus-X 125 is a good general purpose film with many fans due to it's wide processing tolerances and attractive tonal range.
T-Max 100(8), 400(10),

3200p(18) has a wide exposure latitude but needs accurate processing. **Tri-X** 400 is not as sharp but is a favorite of pictorial, sports and news photographers for its beautiful tonal range and high speed.

Ilford
SFX 200 is a new film with

extended infra-red, good with deep red filters.
400 Delta is highly praised. **XP2 400** can be developed by a one-hour lab.
Pan F Plus 50 has tremendous exposure latitude, grain and sharpness.
FP4 Plus 125 is easy to work with.
HP5 is a 400 ISO film.

Acamera **is your media**, so the better you understand the media, the better your pictures are likely to be. The two most useful controls are:

1. **Focal Length** (the zoom of your lens), which affects how much of the view is included in the shot, and;

2. **Depth-Of-Field** (the f-stop of your lens), which affects how much of the foreground and background is in focus.

To use these techniques effectively, you need to understand lenses and exposure.

Lenses

The first thing to play with on most cameras is the lens. A *long* lens (say 210mm), allows you to zoom-in to your subject, to get close to it. A *short* lens (say 35mm), is often called a wide-angle lens because it allows you to zoom-out and get a wider view.

The numbers (e.g. 210mm) represent the *focal length* of the lens. This is the distance between the focal plane (film) and where the light rays appear to originate (when focused on infinity).

You can select the focal length based on what you want included in the shot, and how you want to portray *depth*. A short lens exaggerates depth, combining a close foreground with a deep background. This is a popular pro technique where a close foreground (flowers or roadway) sweeps back into the far horizon. To do this (called *hyperfocal*) you need a wide lens (say 20mm to 28mm) and a wide depth-of-field (small aperture such as f22 - see later).

A long lens on the other hand contracts the image, giving it narrow depth. Distant elements are put on the same focal plane, making them look closer together than they really are. This is useful to create a flat image, or to emphasize the scale of your background relative to your foreground.

Film

Camera film is a strip of material coated with chemicals. When exposed to light (*photos*- in Greek), the chemicals react and produce a defined image (-*graph*). Unlike our eyes, which can see under a variety of conditions, the chemicals are acutely particular about how much light they react to - the *exposure*. Too much light, *overexposed*, and the image will be pale and washed out; too little light, *underexposed*, and the image will be dark and indistinct.

Thus the **correct exposure is essential**. Your camera has controls to obtain the correct exposure.

Exposure - Four Factors

A camera is basically a box with a hole in it. The correct exposure is determined by four factors:

1. How large this hole is (the *aperture*);
2. How long it stays open for (the *shutter speed*);
3. How quickly the film reacts (the *film speed*), and:
4. How much light is reflected off the subject (the *light level*).

Fortunately, most cameras are automatic and will make all these decisions for you. However, higher-end cameras allow you to intervene to create particular effects. Its useful to understand how these four factors interact so that you can use them to your creative advantage.

Let's review each factor in turn (in order of usefulness) and see how it can improve your photography.

1. Aperture

Inside the lens is an adjustable device, the *diaphragm*, which alters the size of the opening - the *aperture*. Changing the aperture is useful as it has a handy side-effect. A very small aperture makes everything (background and foreground) in focus. A large aperture makes only the subject you're focused on in focus. Try squinting your eyes (everything is in focus) and then opening them wide (some things are blurry).

This zone of acceptably sharp focus extends both in front of and behind of the point of focus. It's called the *depth-of-field*. With landscapes, we usually want a *wide depth-of-field* to get both the background (hills or mountains) and the foreground (a flower or your travelling companions) in focus. With portraits, we want to emphasize the foreground (a person's face) so we make the background blurry by using a *narrow depth-of-field*.

How can you tell how much of the image is going to be in focus? The depth-of-field is affected by three things: the size of the aperture; the focal length of the lens; and the distance to the subject you're focused on (the *focal distance*). To make things easier, the first two items are combined to give us a field number, or **f-number**. The bigger the f-number (say f11 or f22), the bigger the depth-of-field (the wider the zone of focus).

2. Shutter Speed

Inside the camera is a mechanism (a **shutter**) which controls how long light is allowed to act on the film. When you take a photograph (by pressing the **shutter-release**), the shutter opens and then closes a fraction of a second later. How quickly this is done is called the **shutter speed** and is measured in seconds (shortened to **s**). A **fast shutter speed** (say 1/500th of a second) is good for action shots as it freezes movement. A **slow shutter speed** (say 1/60s) blurs moving objects, which is useful when you want to emphasize movement and speed.

Most of the time you will select a shutter speed based on the size of your lens. This is because when you hold a camera, you introduce unwanted movement, called **camera shake**, and how much of this shake is noticed on the photograph depends upon how much you are zoomed in.

A good rule of thumb says that you're safe with a shutter speed equal to, or faster than, the length of your lens. For example, with a wide lens of 35mm, you're fine with a shutter speed of 1/60s. But when zoomed in to 210mm, you need a faster shutter speed of 1/250s.

3. Light Level

The amount of light is usually set by mother nature. Generally, the brighter a view is, the better the photograph.

If someone is in the shade, you can add light to their face by using a flash unit. This is called **fill-flash** because it fills in some light. You can do the same thing with a reflective surface, such as white card or a purpose-made **reflector**.

If a sky is too bright, you can reduce the amount of light with a filter (such as a **gradiented neutral-density filter**).

4. Film Speed

How quickly the film's chemicals react is known as the **film speed**. A rating system was developed by the International Standards Organization (**ISO**) so that a film rated 200 ISO is a **faster film** (i.e. it reacts twice as quickly) than a 100 ISO film. (You

may have also heard of ASA or DIN - these were two other standards which were replaced by the ISO.)

Most cameras know which film speed you've put it by reading those silver and black shapes on the casing (**DX coding**), but older cameras will need manual setting.

There is a trade-off between speed and resolution, or **grain**. Generally it is preferable to use a slower film (say 100 ISO) as it gives a sharper image (a **finer grain**). But when there isn't enough light (indoors or at night), you'll need a faster film (say 400 or 1600 ISO) and will have to suffer it's less-distinct image (**coarser grain**).

Combining the Four Factors

To get the optimum exposure, you must consider all four factors - aperture, shutter speed, light level, and film speed. Always remember that these four factors are all interrelated. When you set one, you must juggle the others to get the right exposure. Usually you'll be balancing your preferred aperture with a suitable shutter speed.

For example, say you're shooting a landscape with a 100mm lens set to f5.6. When you activate the light meter in your camera, based on the light level and the film speed, it recommends a shutter speed of 1/125s. So your factors are: f5.6, 1/125s, a fixed light level, and your film speed. The f5.6 aperture is giving you a medium depth-of-field - a blurry foreground to a sharp background.

Now lets say that you want both the background and the foreground elements to be in focus. You therefore select a larger f-number, going **up a stop** from f5.6 to f8. This halves the aperture, so, to compensate, you need to double the shutter-speed from 1/125s to 1/60s. You have successfully juggled your factors.

Unfortunately, this has now taken you past the slowest speed for your lens when hand-held (100mm => 1/100s) and will make a blurry image due to camera shake. So you either need to change to a wider-angle lens (say 50mm), change to a faster film, or find some support for your camera such as a wall or tripod.

Summary

Enhance the creativity of your photographs by intelligently choosing the length of your lens and it's aperture.

Planning Your Trip

Before you leave home, decide where you want to visit. Review this book, other guide books, magazines, tourist information literature, brochures, and other information and find out what you can't miss. Then draw up a preliminary itinerary.

Test your camera and polish your skills by setting yourself some practice assignments. Use the preceding "How To Photograph Anything" section for techniques to work on. Try different lenses (you can borrow from friends or rent from a good camera store) to find out which ones you need. Try out different film types to determine which best suits your style and budget. Then stock up on rolls of film - twice the amount you think you'll use.

While You're Traveling

Start with the end in mind. Always think how your shots will work in an album or journal. You'll be narrating a story at the time so take photographs for 'chapter headings', ones designed to introduce locations and sections. Look out for signs of place names and directions.

Many of the fun times occur *between* sights so capture these with 'ordinary' shots - in a car, waiting at a bus stop or train station, in the hotel room, eating at a restaurant, and with the people you meet. Tell a story with your photography and create a visual variety of views, people shots, and fun stuff.

Collect memorabilia of the trip. Tickets stubs, timetables, postcards, restaurant receipts, napkins with logos, and hotel brochures. You can use these later to liven up your album or journal. Make notes of your travels and sketch a map showing your route. If you might enter some of your shots in photography competitions, keep a note of the camera settings you use (f-stop, shutter speed, film type and lens size).

If you're carrying a lot of film, consider marking the canisters with the subject or location. Use removable labels, then, when you get home, transfer them to the developing bags so that you're films are identified before you even review them.

Keeping A Journal

Decide beforehand how you're going to organize the journal (usually by date) and stock up with enough books or paper to last the trip. Try to write something each day,

Camera Care

You've probably noticed by now that cameras aren't cheap. They particularly hate dirt, sand, vibration, and being dropped. Don't we all. So, as you would for any partner, protect your investment with some regular attention.

Use a good padded case and strap. This protects against the elements, knocks, and theft.

Always replace the lens caps when you remove a lens. Clean the lenses regularly. Start with a soft brush, then finish with a special photographic lens tissue (not one for eyeglasses). Special lens cleaning fluid can help with stubborn smudges. With SLRs, consider adding a UV or skylight filter to each lens for extra protection.

Clean the camera in the same manner. The autofocus, exposure and viewfinder windows need to be clean for correct operation. It's amazing how sand and dirt get so easily inside the camera. A can of compressed air may help but make sure it's suitable for photographic equipment.

When driving in the Summer, put your film canisters in a plastic zip-lock bag and keep them in an ice chest. Replace the ice each day and check the bag so that the film stays cool and dry.

If you're not going to use the camera for sometime, make sure you remove the batteries. Otherwise they'll may leak and corrode the electronic contacts.

Travels with My Camera

You may be wary of X-ray machines but they don't damage film anymore. The exception is sensitive film such as ISO 400 and faster. To rest peacefully, put them in a clear zip-lock bag and drop them in the hand inspection bucket with your wallet or purse.

Always take your camera and film as carry-on. Never check it with the suitcases as rough handling, cold, and opportunistic 'borrowers' may get to it.

Keep your film in a dark, cool place. Good shops store their film in refrigerators but, even if you're away for several months, you don't need to.

particularly funny stories and irreverent remarks people made. Include the date and location. Ask your companions to contribute notes every now and then.

Getting Home

After you've recovered for the trip, put your films in for developing (don't leave them for months as the quality will slowly degrade). Ask for a second set of prints if you want to send copies to other people.

Assign a free evening and edit your shots. Don't be afraid to throw the weak ones out. The more you edit, the higher you're average quality will be. Sort them into subgroups by subject or location, and then sort each subgroup.

Making An Album

Buy a good quality album, with refillable pages and thick paper. You'll need to know your print size (usually 4"x6").

As you install the prints, consider each spread as a single story or subject. Paste in postcards, brochures and other memorabilia to highlight the story. Crop some photographs by cutting out unnecessary elements, or trimming around a figure.

Enlargements

A great way to remember your trip, and to let people admire your photographic skills, is to get enlargements made of the best shots. They come in standard sizes (5x7, 8x10, 11x14). A good tip for some revisionist improvements is to enlarge your shot to one size larger, then crop the print down (use a sharp knife and a metal edge) for an even tighter shot. Or ask your local film processor if they can crop it for you at the development stage.

It takes extra time, cost and effort but enlargements are the most admired result of your skill and art.

Newsletters

Use your shots to illustrate a newsletter of your trip to your friends and family. Cut up spare prints, stick them on paper and make photocopies (black and white, or color). Or get them scanned into a computer (ask at an office-services provider like Kinko's®) and use a word processor (Word®, Wordperfect®) or page layout program (QuarkXPress®, Pagemaker®) for a professional presentation. You could also make your own posters, key rings, refrigerator magnets, note cards, and seasonal cards.

The Digital Domain

There are an increasing number of options to use your photographs with computer applications. Generally you'll need to scan in the shots. You can buy a scanner (Epson, HP, Polaroid, UMax) or use a service bureau such as Kinko's. For top quality, use slides and have them placed onto Photo CD® or drum-scanned. There are several image editing software programs available but the best is Adobe Photoshop®. Use the Kodak Acquire module to import Photo CD®'s into Photoshop®.

For most other applications, a JPEG file format will work best. World Wide Web (Internet) pages accept JPEG and CompuServe GIF™. Macintosh printers like PICT and Windows machines like JPEG and TIFF. For four-color printing in books, magazines or flyers, use EPS (Encapsulated PostScript®). All the pictures in this book were saved as EPS files.

Slide Presentations

There's not a more fun re-union of travel companions than a slide show. The golden rule is to keep it short - less than one hour or else people will drift off. Tightly edit your shots to the best ones (resist showing everything) and arrange them to tell a narrative story. Test out the projector and the focus before the show, and keep the pace moving along. Get in the drinks and food and make an evening out of it, remembering the escapades.

Storage

Keep negatives in the sleeves they came in, or transfer them to special acid-free paper sleeves in a ring binder. Store photos, negatives and slides in a cool, dry place, and don't subject them to pressure with heavy items on top of them. If you're going to send slides away for competitions or magazines, make duplicate copies first so that you keep the original.

Send Us A Copy

If you find something cool we've missed, send us a copy of your photograph and we may include it in the next edition.

Do I Need Permission?

By Dianne Brinson for PhotoSecrets.

Before you take that photo, you may need permission for the following: Photographing buildings, works of art, or other copyrighted items; Photographing people; Photographing on public or private property. In this short article, attorney Dianne Brinson briefly discusses when permission may be required.

Copyright

Under current U.S. law, copyright protection arises automatically when an *"original work of authorship"* is *"fixed in a tangible medium of expression"*. A work is *"original"* in the copyright sense if it owes its origin to the author. For example, a photograph of Yosemite's Bridalveil Fall is original so long as it was created by the photographer, even if it's the zillionth photo to be taken of that scene. Only minimal creativity is required to meet the originality requirement, no artistic merit or beauty is required.

Works of art - sculptures, paintings, and even toys - are protectable by copyright. Furthermore, buildings created on or after December 1, 1990 are protected by copyright. A copyright owner has the exclusive right to reproduce a copyrighted work, and photographing a copyrighted work is considered a way of reproducing it. Thus, you may need permission to photograph a building or an art work.

Here are some guidelines:

Buildings

Only buildings created after December 1, 1990 are protected by copyright. Fortunately for photographers, the copyright in an architectural work does not include the right to prevent others from making and distributing photos of the constructed building, if the building is located in a public place or is visible from a public place. So you don't need permission to stand on a public street and photograph a public building. You don't need permission to photograph a public building from inside the building (although you may need permission to photograph separately-owned decorative objects in the building, such as a statue). You don't need permission to stand on a public street and photograph a private building such as a church or a house.

This *"photographer's exception"* to the copyright-owner's rights applies only to buildings, a category which includes houses, office buildings, churches, gazebos, and garden pavilions. The exception does not apply to monuments (protectable as *"sculptural works"*) or other copyrighted works, such as statues and paintings.

Art

You may need permission to photograph a copyrighted work of art, for example, a statue in a public park, or a painting in a private collection or art museum. And getting permission can be tricky, because, according to copyright law, you need permission from the copyright owner, not from the owner of the work of art itself. In copyright law, ownership of the copyright in a work is distinct from ownership of the copy (the tangible item).

For example, suppose that you are taking photographs of a painting in an art collector's private home collection. The art collector probably does not own the copyright in the painting, the artist does. Unless your photograph of the painting is *"fair use"* (discussed later) you need permission from the artist.

When You Don't Need Permission

You don't need permission to photograph a work that is not protected by copyright (in *"the public domain"*). Works fall into the public domain for several reasons, one of which is expiration of the copyright term. In 1997, works created before January 1, 1922 are in the public domain. Also, works created by federal government officers and employees as part of their official duties are not protected by copyright. (This rule does not apply to works created by state or local government officers and employees).

You don't need permission to use a copyrighted work in two circumstances: (1) if you are only copying facts or ideas from the work; or (2) if your use is *"fair use"*.

You are free to copy facts from a protected work or to copy ideas from a protected work. The copyright on a work does not extend to the work's facts. This is because copyright protection is limited to original works of authorship, and no one can claim originality or authorship for facts. Anyone can use ideas.

Fair Use

It may be that your photograph is *"fair use"* of the art works you photograph. If so, you don't need permission. Whether a use of a copyrighted work is fair use is decided on a case-by-case basis by considering the purpose and character of the use, the nature of the copyrighted work, the amount and substantiality of the portion used, and the effect on the potential market for or value of the protected work.

There is no simple rule to determine when an unauthorized use is *"fair use"*. You are more likely to be able to rely on fair use for photographing copyrighted items if your work serves a traditional fair use purpose (educational, research, news reporting, criticism, or public interest). Fair use is always subject to interpretation.

Publicity and Privacy Rights of Individuals

You may need permission to photograph people due to state laws giving individuals privacy and publicity rights.

Most states in the US recognize that individuals have a right of privacy. The right of privacy gives an individual a legal claim against someone who intrudes on the individual's physical solitude or seclusion, and against those who publicly disclose private facts. Unless you have permission, avoid publishing or distributing any photo of an individual that reveals private facts about the individual (particularly if revealing those private facts might embarrass the individual).

Almost half the states in the US recognize that individuals have a right of publicity. The right of publicity gives an individual a legal claim against one who uses the individual's name, face, image, or voice for commercial benefit without obtaining permission. In case you are wondering how the news media handle this, newspapers and news magazines have a *"fair use"* privilege to publish names or images in connection with reporting a newsworthy event.

Be particularly careful about celebrities. Using a photograph of a celebrity for your own commercial gain - for example, posting a photo you took of Clint Eastwood on your business's marketing material or Web site - is asking for a lawsuit, even if you took the photograph when you ran into Clint on a public street.

Commercial photographers avoid right of publicity/privacy lawsuits by obtaining photographic releases from people shown in the their shots. If you are considering selling your photos or using them on your Web site, you may want to do the same. The *Multimedia Law and Business Handbook* contains a sample release. Experienced performers and models are accustomed to signing these releases.

Permits

If you are going to shoot commercial photographs on public property, you may need to get a permit from the appropriate government authority (usually a local or state film commission). Permission is generally not required for taking the usual *"tourist type"* photos (although you should obey any *"no entry"* signs you see).

If you are going to shoot on private property, get permission to enter and use the location for shooting and to show the premises in your work, in order to avoid trespass and invasion of privacy claims by the property owner.

The Internet

The laws and rules described in this article apply to photos used on the Internet. Copyright law and other laws do apply to the Internet, and posting a photo on the Internet exposes your photos to the eyes of the whole world.

DISCLAIMER: This article is provided with the understanding that neither the author nor the publisher is engaged in rendering legal or other professional service. If legal advice or other expert assistance is required, the services of a competent professional person should be sought.

Dianne Brinson, a copyright attorney, received her law degree from Yale Law School and her B.A. from Duke University. A former law professor, Dianne currently teaches *Law for Internet Users* at San Jose State University's Professional Development Center.

For more information, read the book *Multimedia Law and Business Handbook*, by J. Dianne Brinson and Mark F. Radcliffe (available from Ladera Press for $44.95 plus shipping, ☎800-523-3721).

CREDITS

The Story of this Book

It's been two-and-a-half years now since the idea of PhotoSecrets was born. I was on a round-the-world trip (as you do when you reach 30), sitting in the Indian embassy in Singapore waiting interminably for a visa, and planning a trip through Thailand. I wanted to visit the beach used in the James Bond film *'Goldfinger'*, where a limestone tower rises out of the sea, housing the Golden Gun. I had seen it pictured in magazines and wanted to be somewhere so remote and exotic.

Unfortunately none of the guidebooks I'd brought identified this place. They were excellent for accommodation and transportation, but didn't address a major goal of my trip - seeing the most visually unique sights from the best angles, and taking memorable photographs. Surely I wasn't the only one who enjoyed using a camera to explore? Perhaps there were other people who would appreciate a portable book, cataloging the most distinctive landscapes and giving photography information.

A year later, wishing to pursue new career directions and after persistent encouragement from my love, Jennie, I decided to take this pie-in-the-sky idea more seriously. Because layout and design were so critical to the project, I rashly chose the Tony Wheeler approach (I'm a devout *Lonely Planet* fan) and attempted to publish the book myself. In April 1996, I left the safety of a full-time job and dove headfirst into a world I knew nothing about.

I did five long trips (to cover all the seasons), some of them with Jennie, driving and camping through San Francisco and Northern California, and was astounded by the varied and stunning scenery and exciting history of this much-loved region.

By the miracle of desktop publishing, this book took shape in our spare bedroom. Having grown up an engineer (a degree in Computer Engineering), I had no knowledge of publishing or design and far longer than expected was taken up with computer 'gotchas', as well as printing, marketing, and distribution issues.

Now as we go to press, a year after earnest embarcation, I'm both nervous and exhilarated. It's like giving birth (although, as I'm often told, *'far less painful, so don't complain!'*). I'm sure there are improvements that can be made and places I've overlooked, so please let me know what you think and your suggestions can be used for the next edition.

I hope you enjoy using this book and find that it maximizes your time and alerts you to the best viewing locations. From a fellow fan of travel and photography, have fun!

Andrew Hudson, April, 1997.

"The writer does the most who gives his reader the most knowledge and takes from him the least time." Sydney Smith.

Acknowledgements

This book would never have been more than a daydream without the belief and campaigning of my love, Jennie Van Meter. Thanks for holding me through the tough times, Coco. And I would never have been anything without my wonderful parents, Chris (Ann) & Cy Hudson. Thanks Mumb and Dad for your encouragement and support.

I have to say a special thank you to Bob Krist. With his work in *National Geographic Traveler*, *Travel & Leisure*, and *Islands*, I have long considered Bob to be the pinnacle of travel photography and was greatly honored by his assistance. Bob's lucid Foreword explained the PhotoSecrets concept better than I could and his early support was a great psychological and marketing boost. A special thanks also to Galen Rowell and his staff at Mountain Light. As a fan of Galen's books and his monthly column in *Outdoor Photographer*, I was honored by his endorsement and ecstatic when he enthusiastically agreed to write the foreword to Yosemite.

Thanks go to Karen Cure at Fodor's; Sherry at KC Publications; Dan Poynter and *The Self-Publishing Manual*; Jan Nathan, and the Publisher's Marketing Association; Claire Arias, Bob Goodman and the San Diego Publishers Alliance; everyone who endorsed the book and everyone who visited the PhotoSecrets web site (started August 1996) and gave opinions and feedback. I am indebted to my fabulous distributor National Book Network (NBN) for boldly signing a publisher who had, at the time, no books. Thanks to Jed Lyons, Miriam Bass, James Penfield, Spencer Gale, Rich Freese, Michael Sullivan, Ray Wittrup, Jock Hayward, Linda Biggam and the others for their efforts. Thanks also to Vickie Visa and Marcie Mastercard for financing this extravagant venture.

Special thanks go to our good friends Eduardo and Sylvia Rallo Verdugo (hello to everyone at WorldWrapps!) and Elayne Blair for use of their apartments in San Francisco, as well as their inspiration and enthusiasm. Research benefited from the kind help of: Joyce Blinbo at Hearst Castle™; Ken Peterson at the Monterey Bay Aquarium; Christine Cowles at the Yosemite Press Office; the University of California, San Diego library. Acknowledgements to Professional Color Lab (San Francisco) and Chrome (Sorrento Valley) for film developing; Dale Labs (Florida) for PhotoCD scanning; Kinko's (La Jolla) for computer and office equipment; Jay H. Koo and Doosan Dong-A for printing.

Thanks to good friends who made this possible, including: Tony Jowett for initial inspiration; Maite Agahnia for early design work; Andy Cunningham for invaluable Macintosh help; Mike Brooks for design support; Martin Carrington for photography ideas and proofreading; Andy Harris for moral support and proofreading; Chuck Allen for publishing info; Dan & Sue Miley for publishing info; Jennie's parents, Judy & Jerry Van Meter for encouragement and 'research' at bookstores and coffee houses.

I wouldn't have survived long were it not for the interest and support shown by our many other San Diego friends, including: Dave & Liane Ousley; Mary & Chuck Allen (hello Ben & Katie); Steve Roy & Kelli Burn-Lucht; Alex, Joni and Michael Ratajac; Martin & Cynthia Beck; Paul & Carol Bremner; the Rohr Sailing Club.

Hello also to my brother Patrick and his nutty friends; my family (Gracie; Nan; Ive & Bill; Yve, John, Rich, Jen, Fi & Dan; Sue, John, Sarah & Alex; Olive & Kim; Liz, Malcolm, Rachel & James; Ken, Wendy, Rich & Sylvia); and friends from Redditch, GEC (now GPT) in Coventry and Iraq, Manchester University (especially Sam, Dan, Pom, Lisa, Fran, Mike, Pete, Neil, Sarah, Alison, Amanda, Elbie, Roland, and the *Free Beer* band and it's derivatives), GPT in New York and Stamford, Peirce-Phelps in Philadelphia, and BT in California, Virginia and London.

Production Notes

All photographs were taken with a Minolta X-700 SLR camera (20-35, 50, & 75-300 lenses) using manual or aperture-automatic mode and a Ricoh R-1 compact camera (nothing fancy!). The rich colors are courtesy of the Fuji Velvia™ (ISO 50) slide film and a Tiffen polarizer filter.

Slides were scanned as Kodak Digital Science™ Photo CD™ files and imported to an Apple® Power Macintosh 9500/132 with 48Mb RAM, running System 7.5.5. Basic touch up (levels adjustment and unsharp mask) was performed in Adobe Photoshop® 3.0.5. Layout was performed in QuarkXPress® 3.32. Hand-drawn maps were scanned on a HP ScanJet™ 4c and computer-generated maps made in Adobe Illustrator® 6.0. Basic proofs were made on the excellent HP DeskJet™ 855C. Lots of Ty•Phoo™ and PG Tips tea® was drunk.

The entire book was created digitally and delivered to the printer on six Iomega 1GB Jaz™ disks. The book is printed on 120 gsm gloss paper with a 300 gsm cover, and Smythe sewn to lay flat. Lamination has been added to the outside for extra protection. Printed in Korea.

Distribution

PhotoSecrets books are distributed to the US and Canadian trade by National Book Network (NBN), ☎800-462-6420. US wholesalers include: AMS, Baker & Taylor, Bookazine, Bookpeople, Ingram, LS Distributors and Sunbelt Publications.

Credits

All photographs by Andrew Hudson except where noted. Special thanks to the owners of all the excellent establishments pictured in this book. Particular acknowledgments for image reproductions: The San Francisco Film Commission; Hearst San Simeon State Historic Monument, Dept. of Parks & Recreation, San Simeon, CA 93452; SFMOMA; the Monterey Bay Aquarium; the Pebble Beach Company.

Apologies to anyone we've left out or misnamed - please advise us and you'll be included in the next edition.

Copyright

TRIVIA QUIZ

Something To Pass The Time On A Long Drive

OK. So you've read the book and think you know everything. Let's find out. All the answers are in the main text (and, for the confounded, are on the next page).

1. What color is the Golden Gate Bridge?

2. Under which city are 750 miles of tunnels?

3. Which is longer, Yosemite Valley or San Francisco?

4. Name three places in California with churches painted red.

5. Where can you find: (a) Elvis' Pink Cadillac; (b) the Barbie Hall of Fame; (c) a Scandinavian Castle?

6. Where in San Francisco can you find two full-size windmills?

7. Name the structures derided as (a) The Great Alien Ring Toss; (b) Aqueduct Meets Ventilation Duct.

8. Name the places referred to as: (a) The Athens of the Pacific; (b) The Dead Sea of the West; (c) Bedlam at the Kremlin.

9. What is the tallest single waterfall in Yosemite?

10. What is the windiest place in North America?

11. Name the city based around a lake, and the town based around a baseball diamond.

12. Where did Ansel Adams first learn about artistic photography?

13. Name the buildings modeled after these European treasures: (a) St. Marks Basilica in Venice, Italy; (b) St. Peters Basilica in Vatican City (Rome); (c) Giralda Tower in Seville, Spain; (d) The Palace of the Legion of Honor in Paris.

14. What is the nation's only moving national landmark?

15. Where was *The Birds* filmed?

16. What is the connection between Yosemite's Hetch Hetchy valley and Mono Lake?

17. Which nationality did not help hunt otters to extinction: Americans, British, Russians or Spanish?

18. Name the two men who founded: (a) Apple Computer; (b) the Beat movement.

19. Where was the UN Charter signed?

20. Where was the fortune cookie reputedly invented?

21. Name three differences between Redwoods and Sequoias.

22. Who was California's last Governor to reside at the Governor's Mansion in Sacramento?

23. Who was crowned Castroville's first artichoke queen?

24. Big Sur's Bixby Creek Bridge was mainly built by what group of people?

25. What is the connection between Sutter's Fort in Sacramento and Fort Ross?

26. Name three places in California with full-size operational steam trains.

27. What is the connection between the Fairmont Hotel and Hearst Castle?

28. Where is California's only 'old faithful' geyser?

29. What was the capital of Spanish and Mexican Alta California?

30. What was the most expensive building ever bought in the US?

31. Millionaire James Lick had which two well-known buildings made?

32. What is the only Frank Lloyd Wright building in San Francisco?

33. What is the tallest lighthouse on the West Coast?

You can:

- Add your name to our mailing list;
- Tell us how to improve this book;

or

- Send us a distinctive or fun shot to be included in the next edition[1];
- Order another book.

☞ Cut out the FREE reply card below, or e-mail to **feedback@photosecrets.com**

--

☞ Send in a stamped envelope to:
Photosecrets Publishing   PO Box 13554
La Jolla CA 92039-3554   USA

Order Form

Please send me: _____ copy/copies of *PhotoSecrets Yosemite* at $7.95 each;
_____ *PhotoSecrets San Francisco & No. California* at $16.95 each;

Add: ❏ 7.75% sales tax if shipping within CA ($0.62 for Yos; $1.32 for SF&NC)
Shipping[2]: ❏ US: $4 first book +$1 for each add'l; ❏ CAN: $5 first +$1 ea. add'l;
❏ Europe & Mexico: $6.95 per book; ❏ Pacific Rim & elsewhere: $8.95 per book
Please mail your check (payable to *Photosecrets Publications*) to the address above.

Feedback

[1] When submitting photos, include a stamped addressed return envelope if you want them returned. Not responsible for any loss or damage. Orders and submissions require a stamped envelope.
[2] For each pair (Yosemite + SF&NC) the second book ships for free.

To use this FREE card, please cut along line exactly.

Comments/Suggestions/Compliments/Changes:

1. **Where did you buy this book?**

2. **What city/area/country would you like our next book to be about?**

3. **What camera do you use?**   ❏ Compact;   ❏ SLR;   ❏ Other format

4. **If you would like to be informed of future books and improvements, please add your contact information here:**

Name: _____

E-mail Address: _____

Street: _____

City & Zip/Postcode: _____

Country: _____

☺ Please **CUT EXACTLY - DO NOT TEAR**.
Because it's barcoded reply mail, the Post
Office will only deliver this card if it is cut
to the exact size. They're funny like that. ☝

✉ Send other correspondence to:
Photosecrets Publishing
PO Box 13554
La Jolla CA 92039-3554
USA

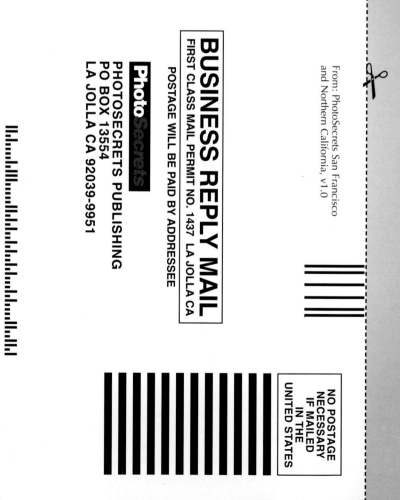

From: PhotoSecrets San Francisco
and Northern California, v1.0

BUSINESS REPLY MAIL

FIRST CLASS MAIL PERMIT NO. 1437 LA JOLLA CA

POSTAGE WILL BE PAID BY ADDRESSEE

PhotoSecrets

PHOTOSECRETS PUBLISHING
PO BOX 13554
LA JOLLA CA 92039-9951

NO POSTAGE
NECESSARY
IF MAILED
IN THE
UNITED STATES

BIBLIOGRAPHY

Books on Travel Photography:

Kodak Pocket Guide to Travel Photography. Eastman Kodak Company Staff. $6.95.

Berlitz Travel Photography. Jon Davison and Jerry Burman. $9.95.

Vacation and Travel Photography (Point & Shoot Series). Sean Hargrave. $11.95.

Photography Outdoors: A Field Guide for Travel & Adventure Photographers. Art Wolfe and Gardner Mark. $12.95.

Pocket Guide to Outdoor Photography. Mary Mather. $12.95.

Kodak Guide to Shooting Great Travel Pictures. Jeff Wignall. $16.50.

The L.L. Bean Guide to Outdoor Photography. Lefty Kreh. $16.95.

The Backpacker's Photography Handbook: How to Take Great Wilderness Pictures While Hiking, Climbing, and Skiing; Charles Campbell. $19.95.

The Art of Outdoor Photography: Techniques for the Advanced Amateur and Professional. Boyd Norton. $36/22.

Guide to Travel Writing and Photography. Ann and Carl Purcell. $22.95.

Travel Photography: A Complete Guide to How to Shoot and Sell. Susan McCartney. $22.95.

Mountain Light: In Search of the Dynamic Landscape. Galen Rowell. $40/$25.

Galen Rowell's Vision: The Art of Adventure Photography. Galen Rowell. $30.

The Art of Adventure. Galen Rowell. $33.

Bay Area Wild. Galen Rowell.

Focus on Travel: Photographing Memorable Pictures of Journeys to New Places. Anne Millman and Allen Rokach. $44.

National Geographic the Photographs. Leah Bendavid-Val. $50.

Quiz Answers: **1:** International Orange -it's best seen in fog; **2:** Virginia City, NV. They were digging for silver; **3:** They're both the same length. Yosemite Valley is 7 miles long and 3/4 mile wide - San Francisco is 7 miles long and 7 miles wide; **4:** Mendocino, Santa Rosa, Sonora; **5:** (a) Reno; (b) Palo Alto; (c) Emerald Bay in Lake Tahoe; **6:** Golden Gate Park (west end); **7:** (a) The Transamerica Pyramid; (b) Vaillancourt Fountain in the Embarcadero Center; **8:** (a) University of California, Berkeley; (b) Mono Lake; (c) Mad Magda's Russian Tea Shop; **9:** Ribbon Fall at 1,000-feet. Yosemite Falls is taller at 2,645-feet but is a combined (three-part) fall; **10:** Point Reyes - the trees grow diagonally; **11:** Oakland is based around Lake Merritt, and Nicasio in Marin County is based around a baseball diamond; **12:** At the 1915 Panama-Pacific Exposition, the only remains of which is the Palace of Fine Arts; **13:** (a) Sather Tower (aka The Campanile) in UC Berkeley; (b) City Hall; (c) the Ferry Building; (d) The California Palace of the Legion of Honor in Lincoln Park; **14:** Cable Cars; **15:** Bodega, not Bodega Bay which is a separate town; **16:** Hetch Hetchy was damned in 1919 to supply water to San Francisco (it is now a reservoir), and Mono Lake was tapped (its tributaries were diverted) in 1941 to provide water to Los Angeles; **17:** The Spanish. Their laws prohibited catching fur-bearing animals; **18:** (a) Steve Jobs and Stephen Wozniak; (b) Allen Ginsberg and Jack Kerouac; **19:** The Veteran's Building, near City Hall; **20:** The Japanese Tea Garden in Golden Gate Park; **21:** Redwoods are taller; thinner; have thinner bark; have less-spongy bark; have orange/gray bark instead of Sequoia's cinnamon-colored bark; **22:** Ronald Reagan; **23:** Marilyn Monroe; **24:** Prisoners - much of Route 1 was built with convict labor; **25:** In 1841 Captain John Sutter bought most of Fort Ross from the Russians to equip Sutter's Fort in present-day Sacramento; **26:** Fort Bragg and Willits share the Skunk Train; Roaring Camp at Felton goes to Santa Cruz; Jamestown on Rt 49; Sugar Pine near Yosemite. Virginia City has the V&T but that's in Nevada; **27:** Architect Julia Morgan designed them both; **28:** Calistoga. There are only three known 'faithful' geysers in the world. **29:** Monterey. The old customs house still stands; **30:** The Bank of America building in San Francisco was sold for $660M in 1985; **31:** The Conservatory of Flowers in Golden Gate Park and Lick Observatory east of San Jose; **32:** Circle Gallery on Maiden Lane near Union Square; **33:** Point Arena.

INDEX

Andrew Hudson (author) loves to travel and take photographs. *"A camera is the perfect tool for travel"* he says, *"it pushes us to explore a location, to capture its essence, and to view the ordinary in an extraordinary way."*

Born in England, Andrew received his first camera from his parents on his 21st birthday and learned it's art on trips through Europe and Africa. He graduated from Manchester University with a degree in Computer Engineering, and became a Field Engineer in London and Iraq. In 1988 he moved to the US, living in New York, Stamford, Philadelphia and San Diego. His last position was a Sales Manager for British Telecom.

On business and vacation trips he always sought out the perfect shots, scouring travel books and postcard racks for ideas. He wondered why there wasn't a book that did this for him. *"For many travelers, coming home with a good set of photographs is a major objective of the trip."* Finally, on a trip through Asia, he decided to develop such a book himself. The PhotoSecrets series was born.

Andrew has spent two years researching, photographing, and designing this, his first, book. He lives with his partner Jennie in San Diego, California.

Near right: **Bob Krist** (Foreword) is a respected travel photographer. He writes the photography column for *National Geographic Traveler* and his photographs regularly appear in *National Geographic*, *National Geographic Traveler*, *Islands*, *Travel/Holiday*, and *Travel & Leisure*. Bob lives with his wife Peggy and three sons in Ridgewood, New Jersey.

Far right: **Galen Rowell** (Introduction to Yosemite) is a renowned wilderness photographer and author. He writes a monthly column for *Outdoor Photographer* and his writings and photographs regularly appear in *National Geographic*, *Life*, *Sports Illustrated*, and *Outdoor Photographer*. Galen lives with his wife Barbara in Berkeley, California.

Visit the web site:
http://www.photosecrets.com

PhotoSecrets will return in:
PhotoSecrets Los Angeles and Southern California.